Zalkin's Handbook
of
Thimbles
and
Sewing Implements

Zalkin's Handbook
of
Thimbles
and
Sewing Implements

A Complete Collector's Guide
with Current Prices

1st Edition

by
Estelle Zalkin

Warman Publishing Co., Inc.
a division of
Wallace-Homestead Book Company
Radnor, Pennsylvania

ISBN 0-911594-14-0
Library of Congress Catalog Card No. 88-50383

Manufactured in the United States of America

3 4 5 6 7 8 9 0   7 6 5 4 3

DEDICATION

To Julie

Contents

PART IV: SEWING TOOLS —NEW APPROACHES

PART V: ADDITIONAL INFORMATION

PREFACE

This is a book for collectors written by an active, aggressive collector of thimbles and other sewing collectibles.

Estelle Zalkin, the author, is an enthusiastic person who's warmth and energetic spirit spills over onto every page of her writing. The text is comfortable to read with sufficient color and humor to captivate the reader's interest.

Estelle Zalkin is a charter member of Thimble Collectors International. She served on the Board of Directors from 1978 to 1982, and was Ways and Means Vice President from 1982 to 1984. She is an active member of Thimble Guild and The Gold Coast Thimblers of Florida. Her articles about thimbles and sewing tools have appeared in various antiques publications, as well as the *Bulletin* of Thimble Collectors International and *Thimbletter*. Her knowledge and warmth has made her a welcomed keynote speaker at various thimble conventions and meetings.

The author has shared a rich background of thimble history and brief biographical sketches of the craftsmen who have created our sewing treasures. Aside from her verbal pictures, the author has generously shared excellent photographs of items to whet the appetite of the most lukewarm collector.

The field of thimbling has been cradled from the most precious metal and porcelain to the frequently overlooked items in the "Twenty Pockets" collectibles. The author has explored and written over a broad range, extending from museum quality items to advertising, native American and Black memorabilia, to souvenir and commemorative sewing collectibles.

She has done her homework and has challenged us to do the same. This is one book every thimble collector will enjoy reading as well as using as a reference.

Lahoma Haddock Goldsmith, first editor,
the *Bulletin*, Thimble Collectors International.

PREFACE

When Myrtle Lundquist's *Book of a Thousand Thimbles* was published in 1970, it heralded the appearance of the first book devoted solely to thimbles and thimble collecting. Lundquist's second and third books appeared in 1975 and 1980. Other authors contributed seven additional books between 1979 and 1986. Books about needlework tools and accessories have a similar history. The earlier efforts by Gertrude Whiting in 1928 and Sylvia Groves in 1966 were not followed by another publication until Gay Ann Rogers' book in 1983.

Estelle Zalkin's book is devoted to the thimbles and sewing accessories that have been available in the antiques market during the last twenty years. Her photographs are mainly of items in her own collection, painstakingly gathered by Julius, her husband, and herself during a wealth of excursions to a wide variety of marketplaces. Their primary source is the well-stocked winter antiques shows of the eastern Florida coast. Additionally, they have made many trips to shows and shops of the Carolinas, Tennessee, Pennsylvania, New York, Connecticut, and especially the unique outdoor shows at Brimfield, Massachusetts. Their trips abroad to England, France, and Italy have yielded classical examples of the thimbles and sewing tools of these countries.

Estelle's chapter on Dorcas thimbles is a very thorough treatment of this highly collectible thimble. She was encouraged and supported during the early stages of her research by Edwin Holmes. Equally impressive is the chapter on souvenir thimbles. Estelle has found seven additional souvenir thimbles to add to the current list of sixty-eight known types. A highlight of this section is the World's Fairs thimbles, a unique subgroup. The section on early American thimbles, certainly steel tops, introduces the collector to an era of thimble manufacturing that has not been thoroughly researched or its products systematically identified. It is hoped that the present complement will stimulate additional investigations into this period of American thimble manufacturing.

The enthusiasm and energy that Estelle brings to her hobby is evident throughout the book along with the wealth of information she has acquired during her many years of collecting. She is probably the most prolific author in the field of thimble and sewing accessories. Her articles have appeared in a variety of antiques journals, e.g. the *Bulletin* of Thimble Collectors International and newsletters written exclusively for thimble collectors. These articles range from discussions of antique items to warning the collector of the appearance of modern reproductions of some classical silver thimbles.

Estelle Zalkin makes a significant contribution to our knowledge of sewing accessories and thimbles available in the American antiques market. Both the new and seasoned collector will find a wealth of information not readily available in any other source. This will not only enhance the collectors' understanding and enjoyment of their hobby, but also will help tremendously in their becoming knowledgeable buyers.

Milton Mager, past vice president,
Thimble Collectors International

FOREWORD - ACKNOWLEDGMENT

My earliest recollection of developing an interest in needlework tools was when my grandmother permitted me to rummage through her Martha Washington sewing cabinet. It held many fascinating gadgets, some of which she may have brought with her when she emigrated from her native Finland.

The idea to seriously collect sewing tools occurred when I started to travel to faraway places. Souvenirs and gifts for friends and family back home had to be small, lightweight, and unbreakable. A fancy thimble fitted all of these criteria. Of course, I always managed to keep one for myself. A pretty applied wire work silver thimble from Mexico, Spanish black and golden damascened thimble marked "TOLEDO", and a silver one with allover pounced flowers from England found their way into my sewing box. Each represented memories of a past trip. When I have three of anything, it is the start of a collection.

I wanted to learn about the history of thimbles and sewing tools. Prior to 1970 there was very little published on this subject. Gertrude Whiting's *Tools and Toys of Stitchery* was published in 1928. I was delighted to find a copy at my local library. When the Dover reprint became available in 1971, I became the proud owner of one of the first copies. Sylvia Groves' *The History of Needlework Tools and Accessories* was the only other book available in the 1960s. Other than a few paragraphs in needlework and collectibles books, these books were my principal source for information on old thimbles and sewing tools. Myrtle Lundquist's *The Book of a Thousand Thimbles* became my collecting guide when it was published in 1970.

In the last fifteen years, other books became available. Each added to the research knowledge, but none focused adequately on how to collect. When *THIMBLETTER,* a newsletter for collectors, was published in 1973, it gave me the opportunity to meet other collectors, if only by mail. Eventually, Thimble Collectors International, a non-profit club for collectors, was established, and collecting thimbles and sewing tools achieved national recognition.

I meet many collectors through the mail, at meetings, and conventions. All are willing to share whatever knowledge and research they have acquired; they also are eager to learn more about their collections. Many ask the same questions: how to display, how to catalog, how to date a piece, what to look for when shopping, and what is a fair price to pay? No matter how long someone collects, there are always unanswered questions.

This book attempts to answer some of the more common questions about collecting sewing tools and thimbles. It is like a game because it is fun and rewarding. My book is basically a handbook on collecting, with points of historical significance included with each tool.

The history of needlework tools is linked with the needlework itself. Many tools were designed and created for a specific purpose or fashion of the day. When this became passé, the tool was relegated to the bottom of the sewing basket. The cording tool, used to make fancy cording for drapery ties and other corded trimmings, is an example.

There are many facets and approaches to collecting thimbles and needlework tools. Some can be assembled for a minimum investment. "Twenty Pocket" collectibles and "Paper Memorabilia" collectibles fall into this area. These can be stored in plastic pocket pages in a loose leaf binder. There also is plenty to attract the individual with a larger spending budget.

Though I concentrate on antique sewing tools and thimbles that are available in today's antiques market, a few of the photographed pieces are from museum collections. This does not mean that collectors will never see similar pieces available for sale. Individuals should study the museum pictures so that they can recognize a "museum quality" piece when it does surface at an antiques show. A perfect example is a needle case in my own collection. A picture appeared in the Dover reprint of Gertrude Whiting's *Old-Time Tools and Toys of Needlework* of a seventeenth century needle case that is in the Baron Henri Le Secq Des Tournelles collection of rare old steel needle cases in the Museum in Rouen, France. From the picture in the Dover book, I was able to recognize this rare key-shaped steel needle case that was mixed in with an assortment of cork screws in a show case at an antiques show. Needless to say, I bought it at a fraction of its true value. Opportunities like this do not happen often. The skilled collector recognizes the opportunity when it arises.

Many museum collections were private collections at one time. For example, the Eugenie Bijur collection of sewing clamps at the Monmouth Museum in New Jersey was once the prized private collection of Mrs. Bijur, who collected sewing clamps during the 1930s and 40s.

I would like to express my grateful thanks to the many collectors who offered their opinions on the various topics covered in this book. The list is lengthy and to avoid omitting one name, I offer my gratitude to all.

Many collectors loaned prized pieces from their personal collections to be photographed for this book. A credit line appears at the appropriate photograph. Unless otherwise noted, I took the pictures that appear in this book. Now that I am done, Julie and I will be able to enjoy our Florida room again rather than have its use restricted to my photo studio.

My gratitude also goes to Lahoma Goldsmith, who checked my chapters for facts, and to Lora Lee Cordes, who did the art work in this book. This book could not be completed without their special talents. A special "Thank You" goes to Harry L. Rinker, my editor, whose professional writing expertise made this a better book. Terese Oswald did an excellent job preparing the final manuscript.

My sincere appreciation is extended to the museums and private corporations that contributed photographs and information. The interest and cooperation in sharing will be greatly appreciated by today's collectors, and those in the future.

Estelle Zalkin

PART I

INTRODUCTION

CHAPTER 1

The History of Thimbles and Sewing Tools

Possibly, the first "thimble," or finger protector, was fashioned by the cave woman who said "ouch" when trying to stitch on leather with her bone needle.

By the Middle Ages, thimbles were hand made by metal craftsmen. Craftsmen in Nuremburg, Germany, the center for the thimblemaker's trade, made metal thimbles more than a hundred years before Columbus discovered America. Sabastian Prawn, the first thimblemarker, worked as early as 1373. He died in 1414.

The modern mass production era began in 1695 when John Lofting, a Dutch mechanic, set up his thimble factory near London. He was granted British patent number 319 for his "Engine for Making Thimbles." This machine could produce over one million brass thimbles a year.

In America, colonial silversmiths produced custom made thimbles for their customers. Paul Revere, the famous American silversmith, made a gold thimble for his daughter,now part of the collection of the Boston Museum of Fine Arts. Few early American thimbles were marked, either with the maker's mark or a mark signifying the quality of the metal. Metal quality markings on gold and silver thimbles were not required in the United States until 1860. Some early American silver thimbles were marked "COIN" or "DOLLAR" to describe the silver contents.

Other early American thimble makers were Ezra Prime, Benjamin Halstead, and David Platt. A gold thimble that Platt made for his wife is now in the collection of the Huntington Historical Society, Huntington, Long Island, New York. A gold thimble made by Jacob Hurd (1702-1758) is in the archives of Yale University Art Gallery.

Historical thimbles have been sold at auction in the four and five figure price. An early American gold thimble, circa 1700, was offered by Sotheby's, New York in 1983. It brought over $6,000, well above the $2,000-3,000 pre-auction estimate. What made this thimble rarer than other early American gold thimbles was the fact it was signed by Samuel Vernon, a Newport, Rhode Island, silversmith.

Antique Meissen porcelain thimbles command high prices every time they are offered for sale. Thimble collectors compete with porcelain and Meissen collectors for pieces, exerting unusual upward pressure on prices.

The Industrial Revolution brought in the "Golden Age" of thimble making during the nineteenth century. Machinery was created that could produce fine working thimbles. This machinery could make smooth and indented thimbles. Die stamps produced decorations on the band. By the end of the nineteenth century, world production of thimbles was about eighty million per year.

PLAIN AND FANCY

Long before the sewing machine became a permanent member of the household, all sewing and mending was done by hand. Needlework can be divided into two kinds—plain and fancy.

Sewing was considered a major part of a young girl's education. She was expected, as part of her dowry, to fill a hope chest with hand hemmed household linens, quilts, and hand made lingerie and clothes. Tradition required a girl to make 13 quilts for her dower chest. Twelve were for everyday use, while the thirteenth was her bridal quilt. The work on the bride's quilt could not be started until the girl was formally engaged.

The embroidered sampler she was required to complete was preserved, but the many hours she spent making samples of darning for socks have been forgotten. The stitches she learned to do while making her sampler prepared her for the many hours of sewing she would do in the future.

Plain sewing required special, but utilitarian tools: a thimble, measure, darning egg, pin cushion, needle case, and a scissors. These were usually simple tools - sturdy and not ornate. Some, such as the pin cushion, were home made. Others were "store bought." City ladies had no problem finding these tools. A selection was always available at the local dry goods store. The name "dry goods" is strictly American. It assured a lady that no "wet goods," or alcoholic beverages were sold in that store, and it was perfectly proper for her to shop there.

Frontier homemakers could not replace their sewing tools easily. Their principal source was the general store, often miles away in a town. They often had to wait until the traveling peddler came along.

The American pioneer woman worked hard, and sewing was only a small part of it. She bore and raised the children, worked in the fields, and tended the vegetable garden and domestic livestock. She cooked and preserved food, made the soap and candles, and helped defend the family from all perils. Her needlework consisted of creating the necessary family clothing and household linens. When any of these became beyond repair, pieces were salvaged to make a patchwork quilt. Nothing useful was ever discarded.

Those women who were able to find the time to do fancy needlework were of the class that had more leisure time. These ladies preferred the word "genteel" to describe themselves and usually did not include the busy pioneer women. Fancy needlework was a parlor or social activity.

The finest and most ornate sewing tools were saved for this purpose. Sewing tools often were mentioned in personal diaries and journals, as well as in wills. This indicates how important these tools were in the every day lives in years gone by. Unfortunately, detail descriptions of these tools were not always included in the writings. We can only speculate that they were fine and ornate tools, often made of precious metals.

Our ancestors were more frugal than we are today. We have become a disposable society. When something becomes damaged or worn, we throw it away. Our ancestors mended and repaired their sewing tools. When a silver thimble became pierced from constant use, it was taken to the local silversmith to be mended. When a small round mirror on a wood sewing clamp was broken, it was replaced with something of a similar size - often a pearl button. Pin cushions were re-stuffed and recovered many times. The thought of disposing of it when it became worn was almost unthinkable in earlier days.

Many thimbles and sewing tools that were made of precious metals were received as gifts. In years past proper etiquette did not permit a young man to give his lady any gift that was personal, such as jewelry or clothing. Flowers, books, or sweets were considered proper gifts. The thimble or sewing tool somehow bridged this rule of etiquette. A fancy gold or silver thimble, engraved with a name or intials and date, was a most welcomed gift. Ornate sewing birds or needle cases were also considered acceptable. Hand made tools such as lace bobbins or a hand carved darning egg may have been gifts from a young swain who did not have the means to buy a factory made tool.

Throughout history men also sewed. Even in the Bible there is the reference to the coat of many colors that Jacob made for Joseph. Many needlework crafts were dominated by men. These include tailoring, shoemaking, sailmaking, and leather crafts. Special and specific tools were designed for these crafts.

Tools designed for a specific task became outmoded because of changes in fashions or methods. They were then discarded or relegated to the bottom of the sewing basket.

The lucet, or chain fork, is one example. This lyre-shaped tool with two horns that curved outward was used to make cording or fabric chains. Cording was needed as the drawstring on a purse, or a tie back on drapery, among other uses. Early lucets were made of ivory, horn, mother-of-pearl, or tortoise shell, often inlaid with gold. Others were made of gold and silver. Crude hand carved lucets were made of wood. Machines were invented to produce cording of better quality than hand made, and the lucet became an obsolete tool. Modern lucets are made today for the craft person who wants to revive this lost art.

Needlework produced in centuries past is now considered Folk Art. The tools used to produce this work can document the methods used to produce it. The tools, as well as the old needlework, should be collected and preserved. Fine needlework has not become extinct. It is the antique tools, methods, and lore of needlework from the past that is disappearing.

CHAPTER 2

How to Collect Thimbles and Sewing Tools

COLLECT WHAT YOU LIKE

There are many ways to approach thimble and sewing tool collecting. You can collect by material (silver thimbles), design (cupid thimbles), object (sewing birds), type (advertising thimbles), or limited edition thimbles (modern collectibles). However, in reality, there is one major thing that should determine what you collect. Collect what you like!

There are thousands of thimbles and sewing tools. The wise collector narrows her approach. This saves her money in the long run and enables her to assemble a meaningful collection.

The wonderful thing about thimble and sewing tool collecting is that there is something for everybody's budget. Collectors with unlimited funds can focus on the gold thimbles and elaborate work boxes and chatelaines. The person on a limited budget might look to advertising thimbles or 20 Pocket items.

HINTS FOR EXAMINING THIMBLES AND SEWING TOOLS

First, get the object into good light. The most ideal light is sunlight. But, this is not always available. A second choice is to place the object under a table lamp. Have the light rake the surface of the object. This enables you to see the detail and locate marks.

Second, carry a magnifying glass and loupe. In many cases, an ordinary magnifying glass will suffice. Several models, often available at your local camera store, have built in flashlights. These will enable you to view those hard to light areas, such as the inside of the cap of a thimble.

Many collectors and dealers use a ten power jeweler's loupe. If you are going to buy a loupe, invest money in a triplet loupe that prevents distortion at the end of the viewing area. The average cost for this type of loupe is thirty-five dollars.

When using a loupe, hold the loupe close to your eye, without crossing your face, and bring the object that you wish to view up to it. Have a strong light rake the surface of the object on an angle for maximum viewing detail.

Third, handle objects with great care while examining them. Ask permission from a collector or dealer before you pick up an object from a case or display. You are responsible for the object while you are examining it. If it is damaged or stolen while in your care, you will be required to pay for it.

Fourth, the most damaging element to metal objects is the oil from your skin. After handling metal objects, wipe them with a clean cloth or polishing cloth. In major museums, individuals handling metal objects are required to wear white cotton gloves. This is becoming common among coin collectors and is practical for thimble and sewing tool collectors as well.

4

RULES OF THE ROAD

Rule One: Do your homework. Don't rush out and begin buying immediately. Take time to survey the market; see what is available and at what price. Visit museums and historical societies. Go to your library or bookseller and read the books listed in the bibliography at the end of this book. Finally, find other collectors and talk with them. If you are lucky, they will invite you to look at their collections.

Rule Two: Remember, you have to live with your collection. Earlier I talked about buying things that you like. I cannot stress this enough. Beauty is in the eye of the beholder. What may look like trash to someone else, may be beauty to you. But, don't be dazzled by beauty. Try to develop an objective, rather than subjective buying approach. Buy from the head and only occasionally from the heart.

Rule Three: The major factors that should govern your purchase are age, condition, pattern, and marks. This is true for both sewing tools and thimbles.

Age alone does not make something valuable. It can be a factor, but often is overshadowed by supply and demand. An Old Sleepy Eye aluminum advertising thimble from the 1920s commands approximately two hundred dollars while an ordinary engraved silver thimble from the 1880s has a top value of fifty dollars. Silver thimbles are collected only by thimble collectors. The Old Sleepy Eye thimble also attracts the attention of collectors of products of the Old Sleepy Eye Flour Company in Minnesota in addition to the thimble collectors. Old Sleepy Eye collectors are willing to pay far more for the thimble than the thimble collectors.

This raises an important point. In many cases, the collector of thimbles and sewing tools competes for her material with collectors from other categories. The wise collector analyzes each piece and determines the potential collectors for it and the amount each group is willing to pay. The collector must make certain that the amount she pays falls within the collecting category upon which she is focusing or to whom she might have to sell if she wishes to dispose of her collection.

Age is a key factor when the thimble or tool is associated with some important event, such as a world's fair. However, there is a strong tendency by some to misdate material, usually making it much earlier than it is.

For example, the patent date on a piece indicates the year the design was patented and not the year it was made. Some designs were made for over half a century. The wise collector should apply her knowledge of historical design motifs from china, glass, furniture, and jewelry to thimbles and sewing tools. Developing this ability will enable her to at least date material within in a fifteen to twenty year period.

Condition is everything. Don't assume because a thimble or sewing implement is old that condition can be negated. Unless the item is extremely rare, do not buy anything in less than very good condition. Repaired pieces should sell for sixty to eighty percent less than pieces in excellent condition.

Completeness is also part of condition. If a work box is missing half of its implements, its value is seriously compromised. Mismatched pieces often will be combined to make what appears to be a complete set. Examine anything with parts most carefully. Make certain all parts belong together, i.e., match in material and design.

In thimbles and sewing tools, pattern and design adds value. Sewing clamps featuring birds are rather common. On the other hand, clamps in the form of a dog, butterfly, and dolphin are less common and will command a higher price. The plain pieces were the utilitarian pieces, those used on an every day basis and designed accordingly. The elaborate pieces were used for gifts and special occasions. Their high quality of workmanship was appreciated when they were made, when they were received, and today when they are collected.

A maker's mark adds potential value. Before 1860 most pieces are not marked. A marked piece preceding that date is a treasure. The maker is important. For example, two similar filigree sided thimble holders in the shape of miniwig cases, one made by Unger Brothers and the other by Foster and Bailey, would not be priced the same. The Unger Brothers holder is worth slightly more.

Beware of marks. They can be added at a later date. One of the biggest abuses is the addition of false assay value marks, e.g., adding an "84" to indicate pre-Revolution Russian origin for a piece. The collector's best defense is knowledge of the styles and designs of historical periods.

Rule Four: Do not believe everything you are told by dealers or collectors. There is a great deal of misinformation about thimbles and sewing tools. Research is being done; more and more good information is appearing in print. However, much remains to be done. Unfortunately, many individuals do not know how to say, "I do not know." Instead, they make up highly plausible stories, some of which later appear in print as valid source material. Being a bit skeptical is helpful.

Rule Five: Few names are worth money. Sellers often use recognizable names to help make a sale, ranging from the name of a museum that has a similar piece in its collection to the name of a well known collector who supposedly documented the piece. Another tactic is to claim the object came from the estate of a famous individual.

The real value of a piece is independent of all these stories. If the story is the only thing that makes the piece interesting, do not buy it.

Rule Six: Ask questions. Do not be afraid to challenge a statement made by any collector or dealer, no matter how much of an expert they may appear to be. Keep asking questions until you are satisfied that you have a valid answer. If you are not satisfied, walk away from the potential purchase or trade.

LIMITED AND UNLIMITED EDITION COLLECTIBLES

Many collectors buy modern thimbles and sewing implements. Those that buy them because they like and enjoy them are taking the right approach. Those that are buying them for investment purposes are taking a risk. Harry L. Rinker, editor of *Warman's Americana & Collectibles,* has developed Rinker's Thirty Year's Rule: "For the first thirty years of anything's life, all its value is speculative." Keep this in mind when you buy a newly made collectible.

Learn to read the description of any newly made collectible carefully. A hand decorated thimble might have a decal for the central decorative motif with a hand painted line around the rim. This is enough to qualify the thimble as being "hand decorated." This practice has been going on for centuries. The late nineteenth century German and Austrian potters put the floral and portrait motifs on their plates with decals and added a few brush strokes of color in the background to justify the hand painted label on the back.

Another concern is how limited are limited editions. In many cases, they are limited to the number of people of who sign up for them. A limited edition of 10,000 is not limited. If all those items appeared in the collectors market at one time, they would flood the market and drive the price lower and lower. The true test of value is not the initial purchase price but the price realized when the piece is sold again and again on the collectors market.

At the 1986 convention of Thimble Collectors International a series of forty-one Wedgwood King and Queen collection thimbles was offered for sale at auction. It was withdrawn when it failed to make a minimum bid of five hundred dollars. Their actual cost was in the three hundred dollar range. Bidding stopped well below actual cost.

Every collector must follow the catalogs that list limited and unlimited editions' newly created items. In many cases, the items are found in the antiques market within months of their original issue date. Knowledge is the collectors only method of protection.

WHERE TO BUY THIMBLES

The primary source for old thimbles and sewing tools still remains the antiques shops, shows, and flea markets. Check most every booth. Thimbles and sewing tools are often found in glass cases, rarely out in the open. Always look in the jewelry cases. Many jewelry dealers carry thimbles and sewing tools as important accessories to their jewelry line.

There are a few specialized dealers in this field who do appear at major shows, such as the Chicago O'Hare show, the Washington Armory show, the Miami Beach Convention Hall show, etc. They do not tend to do business through the mail. Once you have become a regular customer, they will attempt to locate material for you and will inform you when they have something you want. You will pay a higher price, but you will also avoid the costs of the hunt.

The best sources are the conventions and meeting of Thimble Collectors International, meetings of regional clubs, and fellow collectors. *Thimbletter* offers subscribers free advertisements for "wants" or "for sale" objects. It also lists names and addresses of antiques dealers and catalog companies that sell by mail. Many of these same people and companies can be found on the membership list from Thimble Collectors International.

Neither Thimble Collectors International or *Thimbletter* endorses or guarantees any of the sources. If you have an unpleasant experience, a letter to the society or editor of *Thimbletter* describing the circumstances will alert other collectors.

Modern thimbles and sewing tools can be ordered from catalogs. Some offer antique thimbles; others offer newly made "collectible" thimbles. If you want to obtain an antique item from one of these catalogs, it pays to order by phone. This insures that the item still is available and places a hold on it for you until your check arrives. Many of the dealers and companies accept credit charges. When calling by phone, keep in mind the time zones. This is especially critical if you are calling abroad.

Be aware that some of these catalogs offer reproductions of antique thimbles and sewing tools. They tend to be clearly marked. Do not trust viewing a photograph alone to place an order. Carefully read the written description so that you know clearly what you are buying.

Save any and all catalogs you receive for future reference. If the material in them is modern, you will have the date when a newly made "collectible" first appeared, a photograph of the piece, and the original price. When you buy from a catalog, make a copy of the photograph on the catalog page. It will save you the time and cost of making a photograph. Don't cut up the catalog unless you have a duplicate.

The collecting of thimbles and sewing tools is international. Therefore, it is likely that you will be buying from one or more firms or dealers from abroad. Some of these accept credit cards; others do not. A few accept personal checks in dollars. But, reality is that you will be entering into the world of international money drafts.

Large city banks sell international drafts payable in foreign currency. The fee for these drafts vary from bank to bank. The United States Postal Service also sells foreign currency money orders. Check both the bank and post office to see which method is cheapest for you to use.

The cost for placing an overseas call is not expensive, especially if you place the call yourself or call at off peak hours. If you are calling Europe, dial the call prior to 7:00 AM. You take advantage of the cheap night rates and reach the European firms and dealers during their regular business hours.

American Mail Order Catalogs

Andre China & Gifts, P. O. Box 6685, Burbank, CA 91510
Eleanor Brand, 5613 Cranberry Place, Dayton, OH 45410
Carradus Collectibles, Route 2, Box 88, Dundee, IA 52038
James Derirjian, 1166 Rosedale Avenue, Glendale, CA 91201
Downs Showcase, 2778 S. 35th Street, Milwaukee, WI 52315
Dine American, Brandywine Hundred 2C7, 400 Foulk Rd., Wilmington, DE 19804
Franklin Mint, Franklin Center, PA 19091
Kit Frobel, 10002 Ney Street, Houston,TX 77034
Gimbel and Sons, P. O. Box 57, Boothbay Harbor, ME 04538
Heritage Crafts, 10966 Sutter Way, Nevada City, CA 95959
P. J. W. Thimbles, P. O. Box 30831, Bethesda, MD 20814
Thimbles Only, 511 West Glenoaks Blvd., Suite 122, Glendale, CA 91202
Thimbles & Things, 5955 S.W. 179th Street, Beaverton, OR 97007
Art Woeltje, 5155 East Farmdale Avenue, Mesa, AZ 85206

Foreign Catalogs

Cashs, St. Patrick Street, Cork, Ireland
Sonia Cordell, 13A St. Peters Street, Ipswich, Suffolk, England
Charterhouse Mint Ltd., 64 Charlotte Street, London, England
De Vingerhoed, Bos En Vaartlaan 34, 1181 AB Amstelveen, Holland
Charles Iles & Gomms Ltds., Tyseley Industrial Estate,
    Seeleys Road, Greet, Birmingham B11 2LF, England
Feldmann, Burgplatz 18, D-4000 Dusseldorf 1, West Germany
Lawleys, Swift House, Liverpool Road, Newcastle, Staffordshire, ST5 9JJ, England
The Thimble Collectors Guild, Thistle Mill Station Road,
    Biggar ML12 6LP, Scotland
Thimble Exchange Circle, 63 Cranbourne Gardens, London
    NW11 0JP, England
Thimble Society of London, Gray's Antique Market,
    58 Davies Street, London W1, England

New catalog sale companies are announced in the *Bulletin* and *Thimbletter.* Some of these catalog companies are short lived. They will cease doing business without any notice.

CATALOGING YOUR COLLECTION

Do not wait to catalog your collection. Begin with the first piece that you buy. The longer you delay, the harder it will be to do. Cataloging requires discipline. It is not as much fun as buying the pieces. But, the long term rewards of a good inventory catalog will be reaped again and again.

A good cataloging system should include the following information: (1) catalog number, (2) object, (3) description of the object including material, size, and other related data, (4) condition, (5) approximate age, (6) country of origin, (7) maker or manufacturer, (8) marks, (9) reference information and provenance, (10) acquisition information (date acquired, from whom acquired, cost, and location of receipt), (11) current value, and (12) where the object is located in your collection.

The size of a catalog sheet can vary, from a three by five card to a full eight by eleven and one-half inch sheet. The key is to be consistent.

When designing your catalog form, it is wise to leave space for a photograph of the object. Photographs are especially valuable when a large collection is involved. They also are a help for insurance purposes. Hints for photographing your collection are found in the next section.

Most collectors use a numbering system to identify their objects. The easiest method is to number the first object you buy as "1" and proceed accordingly. Individuals with larger collections separate them by using a prefix before the number to indicate a grouping, e.g., material or style. Numbers with the prefix "A" can indicate advertising related objects while numbers with a prefix "SS" can indicate Sterling silver. Tailor the system to fit your own collecting needs.

No collector wants the price he paid or the current value of his collection to be public knowledge. Therefore, most use a code on their catalog sheet. One code is to select of one or two words that have nine letters, none of which are repeats. For example:

B A L T I M O R E
1 2 3 4 5 6 7 8 9

A letter that is not included in the secret word, in this case it may be "S" or "Y" can be added to represent the zero. A thimble that cost $35.00 would then be coded to read "LIYY." I do not use a decimal point to indicate dollars and cents. I know by looking whether the object is a $3,500 piece or a $35.00 piece.

Do not forget to pay special attention to recording reference material and provenance in your catalog. If your thimble or sewing object is identical to one pictured in a book or article, record the name of the book and page number.

If your object belonged to a famous person or collector, appeared on exhibit at a museum or historical society, was purchased as part of a famous catalog sale, or was used as an illustration in an article that you or another collector wrote, record this information as part of the object's provenance.

The computer is a modern fact of life. More and more collectors have access to a home computer. If you are going to catalog your collection on a computer, make certain that you obtain a friendly data base software program with enough field and space potential to answer your needs.

Currently, there is only one data base program designed for cataloging antiques and collectibles. This is the "Rink-Rite" system using an MS-DOS operating system. Information about the program can be obtained by writing Rink-Rite, P. O. Box 275, Zionsville, PA 18092. Other programs are currently in design. Keep your eyes on the antiques and trade publications for more information about them.

PHOTOGRAPHING YOUR COLLECTION

Photographs are important both for cataloging and insurance purposes. Photographing small items such as thimbles and sewing tools requires special equipment and skills. The best place to start is your local library followed by your local camera shop.

I use a thirty-five millimeter camera with a macro-lens. I do the bulk of my work in black and white for record purposes and colored slides for lecture purposes. I have both a copy stand and studio setting using a back drop and tripod. I spend a lot of time and money on film. What works for me may not work best for you.

There are two suggestions that may prove helpful. First, do not become involved in developing and printing your own film unless you already are a skill amateur photographer. The time this takes away from your collecting really adds up. Second, check around your neighborhood for a good amateur photographer or club. They often welcome filming challenges. Usually, all you pay for is their film and developing materials. However, check out carefully anyone with whom you intend to work.

Some collectors have turned to the copying machine as a means of making a record of the items in their collection. The copy will suffice for identification purposes. Place the object to be copied on the glass of the copying machine. Cover the objects with a sheet of white paper and gently put the cover down.

Thimbles will tend to roll around on the glass. Use some of the new tape with a minimum sticky surface to hold them in place. Make certain all tape residue is removed from the thimbles after the copying is completed.

Copying will never duplicate the quality of a photograph. The method is best used only for your personal catalog system. If your object is being used as an illustration in a book or article, a photograph is a must.

COLLECTORS' CLUBS - NATIONAL AND REGIONAL

Thimble Collectors International (6411 Montego Bay, Louisville, KY 40228) is the major, non-profit international collectors' club. Membership is open to everyone. Members receive a quarterly newsletter, *Bulletin,* that includes news about events such as meetings of regional collecting groups, regional and national conventions, questions and answers, reproduction alert, and research articles. Thimble Collectors International publishes a membership directory which is most helpful in contacting other collectors in your area.

Thimble Collectors International also maintains a library of books, articles, and other material relating to thimbles and sewing tools. Material can be borrowed from the library by members for the price of postage. When permitted, the librarian will make photocopies of desired material for a collector's private reference library at a nominal cost.

Thimble Collectors International holds biannual conventions lasting anywhere from three to five days. Conventions feature research papers, slide presentations, panels of experts, displays, special forum for new collectors, sales mall, and numerous informal exchange of ideas.

There are approximately twenty regional thimble collectors' clubs. While not formally part of the Thimble Collectors International, they receive guidance from the national organization. Collectors can find the location of the club nearest them by writing Thimble Collectors International. While it is not necessary to be a member of Thimble Collectors International to belong to a regional club, it is highly recommended.

Caution: Some commercial enterprises use the word "Club" as part of their name. Do not confuse this business with a real non-profit collectors' club. Their catalog may be a combination of a newsletter and sales catalog. In this case, a "membership" or "subscription" fee is required to get the catalog. The name "club" is a sales gimmick to give the collector a feeling of joining and camaraderie with other collectors. No officers will be elected; members do not have a vote. Their membership list is the list of their customers; it is their stock and trade. Do not expect a commercial enterprise to share their list with you.

PERIODICAL

Thimbletter (Lorraine Crosby, Editor, 93 Walnut Hill Road, Newton Highlands, MA 02161), a bi-monthly publication available to subscribers, contains articles about thimbles and sewing tools along with announcements of new catalogs and dealers who specialize in sewing implements. A question and answer column and advertisements appear in this publication. A sample copy can be obtained for one dollar.

SELLING DUPLICATES OR A WHOLE COLLECTION

If you have duplicates, you can sell them to obtain money to buy additional pieces for your collection or you can trade them. Among thimble and sewing tool collectors trading is a very important means of enhancing and upgrading a collection.

The skills involved in trading material are learned through experience. When trading on a dollar for dollar value make certain that the dollar level is identical in both cases. Do not value your piece at wholesale when the other piece is valued at retail. The best advice is to put value aside and focus on what the new addition means to your collection. Only you know how it will relate to the other pieces that you own.

Selling material requires persistence, patience, and finesse. Determine a minimum price at which you will sell and do not go below it. A good price is when both the buyer and seller are happy.

Fairly evaluate the material that you have for sale. If you are selling average material, you will have to price it well below market for a quick sale. Most collectors have the basic pieces already as part of their collection. The rarer or choicer a piece, the easier it will be to sell it.

An accurate inventory of the material you want to sell is critical. The listing must be complete, meaning that it should include at least the first nine items from your catalog sheet. Photographs or copies of photographs also are helpful.

More and more sales are taking place through the mail. Thimbles and sewing tools lend themselves to this approach quite well. Place advertisements for them in antiques and collectibles trade papers. There are many fine publications. The largest one is *The Antique Trader Weekly*, P. O. Box 1050, Dubuque, IA 52001. Ask prospective buyers to send an SASE (self addressed, stamped envelope).

Doing business by mail requires attention to detail and trust. Do not send anything on approval. Get the money first. Be prepared to give a money back guarantee, no explanations necessary. The mail order business relies on honesty and reputation for its principal means of success.

The second selling choice is to an established dealer. He has to make a profit, he will not be prepared to pay top dollar. Ideally he will buy at about half of the market value.

There are other choices. Precious metals can be sold to a jeweler by weight. Unfortunately, this removes the thimble or sewing tool from the market on a permanent basis. I don't recommend this.

If you have a truly rare piece, approach museums or historical organizations with strong collections in this area. They may be willing to talk to you about a purchase, especially if the price is well below market. Of course, the museums and historical organizations would be delighted if you donated the material and took a tax benefit.

There is no established method for selling an entire collection. No major collection of thimbles or sewing tools from a leading American collector has been sold by a large auction house. The Lundquist sale was handled by the law firm representing the estate. The final disposition left many collectors disappointed with the results.

Two major collections were sold abroad. In November 1975 the Collection of Baron Seilliere was sold by Christie's in Geneva and in March 1987 the Collection of Mrs. Hilda Tracy was sold by Graves Son & Pilcher in East Sussex, England. The catalogs for these collection sales are difficult to obtain, but they provide a glimpse into the finalized price of material at auction.

CHAPTER 3

Sewing Folklore

"By the pricking of my thumb, something wicked this way comes."

Macbeth, by William Shakespeare.

Folklore superstitions have been associated with needlework and sewing implements over the centuries. Omens have passed from one generation to the next. Many of these old wives tales have survived into the nuclear age.

NEEDLES

Breaking a needle during ordinary sewing is considered bad luck. If it breaks while making a dress, you can expect to be kissed when wearing this dress. This is good luck.

Dropping a needle is a sign of good luck, unless it pierces the floor and stands upright. In that case, it is a sign of bad luck.

PINS

"See a pin and pick it up, and all day you'll have good luck. See a pin and let it lay, bad luck you'll have all day." This ditty has survived through the ages.

The phrase "pin money" dates back to the fifteenth century England. Pins were scarce and expensive. Women saved their pennies all year to buy pins on New Year's Day, the one day of the year that the Crown permitted merchants to sell pins.

QUILTING

To avoid bad luck, quilters deliberately made a mistake on the quilt they were making. Quilters believed that only God can make anything that is perfect.

The name of a quilt pattern was changed from "Wandering Foot" to "Turkey Tracks." It was believed that if a child slept under a quilt with the "Wandering Foot" pattern, he would grow up to be a wanderer and a rover.

A young girl was expected to complete thirteen quilts for her hope chest. Twelve were for every day use, and the thirteenth would be her bridal quilt. This last quilt could not be started until the girl was formally engaged to be married. Some thought it was bad luck for the engaged girl to make her own wedding quilt.

SCISSORS

Picking up a pair of scissors after they were dropped was considered bad luck. Someone else should pick them up for you. If no one is available to do this task, place your foot on the scissors to cancel this bad omen.

Never lay a pair of scissors down open, with the blades forming a cross. This was supposed to bring bad luck to the seamstress.

A gift of a scissors should include a small coin. The coin is returned to the giver to symbolize the purchase of the scissors. It was feared that the sharp blades would cut into the friendship.

SEWING

"As Ye Sew, So Shall Ye Rip"

If you sewed on the wrong side by mistake, and have to rip the seam, don't be upset. This is a good omen.

Never make stitches on a garment you are wearing. Superstition says "just so many stitches as you take on you, just as many lies you'll have told about you."

Any Friday, not only one that fell on the thirteenth of the month, was considered a bad luck day to cut the fabric for a new garment. To cancel this hex, a garment started on a Friday must be completed on the next day. If not, it would not be completed by the date it was to be worn.

Sewing something new on an old garment was considered bad luck. A replaced button was excluded from this hex.

Sewing on Sunday was not a good idea. "Sew on Sunday, rip out stitches on Monday."

THIMBLES

A lost thimble is a sign of bad luck. Observe how a person uses a thimble. Using the side of the thimble rather that the cap to push the needle is a sign of an expert seamstress.

Folklore says that blue bells flowers were witches' thimbles. This may explain why many thimble manufacturers decorated the band of their thimbles with blue bells.

THREAD

If thread knots and tangles while you are sewing, it is a sign that a spat will start.

Use a contrasting color thread for basting, but be sure to remove every bit of it. Superstitious people claim that remaining basting stitches are a sign that the fabric was not paid for.

Matching thread should always be used for permanent stitching. Mismatched thread is a bad omen, resulting in bad luck for the wearer of the garment.

If you are constantly having problems with your needlework, take heed. Old wives tales and superstitions may be casting a spell on you.

CHAPTER 4

Glossary of Terms

Alpacca: A silver colored alloy of copper, nickel, and zinc. Also called German silver or nickel silver.

Bright Cut: A method of engraving with a special beveled tool. Metal is removed to give a faceted sparkle to the surface.

Cartouche: A symmetrical ornamental framework, often in the form of a shield or scroll, to enclose the blank space reserved for the monogram on the band of a thimble.

Chasing: A method of removing metal.

Cloisonne: An enameling process in which colors are separated by wire. A cellular pattern is formed with soldered wire. The compartments formed by this wire are filled with enamel. The wire prevents the colors from running together. This technique was practiced in Eastern Europe, the middle East, Russia, and the Orient. (Note: See Reproduction chapter for description of fake Russian thimbles that are cast to simulate this applied wire technique.)

Coin: Found on American thimbles made before the 1860s. "Coin" usually indicates that the silver quality is between 850/1,000 and 900/1,000 parts silver.

Commemorative: A thimble issued to commemorate a place, person, or event.

Damascene: A method of decoration in which one metal is inlaid into another. A steel thimble made by Gabler in Germany was decorated with a damascene band in Spain. The Spanish "Toledo" work found on modern souvenir thimbles and scissors is damascene.

Embossing: Metal is hammered from the outside against a form with a design. Repousse and embossing produce the same design.

Enameling: Enamel is ground silica mixed with mineral colors to form a powder. This powder, when mixed with water, can be painted on metal and fired in a kiln. Different enameling techniques are practiced in Russia, Norway, and China.

Etui: A small decorative case fitted with sewing and other tools.

Faceted: Smooth surfaces similar to the facets on a gemstone.

Filigree: Open work in the metal. A filigree thimble is created with a wire design that has no metal base. The strands of wire are soldered together at the intersections. The art of filigree work is practiced in the Middle East, the Philippines, South American, and England.

Gold Filled: A method of bonding three layers of metal. The inner and outer layers are gold. The center layer is brass or other common metal. A gold filled thimble will be marked "1/20th 14k (or 10K) GF". This means that 1/20th or 5% of the total weight of the thimble is 14K (or 10K) gold. A gold filled thimble will test gold when rubbed on a testing stone with acid. See Marks chapter for other marks on gold filled thimbles.

Gold Plated: A thin layer of gold is electroplated to silver or other metal. See: Silver Gilt.

Guilloche: The decorative scoring of metal to make the enamel adhere to the metal firmly.

Gutta Percha: A hard rubber substance used to make cases for tape measures and pin cushions.

Hallmark: The mark used in countries that have a government hallmarking system, such as the United Kingdom. No hallmarking system exists in the United States.

Knurling: A method of producing indentations on a thimble by using a knurling wheel.

Indentations: The dimples on top and side of a thimble. Made by a knurling machine.

Maker's Mark: The trademark or initials of a manufacturer on a silver piece.

Mauchline: A transfer print decoration on Scottish wooden ware.

Mother-of-Pearl: The iridescent internal layer of a mollusk sea shell.

Mushroom Cap: A thimble on which the cap extends beyond the side. This shape is common in early South American silver and gold thimbles.

Pewter: Dull metal made from alloy of tin, copper, lead, antimony, or bismuth. Pewter is soft and wears with constant use.

Scrimshaw: Etched decoration on bone or ivory. Practiced by seamen during the nineteenth century. The Alaskan Eskimos and the Indians of the Caribbean also did scrimshaw work.

Silver Gilt: A thin coat of gold is electroplated to silver. Sometimes called "vermeil."

Sterling silver: 925/1000 parts silver. The word "Sterling" was used in the United States after the 1860s.

Stone Cap: Semi-precious stones such as amethyst, carnelian, and moonstone applied to the cap of a thimble to absorb the pressure of the needle.

Trademark: See Maker's mark.

Vegetable Ivory: A hard nut grown in South American. Two kinds of nuts are used to carve thimbles, thimble cases, and other small items such as buttons. The meat of the tagua nut is hard enough to be carved into a thimble or thimble case. The shell of the coroza nut is sized and shaped like a thimble. A gold cap with indentations is often applied to the top of the nut shell along with a gold band applied to the rim.

Vermeil: See Silver Gilt.

THE PARTS OF A THIMBLE

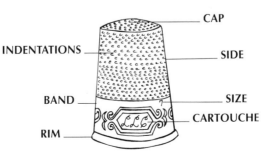

CAP

INDENTATIONS

SIDE

BAND

SIZE

CARTOUCHE

RIM

PART II

Thimbles

CHAPTER 5

Thimble Sizes and Country of Origin

SIZES

Thimbles manufactured before the late nineteenth century were not marked with the size number. Gold and silver thimbles with a size number can be dated as less than one hundred years old.

The major thimble manufacturers in the United States in 1900, i.e., Brogen, Bass, Goldsmith Stern, Gunner, Ketcham and McDougall, Simons, Stern, Waite Thresher and Webster, each had its own sizing system. They were similar, but not exactly the same.

Thimble sizes are not standard. Each country has its own thimble sizing system.

Approximate Thimble Size Comparison

COUNTRY	CHILD	SMALL	MEDIUM	LARGE
United States	1,2,3,4,5	6,7,8	9,10,11	12,13,14
Germany & Holland	1,2	3,4	5,6,7	8,9,10
England	10,11,12	9,8,7	6,5	4,3,2,1
France	4,5,6,7	8	9,10	11,12
Norway		1	2,3	4

Sizes one through five in the United States are children's sizes and often were sold in nests or sets of three graduated sizes. This allowed the child to graduate into the next size thimble as she grew. It is rare to find a child's size thimble that has been pierced by a needle after constant use. A small child would normally outgrow a thimble before it wore out. A child's size thimble that is pierced was probably passed from one child to another as it was outgrown.

Celluloid and plastic thimbles usually were produced in one size. The number that may appear inside the cap is a mold number and not a size number. The interior taper of plastic thimbles made them comfortable on most size fingers.

The taper of the interior of the thimble effects the fit. Occasionally, an old thimble is found with nail polish painted in the interior of the thimble. This was done to make the thimble slightly smaller.

Thimbles were never manufactured in a oval shape. Thimbles with oval openings may have been bent to that shape to create a comfortable fit.

COUNTRY OF ORIGIN

The country of origin of a thimble often can be determined by its shape, decoration, size numbering, and marks. The thimbles illustrated in this book are organized first by country of origin and second by design. To determine the country of origin, carefully consider the following:

In the nineteenth century both the English and American used a dome cap on their thimbles. However, the English thimbles had a taller proportion than their American counterparts. The flat top thimble is a twentieth century American style.

Most French thimbles had a waffle or rectangular indentation pattern on the sides. The German thimbles tended to follow the English style. Marks are critical in separating the two groups. Norwegian thimbles tend to be smooth sided. Indentations appeared only on the cap, either in metal or semi-precious stone.

American thimbles are noted for their scenic presentations, especially waterfronts and agrarian scenes. English thimbles are famous for their overall floral design. The French are renowned for their elaborate gold thimbles, often in more than one color of gold, decorated with enamel or semi-precious stones. Norwegian thimbles often had enameled decoration over guilloche.

The sizing codes for various countries are listed above. Once you have handled a number of thimbles, the size code will become apparent.

When looking at the marks on thimbles, look for two key things. First, find the maker's mark. When you know the maker, the country is obvious. Second, look for the location of the mark. American and Norwegian thimbles normally are marked inside the cap. A few are marked on the band. English and French marks usually appear on the band. German marks are commonly found on the second row of the indentations.

Additional details about maker's marks and their locations are covered in the chapters that follow as well as the mark section in Chapter 32 of this book.

CHAPTER 6

How Precious is the Metal?

Many thimbles and sewing tools made in gold and silver were not marked prior to the mid-nineteenth century. Their low weight exempted them from the required assay mark.

After approximately 1860, gold and silver thimbles and sewing tools were marked with a maker's mark and/or an assay mark. Pieces made in foreign countries usually carry an assay mark. The transition between marking and non-marking took several decades.

If a collector is in doubt about the metallic content of her thimble or sewing tool, a jeweler should be able to test it. Testing involves the use of acid; therefore, I do not recommend that the collector do this on her own at home. It is best to have it done by a professional.

Some thimbles and sewing tools are electroplated or have a layer or layers of precious metal over a base metal interior layer. A jeweler should be asked to determine the method of manufature as well as its composition.

GOLD

There are four popular colors of gold: yellow gold (consisting of a mixture of gold, copper, and silver), white gold (consisting of a mixture of gold, nickel, zinc, and copper), pink gold (consisting of gold and copper), and green gold (consisting of gold, silver, copper, and zinc). Pure gold is too soft to be used alone. Gold is combined with these other metals to make it more durable. The proportion of these metals to gold is measured by karats in the United States and straight decimals in Europe.

Karat gold is measured by 24ths. Twenty-four karat gold is pure. The grades used commercially in the United States are:

18k which is .750 gold and .250 alloy
14k which is .583 gold and .417 alloy
10k which is .416 gold and .584 alloy

The law governing gold in the United States is the National Stamping Act of 1906. This act requires manufacturers to stamp their trademark on gold pieces where the fineness is displayed. An amendment to this act took effect in 1981 requiring that all karat gold must be within .003 (three one-thousandths) of the karat marked on the piece.

Jewelers measure gold weight by pennyweights, abbreviated "dwt." There are twenty-four pennyweights to one troy ounce. In the metric system a penny-weight equals 1.555 grams.

Gold does not tarnish. Sometimes it leaves a black smudge on the skin of some individuals. The problem is not the gold but the alloys in the gold reacting with the acidity level of the individual. The body's acids can react with those alloys, thus creating the black smudge.

SILVER

The United States Stamping Act of 1906 required that any piece marked with the word "STERLING" contain 925 parts of silver out of one thousand; the remaining 75 parts could be alloys. The Sterling mark is not a hallmark system.

The English and several European countries use a hallmark system. When an object is made, it is taken to an assay office to be tested for quality. Pieces that pass the quality test are marked in accordance with the assay system of the country.

In England the mark will be a lion to indicate the quality (Sterling), a maker's mark or initials, the assay office mark, and a letter mark to indicate the year of assay. An English silver marks chart is needed to translate these marks.

The French assay mark is a Mercury head. The boar's head mark indicates it was assayed at the Paris office, and the crab mark means that it was assayed in the provinces. A maker's touchmark is added.

The Swedish assay mark consists of three crowns. The letter "S" indicates silver. Swedish silver is well below the Sterling standard. Initials identify the maker. Assay office and date marks can be interpreted through a chart.

German marks appear on the second row of the indentations on the outside of thimbles. Most other countries require marks to be stamped inside the cap or on the band of a thimble. The German mark will indicate the quality level of the silver, either "800" or "830." This is lower than the Sterling standard of England and the United States. Thimbles with the word "Germany" date between 1891 and 1941. Thimbles marked "West Germany" date from 1945.

CHAPTER 7

Gold Thimbles

Thimbles sometimes symbolized a secret kiss. Barrie enthusiasts will recall the misunderstanding which arose between Peter Pan and Little Wendy, which resulted in Peter giving her "thimbles," meaning kisses. Thimbles were always considered an appropriate gift for a gentleman to give to a lady. A thimble made of gold was a very special gift.

HISTORIC GOLD THIMBLES

Early American gold thimbles were hand made by local silversmiths. Few of these were marked with the maker's mark or gold content, as there was no marking law in the United States until the last quarter of the nineteenth century. Customers had to rely on the integrity of the craftsman.

Early, unmarked gold thimbles are difficult to date. The shape of a thimble and its decoration give clues to the era it was made. American thimbles made during the seventeenth and eighteenth centuries were hand made. Early ones were flat and seamed like a lamp shade. The cap was applied and hand punched. The seam may be visible on the inside of the thimble. During the eighteenth century, a thimble was made from a disk of metal that was hammered into shape with a thimble stamp. Engraved hearts and flowers were popular decorations during this period.

Shapes and decorations on the early American thimbles are different from the machine made thimbles of the late nineteenth and twentieth centuries. Many fine examples of both eras are on display at leading museums or recent auctions.

Gold thimbles made by Samuel Vernon of Newport, Rhode Island, were marked. His mark, "S.V." enclosed in a heart, appeared on a gold thimble that was sold at auction by Sotheby's, New York, in 1983. It can be dated circa 1720. The final sales price was $6,000, well over the original estimate of $2,000-3,000. This thimble is presently in a private collection.

A gold thimble made by the Boston silversmith, John Hurd, is in the archives of Yale University Art Gallery. It is marked "Hurd" enclosed in an oval and engraved with the name of Elizabeth Gooch. It was made during the 1730s.

The gold thimble Paul Revere made for his daughter is in the Boston Museum of Fine Arts. It is tall and tapered, with a dome cap, and engraved with her name in fine script.

A tall French gold thimble is in the collection of the Metropolitan Museum of Art, New York. The thimble has two garlands of arrow shaped leaves. The thimble is too tall to be used for sewing. Thimble collectors refer to this style as a "wedding band" thimble. One garland can be removed to make a wedding band. The thimble then becomes a normal usable size.

The Metropolitan Museum of Art offers a reproduction of this thimble in its gift shop. The reproduction is made of gold plated silver and clearly marked "M.M.A. 925."

In 1913, the King of Siam, (now known as Thailand), commissioned a Paris jeweler to design a thimble as a wedding anniversary gift to the Queen. This thimble was made of pure gold in the shape of a half open lotus blossom, the emblem of the Royal House. It was encrusted with diamonds and other precious stones, arranged to form the Queen's name. The thimble cost $5,000, an enormous sum at that time.

COLLECTIBLE GOLD THIMBLES

The average gold thimble weighs between 2 and 3 pennyweights (dwt.). There are 20 dwt. to a troy ounce of gold. A 14k thimble has slightly more than half its weight in gold: 14/24 or 58% gold. The balance of the metal are different alloys, depending on the color of the gold: green gold, red gold, or yellow gold.

Historical gold thimbles are not likely to surface at antique shows or flea markets. Documented historical gold thimbles are offered by auction houses or donated directly to a museum.

Gold thimbles found in the antiques market today are usually less than 100 years old. Plain, unadorned gold thimbles have less collectible value than an ornate one.

ENAMELED GOLD THIMBLES

Gold thimbles with enameled bands were popular during the second half of the nineteenth century, although enameling on gold thimbles date from the fourteenth century. A transparent enamel was applied over guilloche, a decorative scoring or scratching of the metal. This permitted the enamel to adhere firmly to the metal. The decorative scoring can be seen through the enamel and adds to the design.

Black enamel decorations on gold thimbles were popular during the Victorian era. Black was a symbol for mourning. After the death of Prince Albert, Queen Victoria wore jewelry with black decorations. Black became the vogue during the late Victorian period. It was also the color used on jewelry and buttons, as well as thimbles.

Enamel on metal is very delicate and easily chipped. Check the enamel carefully with a magnifying glass to see if there are any chips or repairs on the enamel. Chipped or repaired enamel detracts from the value considerably.

GOLD WITH APPLIED STONES

Many gold thimbles are decorated with precious and semi-precious stones, e.g., diamonds, rubies, sapphires, seed pearls, coral, and turquoise. Missing or damaged stones detract from the value of the thimble. Likewise, replaced stones that do not match in color or size reduce the value.

DECORATED BANDS

Gold thimbles with bands decorated with engraving or designs in high relief are available. Those with a maker's mark and the karet mark are from the late nineteenth century or twentieth century.

Gold thimbles with no decorations are considered fine sewing tools, but not highly collectible thimbles.

CONDITION

The price of a gold thimble depends on the age, decorations, and condition. The current spot price of gold does not completely control the price of a gold thimble.

A pierced or damaged thimble has less value than one in perfect condition. The fact that it is gold should not dazzle the collector and cause her to ignore the damage. A magnifying glass will help you recognize a repaired thimble. Only a qualified silversmith should repair a thimble that has been pierced by a needle.

GOLD FILLED

The names "gold filled," "gold plated," and "gold washed" are used interchangeable in the antiques trade by people who do not know the correct jewelry vocabulary. No thimble is made of "solid gold", which means 24 karats. The metal would be too soft.

A "gold filled" thimble is made of three layers of metal: two layers of gold, and a "stiffening" center layer of brass or other common metal. This process produced a thimble with all the beauty of gold, but with more durability. The outer layer of gold will test as gold when rubbed on a stone with testing acid. Some nineteenth century thimble makers used a special mark to indicate they were gold filled. (See Marks, Chapter 32). Later, the law required these to be marked: "1/20 10k G.F.", i.e., 5% of the total weight of the thimble is 10k gold. Many older gold filled thimbles have rolled rims, to hide the inner core of "stiffening" metal, but not all thimbles with rolled rims are gold filled.

"Gold plated" thimbles have been electroplated with a thin layer of gold which tends to wear off quickly.

There is no process called "gold wash." The term is used by people who are not familiar with jewelry terminology.

INITIALS AND NAMES

Thimbles may have a cartouche, a blank space on the band where initials or monogram can be engraved. Engraved monogram do not diminish the value of a thimble. A date may be included with the monogram, which will help date the thimble.

Gold thimbles often were received as gifts. Many show no sign of wear from constant use. This may result from the ill fit of the thimble or from it simply being too elegant for mundane work.

7-1: American gold thimble made by Samuel Vernon, Newport, RI, circa 1720. Photo courtesy of Sotheby's, New York.

7-2: French two color gold thimble. Nineteenth century. Photo courtesy of the Metropolitan Museum of Art; 7-3: American gold thimble made by Jacob Hurd, circa 1730–40. Photo courtesy of Yale University Art Gallery.

7-4: English. Rubies on rim. Nineteenth century. 7-5: English. Alternating pearls and rubies on rim. Nineteenth century. 7-6: American. Alternating turquoise and seed pearls on band.

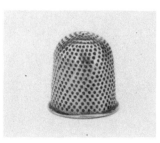

7-7: Dome capped gold. Sixteenth century. Unmarked.

26

7-8, 7-9, 7-10: Typical American gold thimbles. Twentieth century.

7-11, 7-12, 7-13: Typical American gold thimbles. Twentieth century.

7-14, 7-15, 7-16: Typical American gold thimbles. Twentieth century.

7-17, 7-18, 7-19: Typical American gold thimbles. Early twentieth century.

7-20, 7-21, 7-22: Typical American gold thimbles with scenic bands. Twentieth century.

7-23, 7-24, 7-25: American scenic. Late nineteenth, early twentieth centuries.

27

7-26, 7-27, 7-28: Typical American gold thimbles with scenic bands; 7-28: Three masted sailing ship in relief.

7-29, 7-30, 7-31: American gold with birds in relief on band. Late nineteenth, early twentieth centuries.

7-32, 7-33, 7-34: Ornate American gold thimble. Early twentieth century; 7-32 and 7-34: Pierced band.

7-35, 7-36, 7-37: Ornate American. Early twentieth century gold; 7-35: Bluebell flowers, sometimes referred to as "Witches Thimbles" flowers; 7-36: Basket weave with one diamond.

7-38, 7-39, 7-40: Continental. Gold thimble. Late eighteenth, early nineteenth centuries.

7-41, 7-42, 7-43: Typical Continental gold thimbles with scalloped rims.

7-44, 7-45, 7-46: Typical Continental gold thimbles.

7-47, 7-48, 7-49: Typical Continental gold thimbles. Paneled bands. Nineteenth century.

7-50, 7-51, 7-52: Typical Continental gold thimbles. Scenes enclosed in ovals. Nineteenth century. Often unmarked.

7-53, 7-54, 7-55: Typical Continental gold thimbles. Dome caps and shield cartouche. Nineteenth century.

7-56, 7-57, 7-58: Continental. Decorated in high relief; 7-56: Four color gold decorations; 7-57: Four diamonds on band; 7-58: Alternating diamonds and rubies around the band.

7-59, 7-60, 7-61: Continental gold with coral stones on band. Nineteenth century.

29

7-62, 7-63, 7-64: Typical Continental. Nineteenth century; 7-62: "Forget-me-not."

7-65, 7-66, 7-67: Continental, Gold with semi-precious stone caps. 7-67: Four color gold decorated band with pearls and turquoise.

7-68, 7-69, 7-70: Colorful enamel floral bands. Continental. Nineteenth century.

7-71, 7-72, 7-73: Hand made gold. Continental. Eighteenth century.

7-74, 7-75, 7-76: Typical English gold. Twentieth century.

7-77, 7-78, 7-79: Black enamels on band. Typical of the Victorian era.

7-80, 7-81, 7-82: Black enamel
decorations on bands. Typical of
the Victorian era.

7-83: Gold. Commemorating the
coronation of King George and
Queen Mary.

7-84, 7-85, 7-86: Black enamel
decorations on bands. Typical of
the Victorian era.

7-87, 7-88, 7-89: Black enamel
on bands. Typical of the Victorian era.

7-90, 7-91, 7-92: Black enamel
on bands. Typical of the Victorian era.

31

7-93, 7-94, 7-95: Gold. Geometric decorated bands.

7-96, 7-97, 7-98: Gold. Geometric decorated bands.

7-99, 7-100, 7-101: Typical French. Gold decorated in relief. Ninteenth century.

7-102, 7-103, 7-104: Typical French. Gold decorated in relief. Nineteenth century.

7-105, 7-106, 7-107: Typical French. Late nineteenth or early twentieth centuries.

7-108, 7-109, 7-110: Traditional French with dome cap and shield cartouche. Nineteenth century.

7-111, 7-112, 7-113: Scandinavian gold with semi-precious
stone caps. Nineteenth century.

7-114, 7-115, 7-116: Scandinavian, with semi-precious stone
caps.

7-117, 7-118, 7-119: Scandinavian gold with semi-precious
stone caps. Nineteenth century.

7-120: American. Gold, roses in
relief; 7-121: Continental with
medieval warrior's head; 7-122:
American "embroidery" thimble.

7-123: Typical South American
with mushroom cap; 7-124, 7-
125: American gold with applied
cap. Gold. Late eighteenth, early
nineteenth centuries.

7-126, 7-127, 7-128: Handmade
gold thimbles. Unmarked. Unknown origin.

CHAPTER 8

Silver Thimbles

Silver thimbles are the popular choice of many collectors. Prices have doubled during the 1980s. Collectors must be selective and learn the difference between a fine collectible silver thimble and one that is quite ordinary. Age, condition, pattern, and marks are the points that should be considered.

AGE: The age alone does not make a thimble highly collectible. Family history is the weakest link in documentation. The fact that it belonged to someone's grandmother does not add value per se.

CONDITION: The condition of a thimble is critical and strongly influences the value. Any thimble that is bent, pierced, has chipped enamel, has stones missing, or is worn should be avoided whenever possible. A damaged thimble with a scarce or desirable pattern could be added to a collection temporarily with the hopes of eventually finding one in better condition at a later time.

Silver is a soft metal and can be pierced by a needle after constant use. Years ago women took their favorite silver thimble to a silversmith to be mended when it became pierced. Otherwise, it was relegated to the bottom of the sewing basket or the "melting pot," when it was no longer useful.

No thimble was ever manufactured with "vent holes" in the cap or side, as antiques dealers often tell their customers. If a woman wanted a "ventilated" open top thimble, she bought a tailor's or quilter's thimble. These were made by the thimble factory without a cap.

Thimbles were never made in an oval shape. It may have been bent to an oval shape by the original owner to create a comfortable fit. An out-of-round thimble is considered damaged and is difficult to repair. This task should be done by someone who knows how to work on silver and has the proper tools. Even so, there is no guarantee that the thimble will not crack during the attempt to repair it.

PATTERNS: Silver thimbles were made in a wide variety of patterns. Many thimbles that were made as souvenirs of places, people, or events have the same pattern as souvenir spoons. Many highly collectible patterns have been reproduced in recent years. (See Chapter 31 on Reproductions and Fakes.)

Most thimbles have indentations on the cap and side, with the decoration on the band. Thimbles that are decorated on the cap and down the side to the rim are called embroidery thimbles.

Decorations on the band are made in various patterns. Some are in high relief, low relief (similar to a coin), engraved, or bright cut. Foliage, scrolls, cupids, garlands, and scenes can be found on the bands of silver thimbles. Farm scenes and harbor scenes were popular during the early part of this century. A blank space or cartouche often appears on a thimble for engraving initials and dates.

Most silver thimbles were made with a blank band. The decorations were added by hand or machine at the factory. An exception to this was Patent 247,384, issued to Hugh McDougall of the Ketchum and McDougall Company on September 20, 1881. This patent was for a one-step method of making thimbles with the indentations on the cap and side and the decoration on the band. The separate decorating step was eliminated. The patent date, "PAT. SEP.20,'81" appears on many thimbles made by this method. Remember, this is the date the method of manufacturing was patented, not the date the thimble was made.

MARKS: Most thimbles made during the nineteenth century and earlier may have no marks. Marks on thimbles started to appear after the second half of the nineteenth century. The type of mark and its location will give you a rough clue to the country of origin.

American silver thimbles are usually marked inside the cap or on the band. British thimbles will have a series of marks on the band. These will be the maker's mark, the assay mark, and the date mark. German thimbles are marked with the silver content on the second row of the indentations. French thimbles are marked with a tiny punch mark near the rim. This mark will appear as a dent inside the thimble. Russian thimbles have a punch mark on the rim.

Close "in hand" examination of these various thimble marks will tell you where a thimble was made. Always carry a magnifying glass when you are searching for thimbles. The more opportunities you have to closely examine thimbles, the more knowledgeable you will become.

AMERICA

Most silver thimbles were imported during the American colonial era, but some were made in the colonies by local silversmiths. Many of these were tall, tapered, and had a steel cap. Most were unmarked. One of an apprentice silversmith's first task was to make a thimble.

Thimble factories were established in the United States during the second quarter of the nineteenth century. George Washington Simons established his thimble factory in Philadelphia in 1839. George, the American born son of English immigrants, was apprenticed at an early age to the Philadelphia silversmith, Jacob Stockman. It was here that he learned the art of making thimbles. By the time he was twenty years old, he had established his own silversmith shop. The Simons Brothers Company still produces silver and gold thimbles in Philadelphia, Pennsylvania.

In 1832 Ezra Prime and John Rushmore established a thimble factory, later to be known as Ketchum and McDougall, in Huntington, Long Island, New York. The Ketchum and McDougall Company was known as "The Thimble House," as thimble making was their main business and not a sideline. This company still is in business in New Jersey, manufacturing marine instruments. They discontinued the manufacturing of thimbles in 1932.

During the second half of the nineteenth century, two German jewelers left their native land to seek better opportunities in the United States. Both of these immigrants found success in their new country.

Henry Muhr arrived in Philadelphia in 1853 with his wife and eight-year-old son, Simon. He opened a watch repair shop with four hundred dollars he brought with him from Germany. Two more sons were born to the Muhrs. As each became of age, they joined the family firm. In 1892 an advertisement appeared in the Business Directory of Philadelphia listing the company name as H. Muhr's Sons. They manufactured watch cases, jewelry, and thimbles and had offices in New York, Chicago, and Antwerp, Belgium.

In 1863 Nathan Stern arrived in Philadelphia. He worked for Muhr from 1863 to 1868, and then established his own business.

In 1871 he moved his firm to New York. By 1890, the firm was located at 30 Maiden Lane, New York. The catalog issued that year showed forty-six different patterns of thimbles made of gold, gold filled, and silver. Nathan's sons had joined the firm. It was now known as Stern Brothers.

In 1913 the Stern Brothers company merged with the Goldsmith Company, and the new name of the company became Goldsmith, Stern and Company. The trade mark was changed from a small "B" and "C" enclosed in a larger block "S" to a block "G" enclosing a smaller "S" and "C". The Stern Brothers and the Goldsmith Stern mark will appear on the same pattern thimble. The one with the Stern mark is older.

GERMANY

The best known thimbles from Germany were made by the Gabler factory. The factory was established in 1824 when Ferdinand Gabler received a charter from the King of Bruttenburg.

Gabler thimbles can be recognized by the eight pointed daisy that is stamped on the cap of the thimble. They were made in a wide variety of patterns in both silver and gold and are considered very desirable as a collectible thimble.

A silver Gabler thimble will be marked on the second row of the indentations. Silver will be marked 800, or 835S if made for export. This is lower than the 925/1000 silver standard in the United States.

Gabler thimbles were shipped world wide until the beginning of World War I. The company returned to making thimbles at the war's end, but the thimble manufacturers in other countries took away many of their customers. Gabler continued in business on a smaller scale, until it closed it's factory in 1963.

FRANCE

The marks on French thimbles are distinctive. France is the only country that requires the silver marks to be struck with a mallet on an anvil. This process leaves a dent that is visible on the inside of the thimble. The marks are the maker's marks enclosed in a diamond shaped cartouche, and the assay mark. The assay mark will be either a boar's head to indicate it was made in Paris or a crab for the provinces. These tiny marks are difficult to see even with a magnifying glass.

The French thimble maker P. Lenain made a series of thimbles commemorating the Fables of La Fontaine. This series was first produced during the early decades of this century. A second striking from the original dies was issued during the 1970s. The first series will bear the maker's and assay marks. The second strike will also have the word "France" stamped on the rim. The modern series is gilted inside the thimble.

The Fables of La Fontaine thimbles include "The Two Doves," "The Monkey and the Cat," (Bertrand and Raton), "The Wolf and the Lamb," "The Wolf as a Shepherd," "The Hare and the Tortoise," " The Dairymaid and Her Milk-Pot," plus several others. Several other patterns that were not original Fables were added to the series. Among these are "Little Red Riding Hood" and "The Monkey and the Magic Lantern."

RUSSIA

Many people refer to all Russian thimbles as "Fabergé." The name Fabergé has somehow become the generic term for all Russian silver pieces. It is possible that Carl Fabergé or one of his workmasters did make thimbles, but all Russian thimbles were not made by Fabrege.

Beautiful Russian silver thimbles with enamel or niello were made in Russia before the revolution of 1917. Genuine ones are priced in the three and four figure range. Unfortunately, recast fakes of these thimbles are also being offered for sale at antiques shows and sales.

Both genuine and fake Russian enamel thimbles are marked on the rim with the "84" mark. This means the silver content is 840 out of 1,000 parts silver. This is lower than the 925 out of 1,000 parts silver that is considered Sterling. The "84" mark was used in Russia prior to the revolution. After the 1917 revolution, the silver mark was changed to "875".

Modern Russian enamel on silver thimbles have an 875 silver quality mark and are offered to tourists as souvenirs. The thimbles offered for sale to the Russian seamstress at G.U.M.'s Department Store in Moscow are made of brass with a "4K" mark on the band. This mark is the price: 4 Kopek - or about 5 cents.

Niello is an enameling process. A paste is made of the mixture of silver, copper or zinc, lead, and sulfur. The proportions differ from one silversmith to another. The paste is applied to silver that has been carved in low relief, and fired. After polishing, the black niello appears only in the carved recessed areas. Russian silver thimbles with niello designs were made as souvenirs of seaside resorts for the tourist trade.

ENGLAND

The Atlantic Cable Thimble

Never Underestimate the Power of a Thimble

A sterling silver thimble helped make history in 1866. This thimble was used to make a miniature battery with the power of a modern wrist watch battery to produce power to send the first message through the newly completed Atlantic Cable.

After several failures, the Atlantic Cable was laid across the bottom of the Atlantic Ocean. It stretched from Newfoundland to the Irish coast, terminating on the land owned by the Knight of Kerry. A miniature battery was created by putting a few drops of acid and some zinc in a silver thimble that belonged to Miss Emily Fitzgerald, the daughter of the Knight of Kerry.

Miss Fitzgerald's silver thimble, with an applied rim and engraved band, is presently on display in the London Museum of Science. The pattern has come to be known as the Atlantic Cable Thimble.

This was the Telstar event of the nineteenth century. Women here and overseas wanted a thimble like the one used to complete this historic event. Similar thimbles were produced, some with slight variations in the pattern. The silversmith did not mark these thimbles, but it is assumed that all were made by one silversmith. Lightweight silver pieces were exempt from the assay law, and the early ones will not have marks on them. The later version, made after circa 1880, will have British assay marks.

English thimbles made during the sixteenth and seventeenth centuries were heavy and had a domed cap. The common decorations were strap work and chevron designs. Mottos, such as "God Save The Queen," appeared on some early British thimbles. It is difficult to find one of these early British thimbles in the antiques market today, especially in the United States. Most of the fine examples are in the collections of British museums.

English thimbles made during the eighteenth and part of the nineteenth centuries bear no hallmarks. Some have a silversmith's mark. Hallmarks appear on English thimbles that were made during the second and third quarter of the nineteenth century. The mark can be dated with the use of a British hallmarking dating chart. Most English thimbles found in the American antiques market today were made during the 1950s and later.

English thimbles can be recognized by their all-over pattern on the cap and side. This is often a floral pattern and replaces the indentations found on American thimbles. Each flower is struck individually rather than rolled on with a machine.

As labor became more expensive, hand struck decoration moved to the band. Indentations appeared on the cap and side of the thimble. Eventually machines replaced the hand labor method in the twentieth century.

SCANDINAVIA

Thimbles made in Norway and Sweden are distinctive in their shape. Scandinavian thimbles have smooth sides and are capped with either a semi-precious stone or a steel or silver cap with a square waffle pattern instead of indentations. The decoration on the side may be a simple engraved floral pattern or just a monogram.

The stone cap may be moonstone or amethyst. Scandinavian thimbles with silver or steel caps are of more recent production.

Swedish thimbles have been marked with a three crown mark since 1912. The letter "S" is included in the mark to indicate it is Sterling. A date code mark to indicate the year it was made. These marks appear inside the cap of the thimble.

Thimbles have been marked in Norway since 1891. The silver mark "830S" will be inside the cap. Enamel on silver thimbles will have a "925S" mark.

8-1: Silver, circa seventeenth century. Recovered from the ship *Margarita,* which sunk off the coast of Key West, Florida, September, 1622.

8-2, 8-3, 8-4: American. Nineteenth century. Unmarked.

8-5, 8-6, 8-7: American, marked "COIN." Mid-nineteenth century.

8-8, 8-9, 8-10: 8-8: American. "Stitch in Time Saves Nine," Simons; 8-9: Louis XV pattern band, Ketcham and McDougall; 8-10: "Queen Tiere," Ketcham and McDougall.

8-11, 8-12, 8-13: American, with ornate bands. Twentieth century.

8-14: American. Dropped rim with holly berries and leaves around cartouche. Ruby set on cartouche. Ketcham and Mc-Dougall.

8-15, 8-16, 8-17: American. Ornate bands. Twentieth century.

8-18, 8-19, 8-20: Typical American scenic bands. Early twentieth century.

8-21, 8-22, 8-23: American. Embroidery thimbles.

8-24, 8-25, 8-26: American. Bird decorations on bands.

8-27, 8-28, 8-29: Bird decoration on band; 8-27: Ketcham and McDougall; 8-28: Unmarked; 8-29: French.

8-30, 8-31, 8-32: Bird decorations on bands; 8-30: South American; 8-31: Unmarked; 8-32: Germany, Gabler. Applied gold bird, scalloped rim.

8-33, 8-34, 8-35: Continental. Tall compendiums. Late eighteenth, early nineteenth centuries.

8-36, 8-37, 8-38, 8-39: Parts of tall compendiums; 8-36: Needle case; 8-37: alum powder shaker; 8-38: thread reel; 8-39: Thimble.

8-40, 8-41, 8-42: The base of compendiums engraved for wax letter seals.

41

8-43: Russian. Silver compendium. First half of nineteenth century. Photo courtesy of the City Museum, Moscow, U.S.S.R.

8-44: Short compendium; 8-45: Alum powder shaker; 8-46: thread reel; 8-47: Thimble.

8-48, 8-49, 8-50: Continental. Silver. Ornate bands. Twentieth century.

8-51, 8-52, 8-53: Cupid thimbles; 8-51: Cupid towing the banner, made by Goldsmith Stern; 8-52: Cupid and garlands, made by Simons Brothers; 8-53: Cupid seated, made by Webster Company. All early twentieth century.

42

8-54: Cupid and garlands, made by Simons Brothers Company. Design patented November 21, 1905. Artwork by Lora Lee Cordes.

8-55: Small cupid faces around the band of thimble made by Stern Brothers. Early twentieth century. Artwork by Lora Lee Cordes.

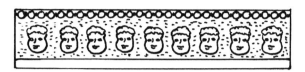

8-56: Cupid seated, made by Webster Company. Early twentieth century. Artwork by Lora Lee Cordes.

8-57: Cupid in different poses, made by Ketcham and Mc-Dougall. Early twentieth century. Artwork by Lora Lee Cordes.

8-58: Cupid with bow and arrow, made by Stern Brothers. Early twentieth century. Artwork by Lora Lee Cordes.

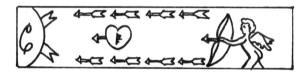

8-59: Cupid towing the banner, made by Goldsmith Stern. Early twentieth century. Artwork by Lora Lee Cordes.

8-60, 8-61, 8-62: Cupid thimbles; 8-60: Cupid in different poses, made by Ketcham and Mc-Dougall; 8-61: Cupid face and wings, made by Gabler, Germany; 8-62: Cupid face with wings. French touchmark. All early twentieth century.

8-63, 8-64, 8-65: Cupid; 8-63: Gold, three diamonds on band. Cupid and garlands, made by Simons Brothers Company; 8-64: Cupid and garlands, made by Simons Brothers Company; 8-65: Cupid towing the banner, made by Stern Brothers. Twentieth century.

8-66, 8-67, 8-68: Typical English silver. Twentieth century.

8-69, 8-70, 8-71: English. Silver, scalloped rim. Nineteenth century.

8-72, 8-73, 8-74: English. Domed cap. Nineteenth century.

8-75: English. Atlantic Cable style. A thimble with this pattern was used to make the final connection of the Atlantic Cable. Nineteenth century.

8-76: Thimble and finger guard screw on to base fitted with emery; 8-77: Filigree thimble screws on the base fitted with a scent bottle. English, silver. Early nineteenth century.

8-78, 8-79: English. Silver filigree thimble with scent bottle and tape. Circa 1830.

8-80, 8-81, 8-82: English. Finger shields to be worn on left index finger. Nineteenth century; 8-81: "Forget-me-not" in relief on band.

8-83, 8-84, 8-85: Finger shields to be worn on left index finger; 8-83: English; 8-84, 8-85: American.

8-86, 8-87, 8-88: French. "Fables of Fontaine." Made by Lenain in the 1970s, using original turn of the century dies; 8-86: The Monkey and the Magic Lantern; 8-87: The Hare and the Tortoise; 8-88: The Wolf and the Stork.

8-89, 8-90, 8-91: French. "Fables of Fontaine." Made by Lenain in the 1970s using original turn of the century dies; 8-89: The Fox and the Raven; 8-90: The Wolf and the Stork; 8-91: Joan of Arc.

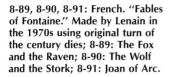

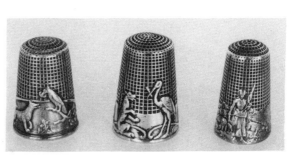

8-92, 8-93, 8-94: French. Made by Lenain in the 1970s, using original turn of the century dies; 8-92: The Dancing Graces; 8-93: Vanity; 8-94: Girl crocheting.

8-95: German. Silver thimble, dated 1577. Photo courtesy of the Metropolitan Museum of Art.

8-96, 8-97, 8-98: German. Twentieth century.

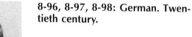

8-99, 8-100, 8-101: German. Applied turquoise and coral on band.

8-102, 8-103: German; 8-102: Children at play; 8-103: mother and daughter sewing, made by Gabler. Early twentieth century.

8-104, 8-105, 8-106: English.
Silver with engraved bands.

8-107, 8-108, 8-109: American.
Silver with engraved bands.

8-110, 8-111, 8-112: American.
Silver with engraved bands.

8-113, 8-114, 8-115: American.
Silver with engraved bands.

8-116, 8-117: Hand chased. India. Nineteenth century; 8-118:
Hand chased silver thimble. India. Nineteenth century.

8-119, 8-120, 8-121: Semi-precious stone caps.

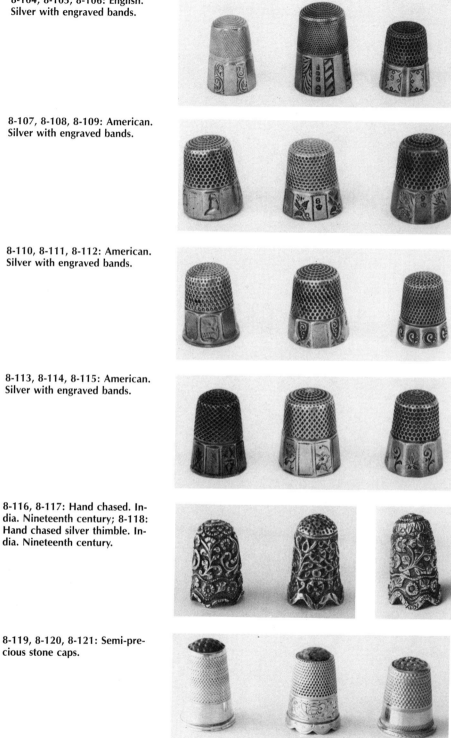

47

8-122, 8-123, 8-124: Semi-precious stone caps.

8-125, 8-126, 8-127: Continental. Semi-precious stone caps.

8-128, 8-129, 8-130: Continental. Semi-precious stone caps, applied shield cartouche.

8-131, 8-132, 8-133: English. Semi-precious stone caps.

8-134, 8-135, 8-136: English. Semi-precious stone caps.

8-137, 8-138, 8-139: Typical English patterns. Semi-precious stone caps.

48

8-140, 8-141, 8-142: Semi-precious stone caps; 8-141, 8-142:
Scandinavian.

8-143, 8-144, 8-145: Typical
Scandinavian silver with steel
caps; 8-143: Signed by Georg
Jensen, Denmark. Twentieth century.

8-146, 8-147, 8-148: South
American. Handmade. Nine-
teenth century.

8-149, 8-150, 8-151: South
American. Hand made with typi-
cal "mushroom" shaped cap.
Nineteenth century.

8-152, 8-153, 8-154: South
American; 8-152: Applied gold
floral garland.

8-155, 8-156, 8-157: South
American; 8-157: Applied gold
cartouche and "wedding band"
gold on rim.

8-158, 8-159, 8-160: Steel capped silver. Nineteenth century.

8-161, 8-162, 8-163: Steel capped silver. Nineteenth century.

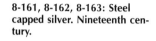

8-164, 8-165, 8-166: Steel capped silver; 8-164: English; 8-165, 8-166: American. Nineteenth century.

8-167, 8-168, 8-169: Typical steel capped silver. American and English. Nineteenth century.

8-170, 8-171, 8-172: Typical steel capped silver. American, nineteenth century; 8-171: Marked "Daniel Low, Salem."

8-173, 8-174, 8-175: Tailor's
thimbles. Silver. Open top.

8-176, 8-177, 8-178: Thailand.
Applied Siamese motifs. Modern.

8-179, 8-180, 8-181: Typical
Mexican silver. Modern.

CHAPTER 9

The Dorcas Thimble
And Other Steel Lined Thimbles

The Dorcas thimble, with its core of hardened steel sandwiched between two layers of Sterling silver, may be Great Britain's best kept secret. Combining steel with silver in the manufacturing of thimbles was done long before the Dorcas thimble was patented. Silver thimbles with steel caps were made in both ladies' and children's sizes. But when the side of the thimble was used for sewing, the silver part of the thimble became pierced by the needle, while the steel cap remained in perfect condition.

Charles Horner received Patent No. 8954 for the Dorcas thimble in England on June 14, 1884. On June 11, 1889, he was granted Letters Patent No. 404,910 from the United States Patent Office for the same thimble design. In his application for this patent, Horner stated, "My invention aims to produce a thimble which shall have the appearance of being made of a precious metal, and shall be durable and as free of danger of puncturing as though made of steel." This was accomplished by making a thimble with a steel core, the outer and inner layers being silver or gold. The thimble produced by this method had the beauty and comfort of a precious metal and the durability of steel.

The original Dorcas patent was for a thimble made of three layers. Each layer was formed separately and the three shells assembled.

Charles Horner gave an honorable name to his new product. He adopted the name Dorcas from the Bible. Dorcas was a seamstress who lived thirty-four miles northwest of Jerusalem at the port of Joppa, today known as Jaffa. She spent her life making clothes for the needy. Her good work is described in the New Testament's Act 9, Verses 36-39. Centuries later church women formed the Dorcas Sewing Circle to continue her good deeds of sewing for the poor.

In 1905, Horner was granted the patent for the "Improved Dorcas" thimble. A sheet of hardened steel was coated on both sides with a sheet of silver prior to forming. The thimble was drawn from this sandwich of metals.

About 1910 a Dorcas thimble was made in the United States. On the outside, the American-made Dorcas appears to be an ordinary sterling silver thimble. It is marked inside the cap, "DORCAS," size number and "PAT. JUNE 11,'89." No other marks appear on this American-made Dorcas thimble.

Two different patterns are known: (1) a connecting letter "S" (on its side) around the band and (2) a "Greek Key" or "Walls of Troy" pattern. Both have a milled rim, scored like the edge of a dime.

At the time the Dorcas thimble was introduced, it was estimated that the world production of sewing thimbles was sixty million. Horner advertised his new product extensively in order to obtain his share of the business.

By the end of the nineteenth century, Horner offered at least ten different Dorcas patterns. These patterns were given names as shown in Horner's advertisements.

A. PLAIN
B. ENGRAVED
D. DAISY
E. DIAMOND
F. STAR

G. LOUISE
H. PERSIAN
J. FLORA
K. SHELL
L. PRINCESS MAY

The Dorcas thimble found a home in a variety of sewing baskets—from those owned by seamstress' apprentices to those of royalty. A gold Dorcas was presented to the Duchess of York, Princess Victoria Mary of Teck, as a wedding gift from the employees of Charles Horner, July 6, 1893. The pattern of this thimble, Registered design #210800, was named "Princess May" in her honor. It became very popular. The border of the thimble presented to the Princess was engraved with wreaths of York roses and May blossoms joined with a true lovers knot. This engraving was not on the "Princess May" pattern that was offered to the public.

Early Dorcas thimbles were not marked with the name. They carried the word "PAT", size number, and sometimes the patent number and the makers initials: "CH". The Improved Dorcas, made after 1906, carried the name "DORCAS" in block letters on the band, plus the makers initials, "CH", and size number.

Horner made the Dorcas thimble in a wide range of sizes, numbering from 1 through 15. His sizing system was in reverse of the thimble sizing system used today in the United States. Size 1 was the largest, size 15 the smallest. The average sizes made and sold were in the middle range: 6 through 11.

Dorcas thimbles were displayed and packaged in an elegant manner. They were delivered to the store in a glass-topped display case or a cardboard box that held one dozen individually boxed thimbles. The store carton had a label printed in bold red and black letters. It proudly announced on a scroll that the Dorcas thimble was guaranteed to last a lifetime. The Dorcas name was printed on the lid of the individual presentation box. The guarantee appeared on the bottom of the box.

The bottom of the individual box for the early Dorcas thimble read: "THE DORCAS THIMBLE. Made in three parts, the inner and outer being Silver, and the intermediate Steel, giving a resisting power not obtained in silver only." Later, the label on the box of the Improved Dorcas read: "GUARANTEE. Exchanged free if rendered useless for any cause whatsoever. Made of Sterling Silver with interlining of hardened steel. None genuine without the name DORCAS, C.H. British made."

Dorcas thimbles never carry the traditional British hallmark. Even though the outer and inner layers were made of thick sterling silver, the steel core disqualifies it for hallmarking.

DORCAS JUNIOR AND LITTLE DORCAS

By 1911 Horner added two other models of Dorcas to his line: the Little Dorcas and the Dorcas Junior. These were advertised as "made on the same principles as the Improved Dorcas, but a little shorter with a slightly flatter top....(which) allows exceptional freedom of the finger joint, a feature highly appreciated by needlewomen." Although the Little Dorcas and the Dorcas Junior were lighter in construction, Horner claimed that they were equal in durability to the Improved Dorcas. The price of these was somewhat less, which appealed to the lower end of the market.

GOLD DORCAS

Horner added a gold Dorcas to his line, which was made in various patterns. It was marked "Dorcas, 9ct, Steel Lined", plus Horner's initials and size number. It was sold in its own distinctive brown leather case, lined with green velvet and white silk. The same guarantee to exchange it free if rendered useless was offered.

IMITATIONS

The reason for the "none genuine" statement that was part of the guarantee of the Improved Dorcas was that imitators had reached the thimble market attempting to emulate the success of Horner's Dorcas. Among these were the Dura, Dreema, and Doris thimbles. All the names of the imitators began with the letter "D," which could confuse the buying public. None of the imitators were produced in the quantity of the Dorcas and are harder to find today. All were British made.

Dura

The Dura was a steel lined thimble made by Walker and Hall. It is marked "Dura" with the company's trade mark of a pennant that enclosed a "W & H". The company used the mark between 1862 and 1919.

Dreema

The Dreema thimble was made by Henry Griffith of Leamington, near Birmingham, England. Griffith began producing thimbles in 1856 and continues today. Dreema was the name of Griffith's niece. Although the label did not include the unconditional guarantee, it did state that the Dreema was made of two layers of solid sterling silver and had the beauty of silver with the strength of steel. The mark on the Dreema is "DREEMA" plus the makers initials, "H.G. & S."

The thimble marked "STEEL CLAD" and "J.W.Ltd," which is the mark of James Walker, a jeweler, has a pattern that is exactly like the one bearing the Griffith mark.

Doris

The Doris thimble is another steel lined Dorcas imitator. The steel core was made by the Iles Thimble Works of Birmingham and sold to other thimble makers, including Horner. The name "DORIS" appears alone on the band. There is no maker's mark. It is possible that it was made by Iles and marketed by the Abel Morrell Company. Morrell, also of Birmingham, was a needle manufacturer. No research has been found to indicate that Morrell ever made thimbles.

ENGRAVED AND MONOGRAM DORCAS

Very few Dorcas thimbles were engraved with a monogram. The Dorcas was considered an elegant workday thimble. One Dorcas was found engraved "To Amy from Robbie and Reggie." It is doubtful that Amy received this thimble from two beaus. Possibly Robbie and Reggie gave this thimble to their sister.

The fact that the Dorcas, and other steel lined imitators, are practically indestructible, may be the reason that so few of these have found their way into the antiques market today. Many of these thimbles are probably still alive and well in sewing baskets.

Production of the Dorcas thimble ceased about 1948. The equipment used to produce the Dorcas thimbles was scrapped by the Horner Company in the 1960s. An era ended.

DORCAS advertisement, circa 1900. Pattern names: A. Plain; B. Engraved; D. Daisy; E. Diamond, F. Star; G. Louise; H. Persian, J. Flora; K. Shell; L. Princess May.

9-1: Gold DORCAS thimble in original leather presentation box.

9-2: The label on the gold DORCAS box.

9-3: DORCAS advertisement, circa 1893. Pattern names: A: Plain. B: Engraved. D: Daisy. E: Diamond. F: Star. G: Louise. H: Persian. J: Flora. K: Shell. L: Princess May.

9-4, 9-5: Salesman's sample of the construction of the DORCAS thimble; 9-4: DORCAS cut in half to reveal sandwich of metals; 9-5: Steel core of the DORCAS.

56

9-6, 9-7, 9-8: DORCAS. Engraved names and initials on band.

9-9, 9-10, 9-11: DORCAS. Engraved names and initials on band.

9-12, 9-13, 9-14: DORCAS thimbles with engraved bands.

9-15, 9-16, 9-17: DORCAS thimbles with Flora combination patterns; 9-15: Early DORCAS marked "PAT."

9-18, 9-19, 9-20: DORCAS patterns; 9-18: Daisy; 9-19: Princess May; 9-20: Louise.

9-21, 9-22, 9-23: DORCAS patterns; 9-21: Star; 9-22: Daisy; 9-23: Louise.

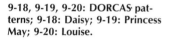

9-24, 9-25, 9-26: Three gold DORCAS thimbles. Marked "9 ct, Steel Lined."

9-27: Partially open cap DOR-CAS for long fingernails; 9-28: Open top tailor's DORCAS.

9-29, 9-30, 9-31: The DORIS thimble.

9-32, 9-33, 9-34: DREEMA thim-ble, made by Henry Griffith.

9-35, 9-36, 9-37: LITTLE DOR-CAS.

9-38, 9-39: DORCAS JUNIOR; 9-40: LITTLE DORCAS.

9-41, 9-42, 9-43: Three patterns of DURA thimble, made by Walker and Hall.

9-44, 9-45: Steel Clad, J. W. Ltd, made for James Walker Jewelers by Henry Griffith.

9-46: Early DORCAS presentation box.

9-47: Guarantee on label of presentation box.

9-48: DORCAS advertisement.

THE "DORCAS" THIMBLE.
(Horner's Patent.)

STERLING SILVER.

The Queen, May 8th, says:—"The 'Dorcas' Thimble is more durable than the generality of these indispensable work-table implements : it is made in three parts, the inner and the outer being Silver, and the intermediate Steel : forming a resisting power not obtained in Silver only. What is more uncomfortable than sewing with a thimble that has seen service to such an extent that it has holes in its sides ? With the 'Dorcas' Thimble this annoyance vanishes." FROM ALL JEWELLERS.

IF YOU CANNOT OBTAIN IT, WRITE TO

C. HORNER, Thimble Manufacturer, HALIFAX.

9-49: Store carton that held one dozen thimbles proudly announces that the DORCAS thimble is guaranteed to last a lifetime.

9-50: "DORCAS the Seamstress" plate by Frankoma Pottery.

9-51: The Singer Sewing Machine Company used the DORCAS theme on their trade card in 1895. The illustration painted by Maude Humphrey, shows children sewing doll clothes and the latest model of the Singer Machine.

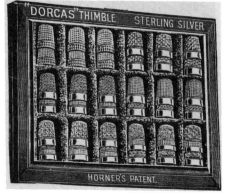

9-52: DORCAS retail display case, circa 1900.

CHAPTER 10

Souvenir and Commemorative Thimbles and Tools

Thimbles were often made as souvenirs and to commemorate people, places, or events. Frequently they contained the same design that appeared on souvenir spoons.

Travel became easier during the nineteenth century with the establishment of the railroad system. A trip away from home was a great event. Travelers bought souvenirs as keepsakes for themselves and as gifts for friends and family. A thimble took little space in the luggage, would not break in transit, and was a useful gift as well as a souvenir.

ENGLISH SOUVENIR THIMBLES

English souvenir thimbles date back to the seventeenth century. Souvenir thimbles commemorated royal events such as coronations, births, and weddings. Royalty commemorative thimbles included a profile picture of the sovereign and the date of the event. An exception is the souvenir thimble of Queen Victoria's coronation. Engraved on the band of this thimble is the entire history of this event:

"QUEEN VICTORIA BORN MAY 24. 1819
ASCENED TO THE THRONE JUNE 20, 1837
CROWNED JUNE 28, 1838
HEAVEN PROTECT OUR SOVEREIGN LADY"

Most royalty commemorative thimbles were produced in silver, but a smaller quantity was made of 18k gold. Others were made of common metal such as brass or nickel. Rich or poor, anyone could afford to buy a souvenir thimble of a royal event.

During the 1930s, the British thimblemaker Henry Griffith made over fifty different souvenir thimbles with names of British towns and seaside resorts. The Griffith factory was located in the city of Leamington Spa, near Birmingham, England. Griffith named his thimble "The Spa," and this name was engraved on the rim of some models. The name of the city or resort appears on the band in relief. This series will have the Birmingham hallmark dates of 1929 (E), 1930 (F) or 1931 (G). The majority were made in 1930. Griffith found that the series was not profitable and ceased production in 1931.

Other thimble manufacturers copied Griffith's souvenir series. These are harder to find since they were made in smaller quantities and discontinued about the same time.

MAUCHLINE AND TARTAN WARE

Scottish mauchlinware or transferware was another popular tourist souvenir. A wide range of objects was made. Some of the sewing items include: bodkin cases, darning eggs, etuis, knitting needle cases, thimble cases, needle books, pin disks, scissor boxes, emeries, waxers, thread barrels and boxes; tatting shuttles, tape measure holders, and yarn ball holders.

The Scottish transfer ware contained pictures, similar to engraved pen and ink drawings, that were transferred to sycamore wood. This wood, plentiful along the banks of the Doon and Ayr Rivers, was knot free and did not warp. Many of these pieces were marked "Made from wood grown along the banks of the Doon." Several coats of shellac sealed the picture on the wood and kept it in an almost-new appearance for many years.

Pictures of people and places appear on Scottish transfer pieces, including hotels, cathedrals, and tourist attractions. Portraits of Robert Burns and Sir Walter Scott, famous Scottish literary figures, appear on many pieces of mauchlinware.

The souvenirs were so popular, they were made with American scenes and sold in the United States. Pictures of the Cog Railway in the White Mountains (New Hampshire), Niagara Falls (New York), and the Capitol (Washington, D.C.), appear on mauchline transfer ware. Pictures of hotels that were fashionable in the nineteenth century in Saratoga Springs, in New York's Catskill Mountains, and the White Mountains of New Hampshire also appear on these souvenir pieces.

Tartan woodware was first produced in the 1820s. The earliest pieces were hand painted. Later the patterns were printed on paper and glued to the wood. The process was done so perfectly, it is difficult to tell the difference from the hand painted variety. The W. and A. Smith Company perfected the process. No makers name appear on any tartan piece. Over one hundred different clan tartans were used, the Royal Stuart being the most popular. The name of the clan tartan often appears on the piece.

GERMAN SOUVENIR THIMBLES

The Gabler Company of Germany made enamel on silver thimbles with semi-precious stone caps. The decaled pictures depicted the large cities and tourist attractions in Europe. (See Chapter 12, Enameled Thimbles.)

AMERICAN SOUVENIR THIMBLES

World's Fair And Bicentennial Thimbles

Thimbles were among the variety of sewing tools offered for sale at World's Fairs. Finding these today is like looking for a thimble in a haystack. World's Fair souvenirs were offered for sale only in the city where the fair was located and only during the years the fair ran.

The first great international industrial fair of modern times was held in London in 1851. The souvenir thimble shows a panorama of the fair, including Prince Albert's Crystal Palace.

The first fair to be held in the United States was in New York, 1853-54. Demonstrations of the newly invented sewing machine were made at this fair.

The Chicago Columbian Exposition was scheduled to open in 1892 in celebration of the 400th anniversary of Columbus' landing in the New World, but construction problems delayed the opening one year. Chicago was a large metropolitan city at that time, but Easterners considered it to be "far west" and laughed at the thought of a World's Fair there. If Chicago was so metropolitan, why did Chicago men demand three pockets in their suit coats? One pocket was for a watch, one for a purse, and one for a jackknife or revolver. W. L. Judson's new invention of the "Hookless Fastener," now known as the zipper, was first demonstrated at the Columbian Exposition.

The Simons Company of Philadelphia made the thimble for the Columbian Exposition. Production, using dies with an 1892 date, started before the announcement of the date change. Two different thimbles were made, both having the 1892 date, although the fair opened in 1893. One thimble has a panorama view of the fair, including Machinery Hall, plus the words "WORLD'S COLUMBIAN EXPOSITION 1492-1892." The other contained only the wording around the band.

Both Columbian Exposition thimbles were made in Sterling silver and 10K gold. A gold thimble set with forty diamonds, which was on display at the Simons exhibit, was presented at the close of the fair to Mrs. Potter Palmer, a prominent organizer of the fair. She was the wife of the owner of Chicago's Palmer House and one of the first woman's rights activists.

The 1904 St. Louis Fair commemorated the 100th anniversary of the purchase of the Louisiana Territory from France. The official souvenir thimble for this exposition is known as "The Golden Spike." It commemorated the completion and meeting of the Central Pacific and Union Pacific railroads. A golden spike was driven into a railroad tie at Promontory Point, Utah, on May 10, 1869.

Shown on this thimble, in high relief, were several methods of transportation: a locomotive steam engine, a covered wagon, a horse, and a canoe. A buffalo and Indian were included in the design, each facing west towards the setting sun.

The Golden Spike thimble had the markings "official" and "1904" in raised letters on the cartouche. It was made in Sterling silver and 14K gold. Simons Company of Philadelphia, the manufacturer, kept this thimble design in production but omitted the marking "Official" and "1904."

The first electrically operated sewing machine was demonstrated at the 1904 St. Louis World's Fair. It was attached directly to the electric wires that were brought into a house. Electric wall outlets were not available in most homes at that time.

Silver thimbles were made for the 1925 Philadelphia Sesquicentennial and the 1933 Century of Progress World's Fair in Chicago. The Chicago Fair ran for two years, and thimbles were issued for 1933 and 1934. The thimbles also were available in nickel and oride at much lower cost, reflecting the economic hard times during the depression.

Two fairs were held in 1939, one in New York and and other in San Francisco. One of the marvels displayed at these fairs was the DuPont company's new yarn called nylon. Women had only a short time to enjoy stockings made of this new material because the company devoted most of its nylon to war production in the 1940 to 1945 period. After the war, many brides made their wedding dresses of nylon parachute material.

Thimbles issued for the 1939 fairs were the last World's Fair thimbles made of silver from a die. Souvenir thimbles for later fairs were cast in pewter with glass caps or made of porcelain with a decaled logo.

The 1976 Bicentennial was a banner year for the production of souvenir thimbles. Both American factories and those overseas made them. Bicentennial thimbles were made of silver, pewter, nickel, enamel on silver, and porcelain. The Simons Company of Philadelphia reissued their unique shaped Liberty Bell thimble. The original issue was stamped with 13 stars; the bicentennial issue is marked " '76 " on the band.

Another series of souvenir thimbles was made of nickel or silver plate. An applied enameled shield is welded to the side of the thimble. Both are marked "Germany." There is no maker's mark. The series that was produced as United States souvenirs had a thimble for each of the fifty states with the state flag on the shield.

Tourist and Special Thimbles

American thimblemakers produced souvenir thimbles for the tourist market, with cities and resorts appearing on the bands.

The Ketchum and McDougall Company made a series of Sterling silver souvenir thimbles during the late nineteenth and early twentieth centuries. Some did not have the maker's mark inside the cap. The clue to the maker is the patent date that is included in the design on the band. This series served as souvenirs for vacation resorts.

The Florida thimble has an alligator and the Palm Beach souvenir shows a palm tree. Views of the old city appear on the St. Augustine thimble. The Old Point Comfort, Virginia, thimble shows the fort and a turtle. The Adirondacks Mountains, New York, souvenir thimble shows a deer, canoe, and fish touting the hunting and fishing in the area.

The Homestead Hotel is pictured on the Hot Springs, Virginia, thimble. The Atlantic City, New Jersey, thimble shows all the attractions the resort offered before gambling came to the city. The band decoration shows a panorama view of the beach, with people sitting on the sand. The famous Steel Pier, boardwalk, and hotels are in the background.

Ketchum and McDougall's patented method of manufacturing thimbles enabled them to make a thimble with a decorated band in one process. This reduced the cost of manufacturing these souvenir thimbles with the scenes in relief on the band.

The Simons Company made a souvenir thimble in 1984 that was not available to collectors. It was designed for Nancy Reagan, the First Lady, to represent the United States at the European Economic Conference in 1984. The thimble shows the south side of the White House, including the "Truman Balcony." It is the view that appears on the reverse side of the U.S. $20 bill. Mrs. Reagan's initials, N.D.R., are on the cartouche. One hundred thimbles with this design were produced.

A different view of the White House, the north side, plus a view of the Capitol building appears on another Simons thimble. The latest version of this thimble is sold in the gift shop of the Smithsonian Institution. It is made from the original die and is marked inside the cap "S.I. 1981."

American Commemorative Thimbles

"American Bicentennial of Freedom 1776-1976" (Simons, silver.) Applied disc with Liberty Bell.

"American Revolution Bicentennial 1776-1976" (Israel, silver.) Embossed Liberty Bell, Independence Hall, and Statue of Liberty.

"1897 75th Anniversary 1972 First Consolidated School West of Mississippi River at Buffalo Center, Iowa" (unmarked, silver.)

"Bicentennial 1976" (Holland, enamel on silver.) transfer print: Betsy Ross sewing the flag.

"Bicentennial 1776-1976"(unmarked, enamel on silver.) Liberty Bell and drums.

"Century of Progress Chicago 1933" (Also made with 1934 date. Simons. Made in silver and nickel.)

"Christmas 1777 Remembered 1977" (Enamel on silver, hand painted by Peter Swingler, England.) George Washington and his troops at Valley Forge.

"World's Columbian Exposition 1492-1892" (Simons, silver.)

"1492 World's Columbian Exposition 1892" (Simons, silver and 10k gold.) Exposition building in bas relief.

"D.A.R." (Simons, silver, Daughters of the American Revolution.) Constitution Hall and Memorial Centennial Hall in bas relief.

"Friends War Relief Service" (Made by Simons and Ketchum and McDougall, silver) World War I.

"Half a Century of Golden Sound. The Jazz Singer. October 1927" (Enamel on silver, hand painted by Peter Swingler, England.)

"Independence 1776" (Enamel on silver, hand painted by Peter Swingler, England.)

"Molly Pitcher at the Battle of Monmouth 1776" (Silver, bas relief, England.) Molly Pitcher loading a cannon.

"National Thimble Convention - 1976" (Simons, pewter. The same thimble made for the 1978 convention marked "Chicago".)

"New York World's Fair 1939 - 1940" (Simons, Silver.) Trylon and Peresphere. (Note: this is the last World's Fair thimble made of silver from a die. Recent World's Fair thimbles were made of pewter or china.)

"Philadelphia Sesquicentennial 1776-1926" (Simons, silver.)

"Philadelphia, Sesquicentennial 1776-1926" (Goldsmith Stern, silver.) Liberty Bell.

"Proclaim Liberty in the Land and to the Inhabitants. By order of the Assembly of Pennsy. in Phil'a. 1752" (Simons, silver.) Thimble in shape of the Liberty Bell, design patented by Simons, 1892. Reissued in 1926 and 1976. (Note: Original and 1926 issue have stars stamped on band. The 1976 issue is marked "'76" on band. The design could be patented because the wording on the the the thimble is similar, but not exactly the same as the wording on the Liberty Bell.)

"Golden Gate International Exposition, San Francisco, 1939" (Simons, silver) Golden Gate Bridge and skyline of San Francisco.

"Skilled Hands for Independence" (England, enamel on silver, hand painted by Peter Swingler.) Seamstress mending a soldier's uniform.

"George and Martha Washington" (England, enamel on silver, hand painted by Peter Swingler.)

"Signing of the Declaration of Independence 1776-1976 Bicentennial", (England, silver.) Delegates sign the document (bas relief).

"Simons - 100th Anniversary" (Simons, silver.) Circa 1939. Transportation theme showing airplane, boat, and truck.

"Spirit of '76" (Holland, enamel on silver.) Marching drummer boy and fifer.

"Statue of Liberty 1776-1976" (France, silver.) Statue and New York skyline in relief.

"Washington Crossing the Delaware" (England, hand painted enamel on silver by Peter Swingler.)

Thirteen Colony series. (Franklin Mint, silver.) Each thimble commemorates one of the original colonies.

Statue of Liberty (Simons, silver.) Copper statue applied to a silver thimble. Issued in 1986.

"Sweet Land of Freedom" (England, silver.) Thimble in shape of the United States Capitol dome.

American Souvenir Thimbles

"Adirondacks Mountain" (Ketchum and McDougall, silver.) Deer, canoe, and snow shoes on band.

"Atlantic City" (Ketchum and McDougall, silver.) Boardwalk, Steel Pier, hotels and beach.

"Atlantic City" (Simons, enamel on silver.)

"Austin, Texas" (unmarked, silver.)

"Brooklyn Bridge" (Ketchum and McDougall, silver.) Bridge, ship, etc.

"Bucyus, O." (unmarked, silver.)

"Bunker Hill 1775" (Goldsmith Stern, silver, applied enamel disc.)

"Bunker Hill 1775" (unmarked, silver.) Wording on band.

"Chicago, 1898" (Goldsmith Stern, silver.) Raised wording on band.

"The Dorcas Thimblers" (Simons, silver.) Map of Florida. Issued by the west coast Florida thimble collecting group.

"'Florida" (Ketchum and McDougall, silver). Lettering and alligator on band.

"Grand Lake, Colorado" (unmarked, silver). Applied disc with long horned sheep and mountains.

"Garden State Thimblers" (Simons, silver.) Issued by the New Jersey regional thimble collectors group.

"Hawaii 1949" (unmarked, silver.) Applied disc.

"The Homestead, Hot Springs, Va." (Ketchum and McDougall, silver.) Lettering and hotel on band.

"Kenosha 1852 First National Bank" (unmarked. silver.)

"Maniton" (unmarked, silver.)

"Merced General Hospital, Merced, California" (unmarked, silver.)

"Minneapolis" (unmarked, silver.) Engraved on band.

"Michigan" (Simons. silver.) State flower and bird, automobile, and Grand Hotel.

"Mount Vernon" (unmarked, silver.) Applied disc.

"New York Subway" (Paye and Baker, silver.) Subway train.

"Newark, N.J." (Simons, enamel on silver.)

"Niagara Falls" (Waite Thresher. silver.) Applied disc.

"Old Point" (unmarked, silver.) Fort at mouth of the James River, Virginia. Turtle and fort on band.

"Old Stone Mill - Newport, R.I. (Ketchum and McDougall, silver.) Lettering on band.

"Palm Beach" (Ketchum and McDougall. silver.) Lettering and palm tree on band.

"Palm Springs" (unmarked, silver.) Applied disc with palm tree.

"Pasadena" (unmarked, silver.)

"Philadelphia 1682-1982" (Simons, silver.) Indian and William Penn in relief.

"Portland, Oregon 1927" (unmarked, silver.)

"Richfield Springs, N.Y." (Ketchum and McDougall, silver.) Lettering on band.

"Salem - 1692" (Webster, silver.) Witch flying on broom, cat, and moon on band in relief. (Note: same die used on thimble made by Ketcham and McDougall. This is the same design used on souvenir spoon made for Daniel Low, a jeweler in Salem, Ma.)

"St. Augustine, Florida" (Ketchum and McDougall, silver.) Fort Marion, City Gate, and cathedral. (Note: several different versions of the St. Augustine souvenir thimble were made by Ketchum and McDougall.)

"Urbana, O." (unmarked, silver.)
"Valley Forge, Pa." (unmarked, silver.) Applied disc.
"Washington, D.C." (Ketchum and McDougall, silver.)
"Washington, D. C." (Simons, silver.) (Note: This was reissued in 1981 and offered at the
gift shop of the Smithsonian Institution. The reissue is marked "S.I.'81" inside cap.)
"Washington, D.C." (Webster, silver.) Applied enamel disc.
"White Plains, N.Y." (unmarked, silver.)
"Yellowstone Park" (unmarked, silver.) Applied disc.

10-1: Exhibition of All Nations, London, 1851. The Crystal Palace is shown in relief.

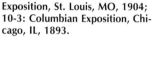

10-2, 10-3: Gold souvenir thimbles; 10-2: Louisiana Purchase Exposition, St. Louis, MO, 1904; 10-3: Columbian Exposition, Chicago, IL, 1893.

10-6: Columbian Exposition, 1893, showing the buildings; 10-7: Louisiana Purchase Exposition, St. Louis, 1904.

10-8: The band of the thimble that was a souvenir of the Louisiana Purchase Exposition, St. Louis, 1904 traces modes of transportation used during the settling of the West. Horses, covered wagon, canoe and steam locomotives are shown. All are heading west towards the setting sun. This thimble is called "The Golden Spike," as the locomotive represents the golden spike that was driven at Promontory Point, Utah, May 20, 1869. The spike commemorates the joining of the Central Pacific and Union Pacific Railroads. Artwork by Lora Lee Cordes.

10-9: French. Paris Exposition, 1889; 10-10: Paris Exposition, 1900; 10-11: Lyon Exposition, 1914.

10-12: Exhibition of All Nations, Crystal Palace, 1851; 10-13: Hyde Park, 1851; 10-14: International Exhibition, Kensington, 1862.

10-15: Century of Progress, Chicago, 1933; 10-16: Philadelphia Sesquicentennial, 1926; 10-17: Knoxville, TN. 1982.

10-18: Century of Progress, Chicago, 1933; 10-19: World of Tomorrow, New York, 1939; 10-20: Golden Gate Exposition, San Francisco, 1939.

10-21, 10-22, 10-23: Transfer prints, enamel on silver. English. Modern; 10-21, 10-22: Westminster Cathedral; 10-23: London.

10-24, 10-25, 10-26: Applied enamel shields on plated thimble; 10-24: Rio de Janeiro; 10-25: British Columbia; 10-26: Jasper National Park, Canada. Modern.

10-27, 10-28, 10-29: Applied enamel shields on plated thimbles. Modern; 10-27: Ohio; 10-28: Florida; 10-29: New Orleans.

10-30, 10-31, 10-32: American City Souvenirs; 10-30: St. Augustine, FL, made by Ketcham and McDougall; 10-31: Salem, MA, made by Ketcham and Mc-Dougall; 10-32: Washington, DC, made by Simons Brothers Company.

10-34: Constitution Hall, Daughters of the American Revolution; 10-35: Bunker Hill; 10-36: Salem, MA.

10-37: Atlantic City, NJ; 10-38: Old Point Comfort, VA; 10-39: Adirondack Mountains, NY.

10-40: Niagara Falls, NY; 10-41: Austin, TX; 10-42: White Plains, NY.

10-43: Philadelphia, PA; 10-44: Liberty Bell; 10-45: Liberty Bell, 1976 issue.

10-46: Statue of Liberty. France;
10-47: Statue of Liberty, made by
Simons Brothers Company.

10-48: Liberty Bell, early twentieth century issue with stars on
band; 10-49: Liberty Bell, 1976
issue, with copy of original loop
on top; 10-50: Liberty Bell, 1976
issue. '76 on band. Simons.

10-51: Michigan. Simons. Mod-
ern; 10-52: California. Simons.
Modern; 10-53: Hot Springs, VA.
Ketcham and McDougall.

10-54: St. Augustine, FL; 10-55:
Florida; 10-56: Palm Beach, FL.
All made by Ketcham and Mc-
Dougall.

10-57: Washington, DC, Capitol;
10-58: Washington, DC, White
House. Both made by Simons
Brothers Company; 10-59: Washington, DC, made by Ketcham
and McDougall.

10-60, 10-61, 10-62: Bicentennial souvenirs. Transfer prints; 10-60: Drum and Fife; 10-61: Betsy Ross. Both enamel on silver, Holland; 10-62: Molly Pitcher, silver, English.

Henry Griffith of Birmingham, England, produce a series of souvenir thimbles with the names of English cities in high relief around the bands. This series was made for only three years—1930 through 1932. Other thimblemakers made some of these, but in smaller quantities.

10-63: Aylesbury; 10-64: Birmingham; 10-65: Blackpool.

10-66: Bournemouth; 10-67: Brighton; 10-68: Bristol.

10-69: Colechester; 10-70: Combe Martin; 10-71: Dewsbury.

10-72: Dickenson Newcastle; 10-73: Eastborne; 10-74: Edinburgh.

10-75: Falmouth; 10-76: Felix-
towe; 10-77: Glastonbury.

10-78: Great Yarmouth; 10-79:
Halifax; 10-80: Ilfracombe.

10-81:Inverness; 10-82: Ipswich;
10-83: Isle of Man.

10-84: Lemington Spa; 10-85:
Leigh on Sea; 10-86: Leven.

10-87: Llandudno; 10-88:
Llanrwst; 10-89: London.

10-90: Minehead; 10-91: Penrith;
10-92: Plymouth.

10-93: Portsmouth; 10-94: St. Leonards; 10-95: Sandown.

10-96: Scarborough; 10-97: Southend on Sea; 10-98: Stratford on Avon.

10-99: Teighmouth; 10-100: Tenby; 10-101: Torquay.

10-102: Westcliff on Sea; 10-103: Weston Super Mare; 10-104: Whitley Bay.

10-105, 10-106, 10-107: English, sterling silver. Modern; 10-105: U. S. Capitol, Washington, DC; 10-106: St. Paul's, London; 10-107: St. Peter's, Rome.

10-108, 10-109, 10-110: Enamel on silver, with transfer prints. Semi-precious stone caps; 10-108: St. Peters, Rome; 10-109: Cathedral, Florence, Italy; 10-110: Gravenhage.

10-111: Coronation of Queen
Victoria, 1838; 10-112: Diamond
Jubilee of Queen Victoria, 1891;
10-113: Queen Victoria commemorative.

10-114: Marriage of Edward,
Prince of Wales and Alexandra;
10-115: Coronation of Edward
and Alexandra, 1902; 10-116:
Silver Jubilee of King George and
Queen Mary, 1935.

10-117: Coronation of Queen
Elizabeth, 1952; 10-118: Queen
Elizabeth's Jubilee, 1977; 10-119:
Queen Elizabeth's 60th Birthday,
1986.

10-120, 10-121, 10-122: English;
10-120: Princess Anne and Mark
Philip; 10-121: Prince Charles
and Princess Diana. Both enamel
on silver, hand painted by Peter
Swingler; 10-122: Birth of Prince
William. Porcelain.

10-123: Prince Willem of Holland; 10-124: Queen Beatrix; 10-
125: Queen Willamina and
Queen Beatrix. Holland, 1980.

10-126: Lord Byron's Home; 10-127: Windsor Castle; 10-128: Balmoral, the Queen's Highland Castle.

10-129, 10-130, 10-131: Modern silver commemorative thimbles. Israel; 10-129: Last Supper; 10-130: Statue of Liberty; 10-131: Sphinx.

10-132, 10-133: Darning eggs; 10-134: Olive wood, marked "Jerusalem" in both English and Hebrew; 10-132: Stickware egg marked "Grindelwald."

CHAPTER 11

COMMON METAL THIMBLES

BRASS

Poor Man's Gold

Brass and other alloy metal thimbles were made several thousand years ago. The earliest ones were hand made and hand punched. A ring type bronze thimble was found in the ruins of Pompeii, the Italian city buried by lava when Mount Vesuvius erupted in 79 A.D.

Early brass alloys were difficult to work. The combination of copper and calamine that was used until the late seventeenth century had tiny bubbles. The surface of the cast thimble had pitting. It was a mottled color and tended to split. By the end of the eighteenth century lead became available and was added to the alloy. Brass became easier to refine and work and was used more in artwork, jewelry, and thimbles.

Brass thimbles have been recovered from the cargo of many sunken ships. The dates of these sinkings give clues to the age of the thimbles. Brass thimbles have been recovered from the wreck of the *Mary Rose,* one of King Henry VIII's men-of-war. It capsized off the coast of England in 1545. Forty brass thimbles, in four different sizes, were found near a wrecked ship off the coast of Yugoslavia. This is believed to be the wreck of the *Gagina* which disappeared in 1583. Hundreds of brass thimbles in four different designs were recovered from the wreck of the *Sacramento,* which sunk off the coast of Brazil in 1668. These thimbles were most likely made in Germany or Holland. Thimbles were an important item of international trade.

Brass thimbles, needles, thread, and scissors were recovered from the steamboat *Bertrand,* which sunk in a bend of the Missouri River 25 miles upstream from Omaha, Nebraska, in 1865. The steamboat was carrying supplies from St. Louis to merchants in the Montana Territory. Gold had been discovered in the Montana Territory, which attracted thousands of newcomers.

Brass and other metal thimbles were made in Nuremberg, Germany, since the Middle Ages. By the end of the seventeenth century, a Dutchman named John Lofting established a thimble factory in Marlow, England, near London. His factory produced 140 gross of thimbles per week, almost a million per year. Some of these thimbles were exported to the American colonies.

Early brass thimbles were cast. The indentations were punched by hand after the thimble was removed from the mold. By the eighteen century, machine-made thimbles were shaped from a disk of metal. Indentations were rolled on by a knurling machine.

By the mid-nineteenth century brass and other common metal thimbles were made by the millions in the United States and overseas. Few of these were marked with the maker's name or trademark.

Precious metal thimbles were considered a luxury and were priced beyond the reach of the average nineteenth century homemaker. Even if a homemaker had a precious metal thimble, it was considered too elegant for mundane mending. She saved it to use at the sewing circle or to do fancy work in the parlor. She used her brass thimbles and other "common" thimbles for everyday work.

The Simons Brothers Company of Philadelphia marked their nickel plated and oride thimble with "S.B.C." enclosed in a keystone. This mark appears inside the cap of the thimble.

Several thimble manufacturers were located in Waterbury and Bridgeport, Connecticut, and Huntington, New York, during the nineteenth century. It is difficult to distinguish these brass thimbles from recently made examples. The size and shape has stayed the same for a century. Except for the size number, they are unmarked.

Modern imported brass thimbles are marked with the name of the country where they were manufactured. These include Austria, Czechoslovakia, England, Germany, Japan, and Taiwan.

Charles Iles and Gomms of England marked their brass thimbles with the name ILES and their trademark on the band. One of their trademarks is three thimbles enclosed in a shield. It also was used on their cupro-nickel and silver plated thimbles. Abel Morall Company of Redditch, England, marked their name on the bands of their thimbles. Morall made thimbles during the nineteenth century. Later the Iles Company made thimbles for Morall, but the Morall name continued to appear on the band.

The Gabler factory in Germany closed in 1963. It had been operated by the same family for 140 years. The factory made common metal thimbles for everyday use in many different patterns and in fourteen to eighteen different sizes.

"HER MAJESTY'S THIMBLE" is a British brand name and not a commemorative thimble. The thimble is nickel plated on brass. The plating was not durable. These have appeared on the antiques market as brass thimbles with the plating worn off.

Decorations

Decorative patterns to delight the eye were applied to the band of brass thimbles. These include a variety of floral designs, palmate shield, Greek key, Christmas bells and holly, and hearts.

Sentimental sayings also appear on the bands of brass thimbles. "Mitzpah," "Esteem," "Forget Me Not," "From a Friend," "Love," and "Industry" are among those found on bands. A child's size brass thimble with "Reward" on the band may have been given to a young girl when she completed her required sampler.

Indian Trade Thimbles

Thimbles made of brass, referred to as "trade thimbles," have been found in Indian burial grounds. The fur traders gave the Indians common metal thimbles as part of the trade for animal skins. The Indians used thimbles for decorations on their garments, and not for sewing. Holes were drilled on the cap of the thimble to enable them to be strung on rawhide thongs. The Indians called the thimbles "tinklers".

Children's Brass Thimbles

Brass thimbles were made in small sizes for children—sizes one through four. Children's thimbles were often purchased in sets of graduated sizes of the same pattern. It is unusual to find a child's size thimble that has been pierced by a needle from constant use. A child would normally outgrow the thimble long before it was pierced.

An exception to this rule are brass thimbles that were used by children enrolled in an "infant school" or "dame's school" during the nineteenth century. Children as young as twenty-four months attended this early version of today's day-care nursery. Laura Russell, born in Plymouth, Massachusetts, in 1827, wrote a handwritten description of her childhood memories. The school was in the home of a neighborhood widow, whom the children always addressed as "Marm." "Marm" started each morning by reading a chapter from the Bible, "rapping on its cover with her steel tailor's thimble as a signal for us to range ourselves in a semi-circle about her chair and listen to the Holy Word." Both girls and boys were required to learn to sew in the dame's school. There was a small wooden box, "into which at the close of each day we dropped our little brass thimbles and our bits of patchwork with its irregular blackened stitches piled one upon another after having been many times picked out and re-sewn with squeaking, crooked needle and tear-dimmed eyes."

OTHER ALLOYS

Pure copper has been used to make thimbles, but it is not durable. Copper thimbles have more reddish color than brass and are scarce.

Brass is an alloy of copper and zinc. The color of the brass depends on the amount of zinc that is added. Lead, block tin, and nickel are sometimes added to copper. Bronze is the oldest alloy known to man. It is an alloy of copper and tin.

"Latten" is an early form of brass with a bright golden color. The sixteenth and seventeenth century thimbles that were found in the archaeological digs at the London Wall and on the banks of the Thames were made of latten.

Some alloys have the word "Silver" in the name, but no silver is included in the alloy. "Nickel Silver," "German Silver," and "Alaska Silver" are alloys of copper, zinc, and nickel. They are silver in color only. The name German Silver should not be confused with the 800/1000 or 835/1000 quality of silver that comes from Germany. Silver colored thimbles from Mexico are sometimes marked "Alpacca," which also is an alloy of copper, nickel, and zinc.

"Diragold" thimbles are marked with the name near the rim. This alloy is also referred to as Scandinavian gold. It is bronze, an alloy of brass, nickel and tin. It shines to a bright golden color and is extremely durable.

Pot Metal

Early versions of the *Monopoly©* board game had pot metal markers, including one shaped like a thimble. This child size molded common metal thimble was unmarked.

Another molded pot metal child size thimble was marked "For a Good Girl" around the band. The originals of this thimble were gum-ball machine prizes rather than a working sewing tool. It is being reproduced today and offered for sale by the dozen at flea markets.

Pewter

Pewter is an alloy of block tin and copper, or any alloy of a low melting point. Modern pewter thimbles are made as souvenirs of places or events, but are not designed as working sewing tools. The picture or wording appears on the cap of the thimble, which is covered by clear dome shaped acrylic. Some have "Treasured Keepsake Thimble" stamped on the band. Several manufacturers produce these gift shop souvenirs, including Fort, Inc. of East Providence, Rhode Island. These are marked Fort (c) inside the cap.

Collecting brass and other alloy thimbles may not be as difficult as it may seem. Antiques dealers keep their gold and silver thimbles locked in display cases. The neglected common metal gems are relegated to jars of old buttons or boxes of miscellaneous odds and ends.

11-1: Old brass thimble and needles. Photo courtesy of The Cairo Museum, Cairo, Egypt.

11-2, 11-3, 11-4: Early brass thimbles. Unmarked.

11-5, 11-6, 11-7: Brass thimbles. Recovered from "digs" in England. Note: indentations were rolled onto thimble in a spiral.

11-8: Brass thimbles. Photo courtesy of Zavicajni Museum, Yugoslavia.

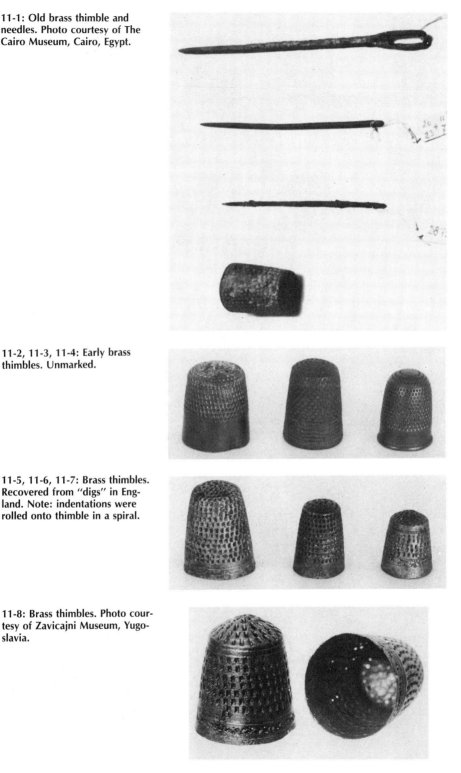

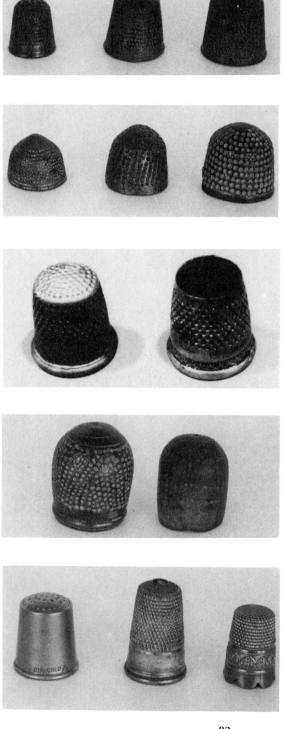

11-9, 11-10, 11-11: Brass thimbles. English. Recovered from archaeological "digs." Eighteenth and nineteenth centuries.

11-12, 11-13, 11-14: Early cast brass thimbles recovered from "digs" in England.

11-15: Brass thimbles recovered from the wreck of the Steamboat *Bertrand,* which sunk in a bend of the Missouri River, 1865. Photo courtesy of De Soto Wildlife Refuge.

11-16, 11-17: Bronze rug makers' thimbles. Turkey. Circa thirteenth century.

11-18: Diragold, sometimes referred to as Scandinavian Gold. This bronze thimble has no gold in the alloy. It is very durable and polished to a high luster; 11-19: Stanhope "peep" inserted in cap of brass thimble. Patented by William Pursall in 1880; 11-20: Ornate brass thimble with scalloped rim.

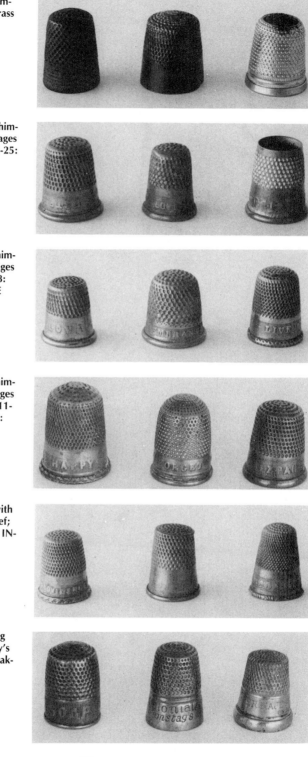

11-21, 11-22: Early brass thimbles; 11-23: Nickel plated brass with magnetic cap. Modern.

11-24, 11-25, 11-26: Brass thimbles with "love token" messages on band; 11-24: ESTEEM; 11-25: LOVE; 11-26: A PRESENT.

11-27, 11-28, 11-29: Brass thimbles with "love token" messages on band; 11-27: LOVE; 11-28: REMEMBRANCE; 11-29: LIVE AND LET LIVE.

11-30, 11-31, 11-32: Brass thimbles with "love token" messages on band; 11-30: BE HAPPY; 11-31: FORGET ME NOT; 11-32: MITZPA.

11-33, 11-34, 11-35: Brass, with "love token" messages in relief; 11-33: PROVIDENCE; 11-34: INDUSTRY; 11-35: REGARD.

11-36, 11-37: Brass advertising thimbles; 11-38: "Her Majesty's Thimble." A British thimble maker's trade mark.

11-39, 11-40, 11-41: Brass advertising thimbles; 11-39: "Gold Thimble Scotch."; 11-40: "O.N.T." (Clark's "Our New Thread"); 11-41: "Newhouse."

11-42, 11-43, 11-44: Ornate brass bands; 11-42: Christmas bells and holly; 11-43: Stars against a milled background, German; 11-44: Hearts in relief.

11-45, 11-46, 11-47: Brass. Ornate bands; 11-46: A fish in relief.

11-48: Enamel over guilloche (scoring on metal to make enamel adhere); 11-49, 11-50: Brass with synthetic stone cap.

11-51, 11-52, 11-53: Brass open top "tailor's" thimble; 11-52, 11-53: Oriental brass sewing rings.

11-54, 11-55, 11-56: Open top "tailor's" brass thimbles; 11-54: "LOVE" on band.

84

11-57: Applied American flag; 11-58: Russian. Brass with price stamped on the band: "4K" (4 Kopek, or about 5 cents). Modern; 11-59: "Her Majesty's Thimble," which is a British thimble maker's trade mark.

11-60, 11-61, 11-62: Copper. American. Nineteenth century.

11-63: Steel thimble with damascene decorated band. India. Nineteenth century.

11-64, 11-65, 11-66: Steel thimbles; 11-64: Domed cap, ornate band; 11-65: Dome cap. "Always Faithful" in raised letters around the band; 11-66: Plain. Nineteenth century.

11-67: Walnut shaped brass mending kit. Photo courtesy of American Home Sewing Museum.

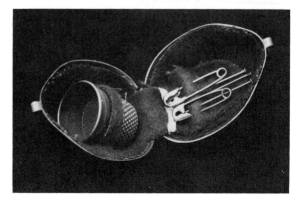

11-68: Assiniboin Indian ceremonial garment decorated with brass thimbles. Circa 1870. Photo courtesy of Buffalo Bill Historical Center, Cody, WY.

11-69, 11-70: Menominee Indians. Thimbles for jingles on stitched and beadwork cloth pieces. Photo courtesy of American Museum of Natural History, NY.

11-71, 11-72, 11-73, 11-74: Brass thimbles found at Indian burial ground fifteen miles from the site of General Custer's battle at Little Big Horn. Nineteenth century.

CHAPTER 12

Enameled Thimbles

Enamel on Sterling silver thimbles are elegant miniature works of art. Most earlier ones were hand painted. Modern ones are either hand painted or decorated with a decal.

RUSSIAN

Pre-revolution Russian enamel thimbles are considered a prize in any collection. It is easy to mistake a modern Greek enamel or a fake modern reproduction as a genuine early Russian enamel thimble.

Early Russian enamel thimbles were made as a genuine sewing tool. Two types of enameling were produced: cloisonne and niello. Cloisonne ("hairnet" or filigree) enamel is sometimes called "Russian Cloisonne." A wirework design of leaves and circles is soldered to the surface of the band of the thimble. The compartments are then filled with enamel, and fired in a kiln. For the niello thimble, the design is carved in low relief. The niello composition adheres to the carved design after firing.

NORWEGIAN

Enamel on silver thimbles have been made in Norway for many years. The older ones have a semi-precious stone cap, usually moonstone. Newer examples have a silver or silver-gilt cap, with waffle pattern indentations. The most famous designs are the Polar Bear, Viking Ship, and Reindeer. These are hand painted against a pink and blue sky, which simulates the midnight sun. Some modern Norwegian enamel thimbles have decaled floral designs.

The David-Andersen Company of Oslo, Norway, has been making enamel on silver thimbles since 1880. The company was founded in 1876 and operated today by the fourth generation of the Andersen family. David-Andersen thimbles were first sold in the United States at the Louisiana Purchase Exposition, held in St. Louis, Missouri, in 1904.

The enameling process used by David-Andersen is called mirror enameling. This is different from the enameling process used in Russia and the Orient, which is called cloisonne enameling. Mirror enameling is free form and hand applied. The translucent enamels on silver produce a mirror effect.

Thimbles made by David-Andersen have the trademark stamped inside the cap. The company artists do not sign their work. The silver contents are marked as 830S or 925S. When the thimbles are gold plated inside and on the cap, it is done by a process called vermeil (pronounced Ver-May).

GERMAN

The Gabler Brothers Company of Germany made many elegant enamel banded silver thimbles, many having a semi-precious stone cap. Because of the stone cap the Gabler mark, the eight pointed daisy flower, is not visible on the cap of the thimble. The German silver mark stamped on the second row of the indentation will give you the clue to the country of origin.

During the 1920s, Gabler made a series of souvenir thimbles with pictures of monuments, cathedrals, and tourist attractions located in countries around the world. These were exported and sold at gift shops near the attractions.

The Delft blue enameled thimbles with pictures of windmills and children wearing Dutch costumes were made in Germany. The early scenes were hand painted. The thimbles made in recent years are decorated with decals.

ENGLISH

Hand decorated enamel on brass thimbles were made in England during the eighteenth century. This craft was produced in two towns located in South Staffordshire, England: Bilston and Battersea. The work done there is often referred to as Bilston and Battersea enamels. These enamel on brass thimbles were never meant to be working sewing tools. The enamel work is fragile. Any that have survived the centuries in perfect condition command a three and four figure price. Excellent examples of this enamel work are in museums, including Colonial Williamsburg Museum in Williamsburg, Virginia.

South Staffordshire enamel thimbles with matching thimble cases were made. The decoration on the egg-shaped thimble case matched the thimble. Tube shaped needle cases had a thimble on one end, which served as a cap for the case.

Caution must be exerted when buying any South Staffordshire enamel pieces. Any repairs on the enamel will detract from the value.

The British miniature artist, Peter Swingler, has been making hand painted enamel on silver thimbles since 1973. In his method each color used to decorate the thimble must be fired in a kiln separately, requiring firing as many times as there are different colors used. Swingler has made a series of thimbles commemorating the Bicentennial of the Independence of the United States. George and Martha Washington appear on one, and the painting of Washington crossing the Delaware River is another.

Other Swingler commemorative or souvenir thimbles are the yearly issues of his Christmas and Bride thimbles. Each thimble of the series is signed and dated.

AMERICAN

Many American thimble makers offered enamel on Sterling thimbles. The labor costs to produce these today is prohibited. It can be assumed that any enamel on silver thimble with an American mark is circa 1920 or older.

GREEK

The enamel on silver thimbles made in Greece today look like Russian enamel at first glance. Closer inspection will reveal that these are of much poorer quality in both workmanship and construction. They are made flat and seamed, with applied caps. They are very light weight and made as tourist souvenirs rather than genuine sewing tools.

12-1: The six steps of the process to make modern Chinese cloisonne.

12-2, 12-3, 12-4: Cloisonne, Chinese. Modern.

12-5, 12-6: Enamel on gold. Continental. Nineteenth century. Scent bottle screws inside thimble. See base below.

12-7: Enamel on gold. Continental. Nineteenth century. The base of the scent bottle serves as a letter seal.

12-8, 12-9, 12-10: Enamel banded silver. German, made by Gabler. Twentieth century.

12-11, 12-12, 12-13: Blue enamel Dutch scenes. German, made by Gabler.

12-14, 12-15, 12-16: Blue enamel Dutch scenes. German, made by Gabler.

12-17, 12-18, 12-19: Greek enamel thimbles. Light weight. Applied cap. Modern.

12-20, 12-21, 12-22: Niello. Middle East. Late nineteenth, early twentieth centuries.

12-23, 12-24, 12-25: Moonstone caps. Enamel over guilloche silver. Norway. Late nineteenth, early twentieth centuries; 12-23: Reindeer; 12-24: Polar Bear; 12-25: Viking ship.

12-26, 12-27, 12-28: Norway, made by David-Andersen. Enamel on silver. Modern; 12-26: Polar Bear; 12-27: Reindeer; 12-28: Viking ship.

12-29, 12-30: Pre-revolution Russian enamel; 12-31: Pre-revolution Russian niello.

12-32, 12-33, 12-34: Pre-revolution Russian enamel thimbles.

12-35, 12-36, 12-37: Pre-revolution Russian enamel thimbles.

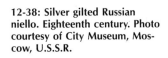

12-38: Silver gilted Russian niello. Eighteenth century. Photo courtesy of City Museum, Moscow, U.S.S.R.

12-39, 12-40, 12-41: Scandinavia. Gilted silver and enamel thimbles. Semi-precious stone caps. Norway. Enamel over guilloche silver. Late nineteenth, early twentieth centuries.

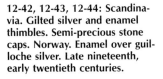

12-42, 12-43, 12-44: Scandinavia. Gilted silver and enamel thimbles. Semi-precious stone caps. Norway. Enamel over guilloche silver. Late nineteenth, early twentieth centuries.

12-45, 12-46, 12-47: English, South Staffordshire. Enamel on brass. Nineteenth century.

12-48, 12-49, 12-50: American. Floral decorated enamel bands. Early twentieth century.

CHAPTER 13

Porcelain Thimbles

The Meissen factory of Germany made thimbles starting in the early eighteenth century. These beautifully hand painted works of art were offered for sale as trinkets and gifts, rather than working sewing tools. About 250 of these early Meissen thimbles are known to have survived. When one of these is offered for sale today, it commands a five figure price.

While early Meissen porcelain thimbles are priced out of the range of the average collector, there are many affordable modern porcelain thimbles on the market today. They are offered for sale in catalogs, gift shops, and by mail subscription. Modern porcelain thimbles also are offered for sale at antiques shops and shows. Do not assume that these are antiques. Occasionally a genuine antique porcelain thimble will surface in the antiques market. Collectors must do their homework and know early porcelain marks.

Porcelain factories such as Meissen and Royal Crown Derby still make thimbles today. They are marked with the company's name, but with an entirely different mark than the one used during the eighteenth and nineteenth centuries.

ENGLISH PORCELAIN THIMBLES

English porcelain factories making hand painted thimbles today include Royal Crown Derby, Spode, and Wedgwood. Decaled thimbles are made by Crown Royal Adderley, Royal Crown Derby, Royal Doulton, and Spode. Wedgwood thimbles are decorated with an applied cameo-type design.

The Royal Worcester factory discontinued making hand painted thimbles during the 1980s, when it merged with the Spode China Company. Thimbles made by this merged company carry the Spode mark. Other lesser known porcelain factories produced thimbles during the third quarter of the twentieth century, primarily as gift items or collectibles and not as working sewing tools.

Early Royal Worcester thimbles were not marked. The shape of the thimble and the fine quality of the decoration are the only clues to the maker and date. A date marking system of a series of dots and circles was used during the first half of the twentieth century. This system was abandoned during the 1960s. Thimbles made after that date were marked "Royal Worcester, Made in England."

It was the custom of artists at the Royal Worcester factory to sign their work. Some of the most highly desirable hand painted Royal Worcester thimbles are signed by William Powell. He was a hunchback dwarf who painted beautiful birds on larger pieces of porcelain as well as on thimbles. He worked for Worcester between 1900 and 1950, where he also conducted tours through the factory. At the end of the tours, the groups were led into the sales room where they could buy some of the pieces they saw being made in the factory. Powell always made a special pitch to encourage the tourists to buy his lovely hand painted bird pieces. His thimbles were equal in quality to that on the larger, more expensive pieces. He sold many of his painted bird thimbles to the tourists at the factory.

The Wedgwood factory marked its 225th anniversary in 1984 with a commemorative thimble marked "Wedgwood 1759-1984." This blue Jasper thimble is decorated with a miniature white bas relief design of a Portland vase. The factory has documented proof that Wedgwood thimbles have been produced since the late 1700s. The Wedgwood Company does not have any examples of these early thimbles, but thimbles appear on a list of pieces fired in the kiln during that period. Drawings of the thimbles are in the old company ledgers. Early Wedgwood thimbles, as well as other small pieces, such as parasol handles and walking stick handles, were not marked with the company's name during this early period.

Jasperware is an unglazed vitreous fine stoneware. Mineral oxides are used to produce the various colors, such as blue, green, yellow, lilac, and black. Blue Jasperware is the most common color used by the Wedgwood factory. The method now used in manufacturing Wedgwood Jasperware is the same as that used in 1774.

CONTINENTAL PORCELAIN THIMBLES

The Meissen factory in East Germany still makes thimbles. This series is of one pattern issued each year, beginning in 1982. The thimbles are marked inside with the date and the company's cross sword trademark.

For centuries the Chinese closely guarded their method of producing hard paste porcelain. The credit for unraveling the mystery belongs to Johann Fredrick Boettger, an apothecary's apprentice in Berlin. In 1709 he produced a formula to make a true hard paste porcelain, and shortly afterwards devised a satisfactory glaze. This was the beginning of the Meissen porcelains.

The Meissen porcelain factory was established in 1710 in the city of Meissen, Germany. Production from this factory was not offered for sale until 1713. Some of the early Meissen pieces were unmarked. The crossed swords mark was first used by the Meissen factory about 1716, and variations of this mark have been used continuously to the present time. Today the Meissen factory in East Germany has a new name—the "People's Own Plant, State China Manufactory, Meissen." It is still producing exquisite china, including thimbles, utilizing its time-honored techniques and using the cross swords mark.

Porcelain factories in Limoges France have been making thimbles for the collectible market. Limoges thimbles that are decorated at the factory have printed or decaled designs. The ones that are sold undecorated are hand painted privately by individual artists. Some of these are signed; others are not.

AMERICAN PORCELAIN THIMBLES

Long before the modern direct mail catalog companies tried to tempt thimble collectors with the newly made thimbles, fine hand painted porcelain thimbles were made in the United States. However, very little research has been compiled on the American porcelain thimbles.

While older American porcelain thimbles are scarce, they do appear in today's antiques market, usually mixed with modern porcelains. With a sharp eye and a little education, a thimble collector can recognize these neglected treasures and buy them for a low price.

Porcelain thimbles attributed to American porcelain makers are usually un-marked. One that is documented was made by the Ott and Brewer Company of Trenton, New Jersey, and is in the collection of the Brooklyn Museum. This unmarked thimble has indentations above the floral hand painted band. The cap is slightly domed. The museum dates this thimble circa 1883–1892. Ott and Brewer was later purchased by the Lenox Company.

The Ceramic Art Company of Trenton, New Jersey, which later became the Lenox China Company, also made porcelain thimbles from Belleek paste. The Belleek clay was imported from Ireland.

Hand painted porcelain thimbles are made today by various artists in the United States. Most of this work is done on blank porcelain thimbles imported from Japan. Some, like the thimbles made by porcelain artist Mildred Kohls, are painted on blank thimbles that are molded by the artist.

Porcelain thimbles make a lovely display. Collectors must be selective in buying them. Many are thick, clumsy, and poorly decorated. Read advertisements carefully and buy from reliable established mail order firms who will refund your money if you are not satisfied with the quality of the thimble.

Price alone will not guarantee a quality porcelain thimble. Some new por-celain thimbles are poor quality, even though they are priced high. Many mod-erately prices ones are fine quality. A series of porcelain thimbles sold by mail by the Royal Crown Derby factory in England is inexpensive—$15 to $20 per thimble, depending upon the international dollar exchange. The quality of the porcelain and the decoration is superior.

13-1, 13-2, 13-3: American.
Hand painted porcelain thimbles.
Late nineteenth, early twentieth
centuries. Unmarked.

13-4, 13-5, 13-6: Modern porcelain thimbles; 13-4: Belleek, Ireland; 13-5: Spode, England; 13-6:
Limoge, France.

13-7: Modern porcelain thimbles.
Wedgwood, England; 13-8: Li-
moge, France; 13-9: Bing &
Grondahl, Denmark.

13-10, 13-11, 13-12: Modern.
American. Bisque thimbles,
signed by Mildred Kohls.

13-13, 13-14, 13-15, 13-16, 13-17, 13-18, 13-19: English. Royal Worcester porcelain thimbles. Nineteenth century.

96

13-20: Meissen eighteenth century. Harbor scene, hand painted, enclosed in gold rimmed cartouche. From the collection of French nobleman, Baron Jean Sielliere.

13-21, 13-22, 13-23: Meissen porcelain thimbles. East Germany. Modern.

13-24, 13-25, 13-26: English. Royal Crown Derby. Modern.

13-27, 13-28, 13-29: Modern English porcelain thimbles. Royal Worcester. Fruit, flowers, and bird.

13-30, 13-31, 13-32: English Royal Worcester porcelain thimbles. Birds, signed by William Powell. Circa 1940.

97

CHAPTER 14

Bone and Ivory
And Other Animal and Vegetable Material

BONE AND IVORY

Most thimbles are made of metal because it is the most durable material, but material derived from animal and vegetable parts also has been used to make thimbles.

Ivory from the tusk of an elephant is the most valuable ivory. Teeth of the hippopotamus, walrus, norwhale, sperm whale, and some types of wild boar and werhogs also are considered ivory. These have less commercial value as they are small compared to elephant ivory tusks, but their size makes them easier to carve into thimbles.

Thimbles made of elephant ivory can be identified by the innumerable criss-crossing lines which produce a pattern similar in appearance to engine turning.

Bone is often mistaken for ivory. The words "bone" and "ivory" are used interchangeable in the antiques trade by people who are not aware of the difference. Bone will not have the telltale markings of ivory. Small black spots will appear on a thimble made of bone. Bone once carried blood, and these black spots are the dried channels. Ivory is much denser and heavier than bone.

One method of determining if a piece is bone or ivory is to do the "hot needle" test. Hold a red hot needle on the piece in an out-of-the-way place. If this produces an odor like burning feathers, it is probably made of bone. Neither bone nor ivory will melt when touched with a hot needle. Imitation ivory will.

Some early celluloid was made to imitate ivory, complete with the wavy lines that appear on genuine ivory. Early versions of this form of imitation ivory were called Xylonite, Ivorine, or Ivoride. These products were developed during the last half of the nineteenth century as a substitute material for genuine ivory in the production of billiard balls. Camphor is one of the ingredients of these products, and a camphor odor will surface when the piece is rubbed. Celluloid is sometimes called "French Ivory".

Scrimshaw

Scrimshaw was once considered just a novelty. Today it is classified as folk art. The crewmen on the whaling ships during the golden era of whaling (1825-1865) whiled away the boring hours between the sightings of whales by carving whale bones and teeth. Many of these thimbles and other scrimshawed pieces were brought home as gifts. Others never found their way back to the United States. They were exchanged for the coin of the realm at the various ports around the world to buy trinkets and pleasures when the seamen were on shore leave.

No one knows the origin of this art. Some link it to the ancient art of the Oriental ivory carvings. Others associate it with the Eskimos working on ivory and bone or the Indians of the Caribbean and South America.

There is said to be an unwritten law that the lower jaw of the sperm whale with its teeth belonged to the crew. A good size sperm had approximately 50 teeth measuring from 4 to 10 inches long, all on the lower jaw. The smallest of the teeth lent themselves in size and shape to be made into thimbles. Few scrimshaw pieces are dated, but it can be assumed they were made during the early and mid-nineteenth century. There were no rules about what a scrimshadler used. Whale bones or shark bones often were used. As long as the bone was not too porous, it was suitable for scrimshawing.

ORIENTAL IVORY

Oriental ivory thimbles were exported to the United States and Europe. These were part of the fitted work box. Oriental carvers worked from pictures. Even though their thimbles looked like thimbles, many were not usable working tools because they were bulky and not tapered inside to fit the finger. Some had indentations on the side and cap, while others were smooth and plain.

OTHER ANIMAL MATERIAL

Tortoise Shell

Tortoise shell thimbles can be dated from the eighteenth and nineteenth centuries. The horny plate of the turtle can be polished to a smooth finish. The shell of the Loggerhead turtle is a mottled yellow and dark brown. This was found in the Pacific and often used in Oriental carvings. The best tortoise shell comes from the Hawkbill turtle, which is found in the Caribbean and South Pacific. The Hawkbill colors range from brown amber to dark mahogany red. The shell from the green turtle was considered an inferior type of shell.

Turtle shell is strong and pliable, but it can be softened by boiling in salt water. After boiling, the shell is so soft it can be inlaid with gold, silver, or other materials. The items to be inlaid were pressed into the shell without the use of glue.

John Piercy of England patented his process, British Patent #4077, for making a thimble made of tortoise shell in 1816. A gold medallion in the shape of a turtle and a banner with "Piercy's Patent" was inlaid on the thimble. The caps were either gold or silver. Other tortoise shell thimbles were made during the nineteenth century. Some had inlaid gold decorations. Others were plain.

Early plastic makers developed a good imitation of tortoise shell. The color and mottle effect can fool the eye, but the camphor odor test will prove it is not a genuine shell. Also, a hot needle applied to the imitation piece will quickly pierce it.

Mother-of-Pearl

Mother-of-Pearl thimbles were made in Paris during the early nineteenth century in a group of shops located near the Royal Palace. Today these thimbles are referred to as Palais Royal thimbles. Some of these were decorated with an enameled medallion with a pansy and had one or two gilted metal rings. Mother-of-pearl thimbles were turned on a lathe from a solid block of material. The inner layers of the pearl oyster shell and other mollusks were the best material for this purpose.

An iridescent glow will appear on only two places on the thimble, where the top and bottom of the block was located. The block of Mother-of-pearl is composed of layer upon layer of shell built up over years by the live oyster. What may appear to be a crack may really be marks of these separate layers. Mother-of-pearl is sometimes used in place of moonstone or other stones on the cap of a silver or gold thimble. The purpose of this stone cap is to absorb the wear of the needle.

Abalone is another type of Mother-of-pearl. It is not suitable for making a thimble, but it is used to decorate them. The glowing red or green abalone shell is inlaid on Mexican silver thimbles today.

Mother-of-pearl should be kept away from direct sunlight. Sunlight will cause it to loose its iridescent glow. This is quite the opposite of ivory, which needs sunlight to keep it in good condition.

VEGETABLE IVORY

Two tropical trees found in South American produce nuts that are hard enough to be carved. The shell of the coquilla nut from the Brazilian palm tree is brown or tan in color and very durable. Thimbles made from the shell of this nut may have a gold cap and gold ring at the rim of the thimble.

Another tropical nut used to make vegetable ivory thimbles is the inner seed of the Coroza nut. The meat of this nut is hard enough to be carved into a thimble and thimble holder. These two pieces were made at the same time as a pair. A collector would be fortunate to find a vegetable ivory thimble holder with the matching thimble inside. The natural color of this nut meat runs from tan to brown. It will not accept dyes and is left in the natural hue of the nut. Buttons also were made of nut meat. Vegetable ivory buttons were first displayed at the Universal Exposition, Paris, in 1862.

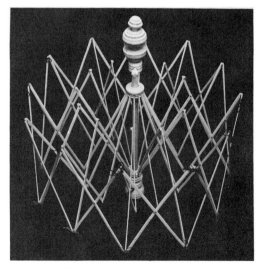

14-1: Whale bone swift for skeining yarns. Circa 1850. Photo courtesy of The American Home Sewing Museum.

14-2, 14-3, 14-4: Coquilla nut shell. Gold cap and rim. South American. Nineteenth century.

14-5: Ivory thimble in original case, circa 1800. Photo courtesy of Museum of the City of New York.

14-6, 14-7, 14-8: Ivory. Nineteenth century.

14-9, 14-10, 14-11: Ivory. Chinese. Nineteenth century. Originally part of fitted Chinese export work box.

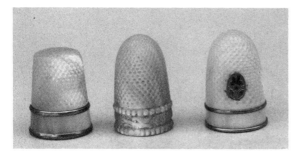

14-12, 14-13, 14-14: Mother of Pearl. French. Early nineteenth century; 14-12: Two gilted rings; 14-13: Dome cap, engraved band; 14-14: Pansy medallion, two gilted rings.

14-15, 14-16, 14-17: Scrimshawed whale bone. American. Nineteenth century; 14-15: Two love birds and hearts; 14-16: Arrow pierces double initialed heart; 14-17: Whale.

14-18, 14-19, 14-20: Tortoise shell; 14-18: Gold inlaid decoration, gold cap, and lining; 14-19, 14-20: Tortoise shell, gold cap and lining.

14-21, 14-22, 14-23: Tortoise shell; 14-21: Piercy's Patent. Gold medallion, gold cap; 14-22: Piercy's Patent. Gold medallion, silver cap; 14-23: Gold inlaid, gold cap and lining.

14-24, 14-25, 14-26: Vegetable Ivory. South American. Nineteenth century.

CHAPTER 15

Patented and Gadget Thimbles

The earliest recorded patent for the manufacture of a thimble was granted to John Lofting in 1693. British Patent, 319 is for the "engine" or "instrument" for the manufacture of a thimble.

Several hundred patents for unusual thimbles have been granted by the United States Patent Office. Although some were never produced commercially, many of these can be found in the antiques markets today. They should be priced low as they are made of common metals. A complete list of patents and copies of the patent drawings are in the library of Thimble Collectors International.

Many large libraries have copies of the patent records, either in printed form or on microfilm. Photo copies of patents can be obtained from the U. S. Patent and Trademark Office, Washington, D. C. 20231. When ordering a copy of a patent from the U.S. Patent office, include the patent number, date of patent (if known), name of patentee, and a brief description of the piece. There is a charge of $1.50 for each patent paper ordered. If you want more information regarding patent searches, write for the Patent and Trademark publication *Obtaining Information from Patents, Patent Classification and Search Services.*

Two different types of patents were issued by the United States Patent office: Utility Patents and Design Patents. The Utility Patented thimble will have a feature included in the design of the thimble. The Design Patent is issued for an original and ornamental design or decoration on a thimble.

DESIGN PATENTS

The Simons Brothers Company of Philadelphia holds several Design Patents. Many of these were patented by Henry Weihman, an employee of Simons Company, with the patents assigned to the Simons company.

The Simons thimble in the shape of the Liberty Bell was patented by Weihman in 1892, Design Patent 21,844. The thimble was unique enough to warrant a design patent. The wording on the thimble is similar to, but not exactly the same as, the wording on the original Liberty Bell.

Design Patent 28,721 was issued to Simons Brothers on May 31, 1898. The design on the band of this thimble is a series of ovals and darts. Simons named this pattern *Priscilla* and marked the pattern name inside the cap. This has become one of the Simons' most popular patterns. It has been produced continually since the turn of the century.

UTILITY PATENTS

A variety of gadgets attached to a thimble or included in the design were patented over the years. Thimbles were designed to accommodate long fingernails. Others had needle pulling devices. Needle threaders and thread cutters were incorporated into the thimble design. Magnets to pick up steel pins were included in the thimble.

Protecting Fingernails

An ordinary thimble would not accommodate a finger with long nails. In 1925, Jesse Baker patented a thimble with a slanted cap, stating in her patent application that this is "a thimble shaped to the natural form of the finger-end that holds it".

Joy Bradly of Sherman Oaks, California, received a patent for a thimble with a disk inside the cap. The ball of the finger would rest on the disk, and the fingernail would extend beyond the disk. Patent 140,525 was issued in 1945. It was manufactured by Shaw and Lucas, Inc. of Glendale, California under the name *Mandarin Thimble*.

Claude Howser of Santa Barbara, California, patented his finger shaped thimble in 1952. This patent had zig-zag grooves instead of indentations on the side of the thimble.

A Michigan housewife became tired of waiting for engineers and inventors to design a comfortable thimble. In 1966 Stella Brophy designed and patented the *Brophy's Nu-Thimble*. She patented, manufactured, and marketed it herself. This pink plastic thimble is open on one side, which permits a long finger nail to extend beyond the top of the thimble. The added feature is that the size is adjustable and will fit any finger. When Brophy assigned her patent to a manufacturer, it was marketed under the name of *Nu-Thimble*.

Magnetic Devices

Magnetic devices have been included in thimble designs to enable a seamstress to pick up steel pins, especially ones that have dropped into a crack in the floor. Theodor Weigle of Germany patented his magnetic thimble in 1909. The horseshoe shaped magnet is incorporated in the side of the thimble, but does not interfere with the use of the thimble.

Other thimbles had the magnet on the cap, complete with the indentations. Pins are made of brass today and will not react to a magnet.

Replaceable Caps

In the days before we became a disposable society, Otto Weber patented a thimble with a replaceable cap. His 1896 patent drawing shows a thimble with a smooth side and cap. Another cap with indentations was designed to screw over this thimble. When the removable cap became worn and pierced from constant use it could be replaced with a new one.

Needle Pullers and Pushers

Pulling and pushing a needle through heavy fabric is a chore. A variety of inventors patented thimbles with devices that make this easier.

Usriah Knauss of Bethlehem, Pennsylvania, received a patent 562,730 in 1896 for a thimble with an attached clamp. This needle gripping clamps made it easier to push the needle through the fabric.

A different needle pusher was patented by Henry Burig of The Bronx, New York, in 1962. A tube-shaped attachment is soldered to the outside of the thimble. The interior of the tube has a spring similar to the piece that is used on the end of a stick pin. Publicity for this thimble stated that is was used by the costume department of the Radio City Music Hall in New York. It permitted the needle-worker to push and pull a needle through the heaviest fabric. This thimble has been available through catalogs and in fabric shops in recent years.

Thread Cutters

A variety of patents have been issued for thimbles with thread cutting and needle threading devices. The thimble with a razor-like knife and wire needle threader on the side is marked "M.T. Patented." This is the "Magic Thimble," patented in 1926, Patent 1,585,936. It was made in huge quantities and marketed heavily.

Another thimble with a thread cutting device was patented by Eugenia King in 1917, Patent 1,221,546. The patent was issued for "a lip" that was punched in the band of the thimble. Thread is cut when passed through this lip.

Collapsible Thimble

A telescoping thimble, which collapsed like a camp cup or "bicycle rider's" drinking cup, was patented by Grace Holden in 1907. The thimble in its compact form could then be carried in a lady's coin or card case.

Finger Guards

The index finger on the left hand needed protection from the needle, too. Fabric was draped over this finger during sewing, and the needle could go through the fabric and prick the skin. Finger guards or shields were invented and patented to protect the left index finger.

In 1870 George Spencer of Cleveland, Ohio, invented a finger guard, Patent 107,420. His finger guard had a small bone roller included in the design. In his patent application, Spencer stated, "By a slight movement of the thumb, imparting an intermittment rotary motion to the roller, the operator is enabled to feed forward the fabric more readily and with greater rapidity than when it rests upon the finger in the usual way." This finger guard is open on top. Thimble collectors call this a hem roller.

The finger guard patented by Mary Connelly of Brooklyn, New York, in 1895 (Patent 525,756) is designed to "protect the finger holding the goods, will permit the finger to be bent to hold the goods, and by means of which the needle will be guided and kept from slipping, with consequent danger of injury to the fingers." The patent attorney who wrote this description of the Connelly finger guard made it seem more complicated than it really is. This finger guard merely had grooves to guide the needle in a straight line.

THIMBLE "QUACKERY"

A patent for a thimble was granted to Marshal Beaty of Cincinnati, Ohio, on June 19, 1883. Although this thimble could be used for sewing, this was not its prime purpose. The thimble was designed to be made in several layers of metal, including copper. The inventor claimed that it was useful as a medical curative agent. "Chloride of sodium" (perspiration) would create "electricity," which in turn would cure almost anything that might ail a person. The same claim was made for rings, bracelets, and corset stays during the late nineteenth century. This is one of the early versions of the copper bracelet that is touted today as a cure for arthritis. It is unknown if this thimble was ever produced commercially.

Another thimble which claimed to have medical curative effect was patented in England on March 16, 1909 by Alfred Constantine. The thimble had a steel lining plus a band of zinc. Copper studs were inserted into the zinc. The inventor claimed that the wearing of this thimble would cure such ailments as rheumatism. Perspiration against the zinc and copper was supposed to create this marvelous cure.

At first glance, this thimble appears to be an ordinary thimble with a pretty English style pattern decorating the side. Although a layer of silver covers the steel, zinc and copper core, it does not qualify to be hallmarked. The maker's mark, "A.C.e." and "PAT." is stamped on the band. The copper studs appear inside the thimble near the rim.

15-1: Spencer's "hem roller" patent, 1870; 15-2: Downer "hem roller," patented 1861; 15-3: Finger guard, patented 1895 by Mary Connelly.

15-4: Single lip thread cutter, patented by W. P. Slensby,1885; 15-5: Double lip thread cutter; 15-6: Needle grabbing clamp, patented by Uriah Knauss, 1896.

15-7: Tobacco stemming thimbles, worn on thumb and index fingers.

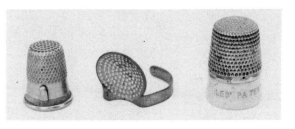

15-8: Needle grabber gadget on band; 15-9: Needle pushing disk, worn on palm of the hand. Patented by Ruby Luse, 1922; 15-10: Metal capped celluloid thimble, patented by Charles Iles, May 8, 1900.

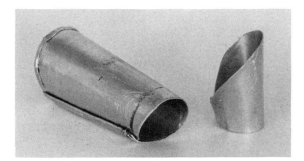

15-11: Needle pushing disk, patented by Ruby Luse, February 7, 1922.

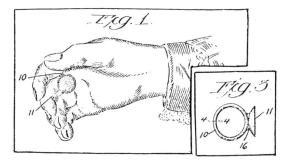

15-12: Needle grabber attachment. Patented by Uriah Knauss, June 23, 1896. Patent #562,730; 15-13: Magnet embedded into side of thimble to pick up stray pins. Patented by Theodor Weigle, June 22, 1909; 15-14: Seam ripper thimble, patented by Kenly Bugg, May 20, 1952. Patent #2,597,564.

15-15, 15-16, 15-17: Patents for long fingernails; 15-15: English. Silver. Open top finger guard. Nineteenth century; 15-16: Celluloid, patented by Stella Brophy, 1967; 15-17: Mandarin thimble, patented by Joy Bradley, 1944.

15-18, 15-19, 15-20: Finger shaped thimbles; 15-19: Patented by Claude Howser, 1948.

15-21, 15-22, 15-23: Finger guards, to be worn on the left hand. Silver. Nineteenth century.

15-24: Patent drawings of Iles ventilated thimble, (below).

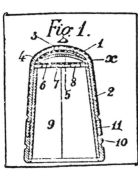

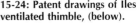

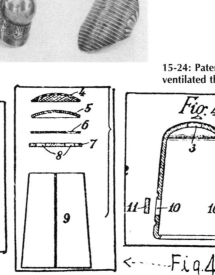

15-25: Burig patent.

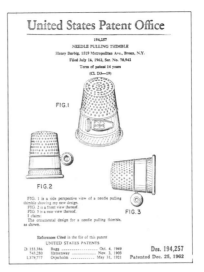

United States Patent Office

194,257
NEEDLE PULLING THIMBLE
Henry Burbig, 1519 Metropolitan Ave., Bronx, N.Y.
Filed July 16, 1962, Ser. No. 70,942
Term of patent 14 years
(Cl. D3—19)

FIG.1

FIG.2

FIG. 1 is a side perspective view of a needle pulling
thimble showing my new design.
FIG. 2 is a front view thereof.
FIG. 3 is a rear view thereof.
I claim:
The ornamental design for a needle pulling thimble,
as shown.

FIG.3

References Cited in the file of this patent
UNITED STATES PATENTS
D. 155,386   Bugg .... Oct. 4, 1949   Des. 194,257
743,280   Hemenway .... Nov. 3, 1903
1,379,777   Orjerholm .... May 31, 1921   Patented Dec. 25, 1962

15-26, 15-27: Needle threading
gadget extends from rim of the
thimble, and thread cutting lip is
cut out on the band. This thimble
was advertised by M. E. Tice,
Brooklyn, NY, in *Modern Priscilla
Magazine*, March, 1907; 15-28:
Needle pulling thimble. Patent by
Henry Burig, 1962.

15-29: The Non-Slip thimble patented by J. Taylor of England;
15-30: The interior of the Iles
Non-Slip is coated.

15-31: Iles ventilated thimble,
patented in England, 1909. It is
lined with celluloid for comfort;
15-32: Thimble with "peep" or
Stanhope in cap. Patented by
William Pursall, 1880. British
patent #118.

CHAPTER 16

Advertising and Political Thimbles
Fingertip Billboards

Advertising thimbles, once considered the step child of collectible thimbles, cover an extensive area of goods and services, both modern and bygone. These little advertising ploys helped many a salesman open a door. Tradesmen knew that these tokens would constantly remind the consumer of their product. Many collectors specialize in collecting only advertising thimbles because they are easy to find and inexpensive to buy.

Advertising thimbles are primarily American. While some have appeared hawking British, French, or German products, the vast majority of them were American.

The list of products and services that appear on the band of advertising thimbles is endless. One that promoted a product that would improve egg production may have come from a rural area. Thimbles from small town merchants would advertise a dress shop or shoe repair. Some products that appear on these thimbles seem bizarre to us today, but they were acceptable at the time. An aluminum thimble that reads, "KIL-VE Destroys Vermin on Children's Heads" was a needed and useful product at one time.

Advertising thimbles made of aluminum or celluloid are older than the modern plastic examples. Aluminum advertising thimbles made their appearance in the early 1900s, and peaked in popularity in the 1930s. They were produced in this country in smaller quantities until the late 1950s.

Other dating clues include the number of digits in a telephone number. If a thimble has wording such as "Victory" or "Buy Bonds," it is from the World War I and II years. Political thimbles range from Presidential campaigns down to all manner of local elections. Presidential thimbles are easy to date, but thimbles naming local candidates who campaigned years ago require research.

The slogan "Holland Furnaces Make Warm Friends" was a campaign to encourage people to install central heat in their homes. "Delco-Light, Lightens the Burden of the Housewife" promoted portable electric generators. This was before power lines were extended to rural areas. Funeral homes and cemeteries that advertised on thimbles probably were the same ones who kept church pews supplied with cardboard fans.

The Delco Light thimble is common and easy to find on the market today. The company was formed in 1908 by two aspiring inventors, Charles Kettering and Edward Deeds. Their company, Dayton (Ohio) Engineering Laboratories, was shortened to the name "Delco." By the late 1930s public utilities had reached most rural areas and the Delco Light generating plants were no longer in great demand. The company turned its resources to home appliances and automobile parts and eventually became part of the General Motors Company.

METAL ADVERTISING THIMBLES

Insurance companies gave away millions of advertising thimbles as reminders of their services. The most common of these are from the Prudential Insurance Company. Two different nickel plated brass thimbles were made. One carried only the name of the company; the other had the name and "Made in U.S.A." in raised letters on the band. A million Prudential thimbles were distributed in 1904. Another million were handed out in 1908. They were extremely durable, although the plating wore off with constant use over the years.

During the 1920s a third Prudential thimble appeared. It had the same wording, but was made of aluminum. It was not as durable and was easily pierced with a needle. Prudential distributed millions of other sewing related complimentary gifts, including wire needle threaders and paper pin holders.

The Prudential giveaway thimbles permitted the insurance salesman to get a toe-hold into homes to sell his policy. One of his other giveaways was not as subtle. It is a oval paper pin card with a picture of a young widow holding an infant. Printed on the reverse is "I don't know how I should have got along without it," and "That's what they tell the Prudential man when he pays a claim."

The advertising messages on the thimbles covered a wide range of services and products. "Lay or Bust," with a picture of a hen laying eggs, promoted a poultry raising product. "Craig's Wife, the Pulitzer Prize Play" was the wording on another thimble. Advertising thimbles were geared to the rural farm woman wearing calico and the sophisticated city lady dressed in brocade.

There was no standard method of distributing advertising thimbles. Most were handed to a potential customer by a salesman. Others were packaged with the product, such as flour or bread, at the factory. The thimble that says "Use Peerless Flour" was inserted into each bag of flour when it was packaged at the mill in Miamisburg, Ohio. The mill closed in 1938.

Most were used for sewing, but others were not. In either case, advertising thimbles found a home in the family sewing basket.

The Old Sleepy Eye flour company distributed many advertising giveaways, including an aluminum thimble. This thimble had a picture of the Indian Chief, Old Sleepy Eye, and the wording around the band. Old Sleepy Eye memorabilia collectors are constantly searching for this thimble and are willing to pay a high price for it. Don't be shocked to see a hundred dollar price tag.

Aluminum is a soft metal that bends easily. Many of the aluminum advertising thimbles offered on the antiques market today are bent, cracked, or pierced. Avoid buying those that are less than perfect. An aluminum advertising thimble with a repainted band detracts rather than adds to the value.

SILVER ADVERTISING THIMBLES

Some advertising thimbles were made of silver and used as premiums or gifts, but not in the quantities as other metal and plastic thimbles.

The Charlmer's Pearl Button Company of Amsterdam, New York, offered their customers a light weight Sterling silver thimble for five empty button cards and a few cents to cover postage.

Pearl buttons were sold loose in a bin until the end of the nineteenth century.

It was difficult to find a set that matched in color in the bin of loose buttons. Charlmer's Pearl buttons were more expensive, but all the buttons on a card matched perfectly. The thimble has "Charlmer's Pearls" engraved on the band.

Needlecraft was a popular needlework magazine published in Augusta, Maine, from 1909 until 1941. It offered a silver thimble with the word "Needlecraft" on the band in exchange for selling five subscriptions to the magazine.

The Domestic Sewing Machine Company gave a silver thimble with the purchase of a sewing machine. The name of the company was engraved around the band.

James Walker, a British jeweler, offered a silver thimble as a gift when a couple purchased a wedding ring. Two different ones were made: "James Walker, the London Jeweller" (British spelling) and "James Walker Wishes You Luck." Other British jewelers adopted this custom. Included were "Hendersons Jewellers, Dundee," "Douglas Jewellers, Storbridge," "Vincent, Vioil," and "Harrol-Ring Shop-Barnsley & Mexbore." All had the wording around the band and were made for the shops by Henry Griffith, a thimble maker from Birmingham, England. The date the thimble was made can be determined by the assay letter mark on the band of the thimble.

Another silver advertising thimble was offered as a premium by a British company, Andrews Liver Salts. This was an over-the-counter digestive product, similar to the American product, Sal Hepatica (Sal = salt, Hepatica = liver).

CELLULOID AND PLASTIC

By the early 1930s plastic advertising thimbles appeared. They were produced in a variety of colors and made in a mold that held ten or more thimbles in a row. The numbers inside the cap are mold numbers, not size numbers.

Plastic thimbles are made in one size, but because of the taper of the interior, they are a comfortable fit to most fingers. Sometimes a rough point appears on the rim of these molded thimbles where the row was snapped apart when taken from the mold. The rough point wears away with use. Plastic thimbles with old fashioned logos that have this rough point may be newly made. Beware of these reproductions.

Plastic thimbles made by Brown and Bigelow of St. Paul, Minnesota, are the only ones marked by the manufacturer. The mark, "B&B St. Paul," appears inside the cap of the thimbles.

Many of Brown and Bigelow's plastic thimbles were painted red on the cap. Other makers of plastic thimbles did not mark their products with a name or trademark. Accurate Molding Company, Long Island City, New York, and Morgan Plastic of Nashville, Tennessee, currently make plastic thimbles.

POLITICAL THIMBLES

The history of political campaign advertising thimbles began with the amendment giving the vote to women, ratified on August 20, 1920, just in time for the 1920 political campaign. The first Presidential candidate to use the advertising thimble was Warren G. Harding.

Early political thimbles were made of aluminum. Modern ones are plastic. The most common older ones are the Hoover and Coolidge thimbles. They were distributed in huge quantities, many of which have survived, but not in the best condition. Hoovers's reads "Hoover * Home * Happiness" in raised letters with a red or blue background. Coolidge's reads, "Coolidge and Dawes," also with raised letters and blue background.

An aluminum thimble-shaped whistle was distributed during the Landon and Knox campaign. It has been told that the delegates in the convention hall blew these little whistles whenever Landon's name was said. The combination of hundreds of these whistles blown at the same time created quite a racket.

A unique collection can be made concentrating only on the Nixon campaign thimbles. A different thimble was made for each of his campaigns. This probably resulted because Mrs. Nixon's personal secretary was an avid thimble collector. Most of the Nixon campaign thimbles are yellow, Mrs. Nixon's favorite color. An exception was the 1952 white thimble with red and blue printing that reads, "Lets Sew It Up for Ike and Dick." The 1946 Nixon thimble reads, "Nixon for Congress. Put The Needle in the P.A.C." This was the Political Action Committee which was campaigning for the opposition candidate.

Advertising thimbles are available at the antiques market today. They are priced from less than one dollar to as high as five dollars. Many collectors limit their collection to certain products, such as foods, services, areas or states.

Political thimbles are priced higher than other advertising thimble. Thimble collectors find they have to compete with the political memorabilia collectors for these.

16-1: Advertising thimbles were made to appeal to the sophisticated city woman. This one encouraged her to see "Craig's Wife," the Pulitzer Prize play.

16-2, 16-3, 16-4: Early political thimbles; 16-2: Coolidge and Dawes; 16-3: Hoover * Home * Happiness; 16-4: Landon and Knox.

16-5: America for Americans. Wilkie for President; 16-6: Vote for Dewey-Brinker; 16-7: For Good Government Vote Republican.

16-8: Nixon for Congress. Put the Needle in the P.A.C; 16-9: Safeguard the American Home. Nixon For U.S. Senator; 16-10: Nixon For Governor.

16-11, 16-12: A collection of Nixon campaign thimbles; 16-11: Ike & Dick; 16-12: Sew It Up For Nixon-Lodge.

16-13: Nixon's The One. Elect Nixon in '68; 16-14: Nixon-Agnew '72; 16-15: President Nixon Now More Than Ever.

16-16, 16-17, 16-18: A collection of Carter campaign thimbles; 16-16: "Grits and Fritz in '78."; 16-17: "The Grin Will Win."; 16-18: "Jimmy Carter for President in '78."

16-19, 16-20, 16-21: The Republican Party appealed to women with advertising thimbles; 16-19: Sew Up The Votes For The G O P; 16-20: Vote Straight Republican; 16-21: Vote The Straight Republican Ticket.

16-22, 16-23, 16-24: Political thimbles promoted candidates for local offices.

16-25, 16-26, 16-27; Thimble whistles. 16-25: The thimble whistle from the Landon and Knox political campaign.

16-28: Feed and Supplies thimble whistle; 16-29: Cities Service Fuel Oil; 16-30: Celluloid. "A Rootin' Tootin' Tarnow Man. Capt. Mac says don't blow in house or school." This is an advertising thimble whistle for children.

16-31, 16-32, 16-33: Advertising thimbles promoted many products and services; 16-31: This thimble with a logo only was attached to a bag of Purina chicken feed. The wording on the bag stated that a thimbleful of a certain product was added to the feed to encourage better egg production; 16-32: Another chicken feed company gave away a thimble that says "Lay Or Bust."; 16-33: Coal Company.

115

PALAIS ROYAL

Workshops located near the Royal Palace in Paris during the eighteenth and nineteenth centuries produced fine sewing tools made of mother-of-pearl. Today these are referred to as Palais Royal pieces.

This gilted metal basket is surrounded by twenty-two tear drop shaped mother-of-pearl disks and topped with glass. Each disk holds a miniature silk flower arrangement. The lid has a silk flower arrangement under the glass dome.

Sewing tools under the domed lid include: A cut glass scent bottle with gold screw on the cap. A glass stopper is under the cap. A mother-of-pearl ripper (a metal blade similar to a jack knife blade, which swings out of the holder). Scissors with mother-of-pearl bows. The scissors shanks have inlaid gold decorations; the unmarked blades are made of steel.

Also a mother-of-pearl snow flake shaped thread winder is stored under the bows of the scissors. A mother-of-pearl thimble rests on the base of the scissors blades. The inlaid gold disk has a hand painted enamel pansy on it. The French word "pensee" means thought, which may account that this particular flower appears on many mother-of-pearl pieces.

Also a mother-of-pearl bodkin or ribbon threader. A carved mother-of-pearl needle case with inlaid gold decorations.

The applied paper label on the bottom of the basket reads:

NAQUIET & CO.

PALAIS-ROYAL No. 152

Md de Nauvenutes

brevetes du Roi Poui

Import de Thuile

de Maiafsav

Paris

116

PRE-REVOLUTION RUSSIAN ENAMEL SILVER AND SILVER GILT THIMBLES

Wirework design of leaves and circles is soldered to the surface of the band of the thimble. The compartments are then filled with enamel and fired in a kiln. Each color is fired separately, starting with the color that will accept the highest degree of heat.

P-2: Modern, Russian Enamel-style, marked "88" inside the cap.

P-1

P-2

P-3

P-4

P-5

P-6

P-7

P-8

PLATE 2

PALAIS ROYAL

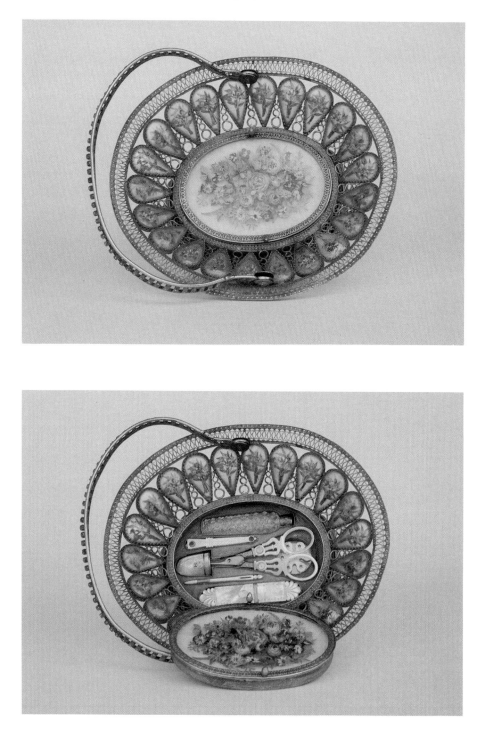

PLATE 1

GENUINE PRE-REVOLUTION RUSSIAN NIELLO THIMBLES

The design is carved on the silver in low relief. The niello composition adheres to the carved design after firing in a kiln.

P-9   P-10   P-11

FAKE REPRODUCTIONS OF RUSSIAN ENAMEL THIMBLES

Fake Russian enamel thimbles with "84" silver quality mark and a deliberately smeared maker's mark. The "wire work" is part of the casting and the indentations are shallow. The rim is thick and interior of the thimble is rough. The enameled colors are painted and not fired in a kiln.

P-12   P-13

GENUINE POST-REVOLUTION RUSSIAN ENAMEL THIMBLES

P-14: Silver.   P-15: Silver with attached chain and finger ring.

PLATE 3

GOLD THIMBLES

P-16: Continental stone capped gold thimbles.

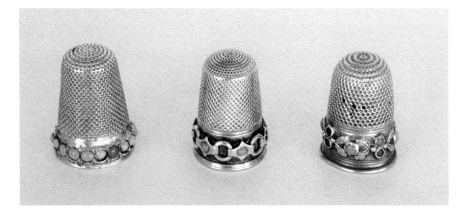

P-17: Gold thimbles with stones on the bands.

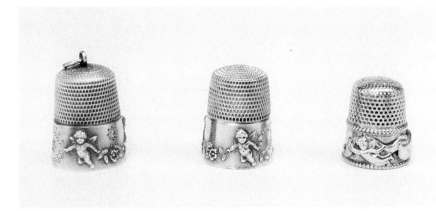

P-18: American gold thimbles with cupids on the bands.

PLATE 4

GOLD THIMBLES

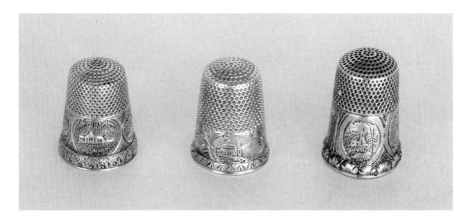

P-19: Gold thimbles with scenes on the bands.

P-20: Gold thimbles with enameled bands.

P-21: French, blue enameled band inscribed "Prefitez du Temps," seed pearls on the rim; P-22: Enamel on gold, Middle East; P-23: Hand chased gold, India.

PLATE 5

GOLD THIMBLES

P-24: "Wedding Band" gold thimbles. French, late eighteenth, early nineteenth centuries. One garland has been removed from each thimble.

P-25, P-26: "Wedding Band" gold thimbles with two garlands. One garland can be removed to make a wedding band. French, late eighteenth, early nineteenth centuries.

P-27: Multi-colored gold bands. French, nineteenth century.

PLATE 6

GOLD THIMBLES

P-28: "Louis IV" band. Ketcham and McDougall.

P-29: Hand made gold thimble with applied cap. American, late eighteenth, early nineteenth centuries.

P-30: Ornate gold thimble with pierced band. American, early twentieth century.

P-31: Continental gold with semi-precious stone cap.

P-32: Gold thimble with enameled band. Scent bottle screws inside the thimble. Base of bottle has initials for wax letter seal. French, nineteenth century.

DORCAS THIMBLES

P-33: Gold Dorcas thimbles. Marked "9 ct. Steel Lined."

PLATE 7

P-34: Columbian Exposition, Chicago, IL, 1893. Simons. 10K gold.

P-35: Liberty Bell, Philadelphia, PA. Simons, circa 1900. 14K gold.

P-36: Louisiana Purchase World's Fair, St. Louis, MO, 1904. Simons. 14K gold.

P-37, P-38, P-39: Bicentennial commemorative thimbles. Enamel on silver. Hand painted by Peter Swingler. England; P-37: George and Martha Washington; P-38: Washington crossing the Delaware River; P-39: "Skilled Hands for Freedom."

P-40, P-41, P-42: British Royalty commemorative thimbles. Enamel on silver. Hand painted by Peter Swingler. England; P-40: Queen Mother; P-41: Queen Elizabeth II; P-42: Prince Charles.

PLATE 8

ENAMEL THIMBLES

P-43: Enamel over Guilloche silver. Moonstone cap. Norway, late nineteenth, early twentieth centuries.

P-44: Enamel on silver. Siamese motif. Thailand, formerly Siam. Modern.

P-45: Enamel on silver. Transfer print. Dutch motif. Gabler, Germany.

P-46: Enamel on silver. "Stitch for the Red, White, and Blue." England, circa 1917.

P-47: Enamel on silver. Swastika. American. Waite Threasher, circa 1920.

P-48: Enamel on brass. China. Modern.

PLATE 9

PORCELAIN THIMBLES

P-49: Derby, England, nineteenth century; P-50: Worcester, England, nineteenth century; P-51: Unmarked, England, nineteenth century.

P-52: Meissen, Germany, eighteenth and nineteenth centuries.

P-53: American Belleek, Ott & Brewer, New Jersey, late nineteenth century. Photo courtesy of the Brooklyn Museum, Brooklyn, NY.

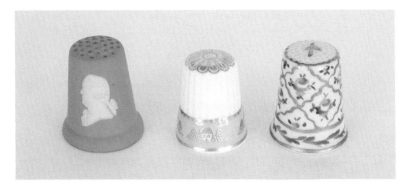

P-54: Wedgwood, England; P-55: Spode, England; P-56: Limoges, France. Modern.

PLATE 10

IVORY AND TORTOISE SHELL THIMBLES

P-57: Tortoise shell. Piercy's Patent. England, early nineteenth century. Gold cap and inlaid gold decoration.

P-58: Tortoise shell. Early nineteenth century. Gold cap and inlaid decoration. Gold lined.

P-59: Vegetable ivory. Coroza nut shell. Gold cap and rim. Applied gold beads. South America.

P-60: Fitted tortoise shell work box with gold tools. Thread winder, bodkin, thimble, scissors, thread waxer, and needle case.

P-61: Tortoise shell Lady's Companion; P-62, P-63: Tortoise shell knife box shaped thimble cases.

PATENT THIMBLES

P-64: Magic Thimble with needle threader and cutter, circa 1920. Gold plated, original box. Band marked "M.T. Patented."

P-65, P-66: Finger shaped thimbles; P-65: Center . Patent by Claude Hower, 1948; P-66: Celluloid. Patent by Stella Brophy, 1967.

PLATE 11

P-67: Porcelain figures holding pin cushions. Knobs on top of their heads are thimble holders. Germany, early twentieth century.

P-68: Porcelain cupid holds a thimble in a thimble shaped quiver on his back. Germany, nineteenth century.

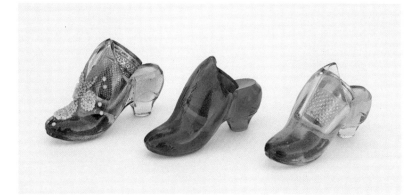

P-69: Glass slipper shaped thimble holders.

P-70: Silver thimble holders with applied enamel college seals on the lids. America, early nineteenth century.

PLATE 12

P-73: Ivory scissors. Double peacock design.

P-71: Gilted brass clamp in shape of a dolphin. Bird in flight perched on top of a crown shaped pin cushion. The turnscrew is a fist holding a bar. England, nineteenth century.

P-74: "End of Day" glass darners.

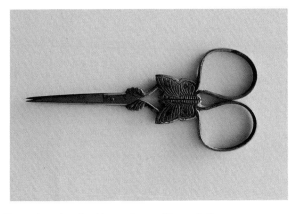

P-72: Painted sycamore clamp. England, circa 1800. Top dome holds thimble, with pin cushion inside base. The left and right knobs turn thread bobbins. The center knob turns the yellow silk tape measure, which is marked in "nails."

P-75: Figural embroidery scissors. "Butterfly."

PLATE 13

PIN CUSHIONS

P-76: Chinese dolls hold hands around a silk pin cushion. The center compartment stores a thimble. China. Modern.

P-77: Seminole Indian princess sits in a sweetgrass basket pin cushion. Modern.

P-78: Tooled red leather boot pin cushion. Japan. Modern.

PIN HOLDERS

P-80

P-79

P-81

TAPES

P-82: Celluloid windmill tape. Sails of the windmill are the winder.

P-83: Brass turtle tape. Back of the turtle marked "Pull My Head and Not My Leg."

PLATE 14

WORKBOXES

P-84: Novelty purse size mending kits. Celluloid. Early twentieth century.

P-85: A surprised miss painted on the wooden cover of a sewing kit that holds needles, thread, and thimble.

P-87: Gilted brass novelty needle cases. Redditch, England, late nineteenth century, early twentieth century.

P-86: Gilted brass novelty needle cases. Redditch, England, late nineteenth and early twentieth centuries.

NEEDLE HOLDERS

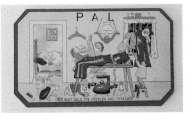

P-89

P-88

P-90

PLATE 15

SOUTH STAFFORDSHIRE ENAMELS

Enameled thimbles, etuis, and other trinkets were made in the South Staffordshire area of England. Today, these pieces are sometimes referred to as Bilston and Battersea enamels, which are the names of the towns noted for this work. This enamel work is done on copper. The decorations were either hand painted or transfer prints. They were produced to meet the demands of the rising middle class, who could not afford the high priced enamels on gold that were made in France during this period.

P-91: South Staffordshire enamel etui.

P-92: Enamel bodkin case with thimble cap.

P-93: Egg shaped thimble holder·

P-94: Enamel egg with matching thimble, scissors, bodkin, tweezers, and embroidery punch. England, nineteenth century.

PLATE 16

16-34: A coal company; 16-35: An Electrician; 16-36: "Delco Light."

16-37: A range company; 16-38: Television antenna company; 16-39: A shoe repairer.

16-40, 16-41, 16-42: Local dress shops advertised on thimbles. Each time a lady used this thimble while mending a garment, she would be reminded where she could buy a new dress.

16-43, 16-44, 16-45: Other wearing apparel are found on advertising thimbles; 16-43: Hosiery; 16-44: Brassieres; 16-45: Millinery.

16-46, 16-47, 16-48: Fabric and needlework shops advertised on thimbles.

16-49, 16-50, 16-51: Food products were advertised on thimbles; 16-49: Coffee; 16-50: Flour; 16-51: Pork Roll.

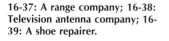

16-52: Coca Cola; 16-53: C.B.S. Radio; 16-54: Kil-Ve, a product to kill nits on children's heads.

16-55, 16-56, 16-57: Brass advertising thimbles; 16-55: Gold Thimble Scotch; 16-56: A jeweler in York, PA; 16-57: Prudential Insurance Company.

16-58, 16-59, 16-60: Other insurance companies followed the Prudential custom of giving away advertising thimbles.

16-61, 16-62, 16-63: Service stations gave advertising thimbles to their customers; 16-61: Shell Oil Company; 16-62: Texaco; 16-63: Gulf.

16-64, 16-65, 16-66: Sewing machine advertising is a natural for thimbles; 16-64: Singer; 16-65: Pfaff; 16-66: New Home.

16-67, 16-68, 16-69: Collectors and collectors groups exchange thimbles. These are referred to as "personals" among collectors.

118

16-70, 16-71, 16-72: Jeweler's silver advertising thimbles. These were given to the customers as gifts with the purchase of a wedding ring. English. Early twentieth century.

16-73, 16-74, 16-75: Jeweler's silver advertising thimbles. English. Early twentieth century.

16-76, 16-77, 16-78: Silver advertising thimbles; 16-76: Andrews Liver Salt. English; 16-77: Rice Sewing Silk; 16-78: Domestic Sewing Machine. Both American. Early twentieth century.

16-79, 16-80, 16-81: Early celluloid thimbles with decaled decoration.

119

CHAPTER 17

Thimble Holders and Cases

Thimbles are small and easily lost or misplaced. The thimble case or holder is designed as a home for the thimble when it is not in use. A wide variety of material was used to make these cases, including vegetable ivory (coroza nut from South America), silver, wood, basketry, leather, glass, tortoise shell, ivory, mother-of-pearl, beaded work, tartan or mauchline transfer ware from Scotland, and cast metal.

Thimble cases were made in a variety of shapes, the most common of which were fruit such as apple, pear, strawberry, and walnut. Other common shapes were the egg and the acorn.

Novelty shapes included a beer stein, boot, glass shoe, and carved wooden figures such as a bird and a bear. The Bilston enamel on brass thimble, made in South Staffordshire, England during the eighteenth century, often had a matching egg-shaped case. Bucket or basket shaped metal cases were made to hang on a chatelain. The metal and decorations matched the other pieces on the chatelain.

The silver thimble case that resembles a miniature wig case, with a post inside to hold the thimble in place is an American design. This round container is decorated with a pierced lacy pattern. It was made by various silver factories during the late nineteenth and early twentieth centuries. Some had chains attached with a ring on the end to slip on a finger.

The Webster Company of North Attleboro, Massachusetts, advertised these cases during the 1920s for $2.25 each. Foster and Bailey of Providence, Rhode Island, produced a series of thimble cases with enameled disks of college seals, such as Lehigh, Princeton, and Yale, applied to the lid of the case. Unger Brothers, Newark, New Jersey, made this style thimble holder.

The three thimbles holders made by Webster, Unger, and Foster Bailey, are very similar in construction and pattern. They are equal in beauty; the difference is the maker's mark on the bottom of the case. While they should be equal in price, the one with the Unger mark brings a higher price because of the mark.

Porcelain figural thimble holders often had a pin cushion and a tape measure included in the design. They were made in Germany and Japan in the form of people. They always had a top hat, the crown of which served as a thimble holder.

Many modern, cast metal, novelty thimble holders are on the market today. These charming newly designed figures are produced in various finishes, such as bronze, dull silver, or pewter. They are made by Rodan Products of Marlboro, New York. Collectors should be aware that these are newly made novelties and not antiques, and should be priced accordingly.

The glass shoe-type thimble holder was made to resemble Cinderella's glass slipper. Made during the early part of this century, they came in a variety of colors: amber, green, clear, and cobalt blue (the rarest). Some were decorated with painted flowers or painted shoe laces. One was made as a souvenir of the Pan American Exposition at Buffalo, New York, 1901.

Other shoe model thimble holders were made of cast metal, covered with velvet, linen, or leather. The colors of the fabric coverings were originally bright, but years have taken their toll on the dyes used to color the fabrics, and they have faded to dull brown and gray.

Dutch style wooden shoes were models for thimble holders. Some were marked as souvenirs of a city or tourist attraction. Another wooden thimble holder is hand carved from Germany. The sitting bear holding the thimble between his paws is one of the most popular figures. A carved eagle with wings spread and an owl with pearl button eyes are other figural thimble holders.

Thimble holders also were made of ivory, bone, and vegetable ivory. Common shapes are an acorn or egg. Ivory thimble holders that were once part of a Chinese fitted work box have carvings in high relief showing Chinese scenes.

Shell is another material used to make thimble cases. Hinged mussel shell thimble cases are lined with silk or velvet, and have an indentation to hold the thimble in place. They are probably French, circa 1900.

Thimble cases in the shape of a miniature knife box are covered on the outside with tortoise shell or mother-of-pearl. A thimble shaped post inside the case is covered with soft fabric. Sometimes there is a slot in the case to store a paper packet of needles.

A miniature sailing ship made of clam and other shells serves as a thimble holder. The shell "sails" are painted with decorations. Many of the miniature ships were souvenirs of sea side resorts, with the name painted on the sail. A bisque figure of a sailor sits on the edge of the boat, and a small metal anchor dangles from a chain. These late nineteenth century novelties were made in Germany.

The sweet grass miniature basket thimble holder was originally part of a set. They were hand woven by American Indians as tourist items. The other pieces in the set include a pin cushion and scissor blade sheath.

Thimble holders have been made in the shape of light bulbs and egg cups. Ivory, vegetable ivory, and ebony were used to make the egg cup design, in which the removable dome cap was made to resemble an egg. Ivory was used for a white egg, and vegetable ivory simulated the color of a brown egg.

One method of preventing a thimble from getting lost was to design a sewing kit where the thimble served as the cap or cover. The kit contains needles and thread, with the thimble on top to make it a complete emergency sewing kit. This idea has been used for centuries. In the eighteenth and nineteenth centuries they were made of silver, many of which have no marks. Those that are marked with maker's or assay marks are from England and the continent.

Celluloid figures that utilized the thimble as a cap for the sewing kit were made during the first half of this century. They are made in novelty shapes of animals and people. The thimble serves as a hat for the figure as well as a cover for the kit. Needles and thread are stored inside the kit. Most were unmarked, but those that are marked were made in Germany or Japan.

Tartan and mauchline transferware thimble holders come from Scotland and were made as souvenirs of tourist attractions. Many have pictures of American resorts. (See Souvenir and Commemorative Thimbles, Chapter 10.)

17-1: American eagle in flight.

17-2: The wise owl with button eyes; 17-3: The brown bear hugs a thimble as though it was a honey pot.

17-4: The knee-high boot holds a thimble; 17-5: The crowing rooster thimble holder.

17-6: Bird; 17-7: Cat holds thimble inside its hunched back.

17-8: Comic strip character, Jiggs; 17-9: Sister Susie of World War I fame.

17-10, 17-11: The acorn is a favorite shape for a thimble holder; 17-10: Wood and vegetable ivory; 17-11: Treen.

17-12, 17-13: Acorn shaped thimble holders; 17-12: Ivory; 17-13: Vegetable ivory. Both have matching thimbles inside.

17-14: Keg shaped thimble holder; 17-15: Miniature beer barrel.

17-16, 17-17: Beer stein thimble holders; 17-16: Leather covered metal with metal cap; 17-17: Brass with a tape measure in the base.

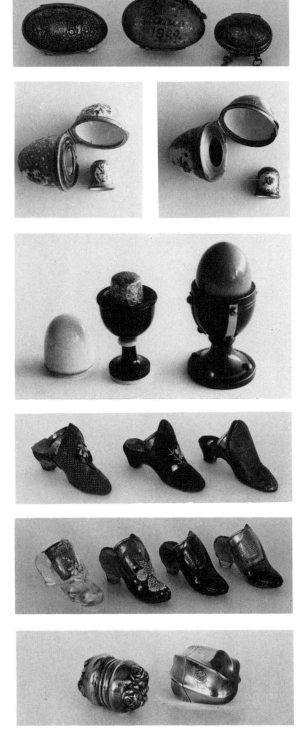

17-18, 17-19, 17-20: Brass, egg shaped thimble purse with chain; 17-19: Marked "Paris 1900."

17-21, 17-22: Enamel on brass, South Staffordshire. Egg shaped thimble holder with matching thimble. Hand painted. English. Nineteenth century; 17-23, 17-24: Enamel on brass, South Staffordshire. Egg shaped thimble holder with matching thimble. Hand painted. English. Nineteenth century.

17-25, 17-26: Egg cup thimble holders; 17-25: White ivory egg and treen base; 17-26: Brown vegetable ivory egg and treen base.

17-27, 17-28, 17-29: Slipper shaped thimble holders; 17-27: Linen covered metal; 17-28: Velvet covered metal; 17-29: Leather covered metal.

17-30, 17-31, 17-32, 17-33: Cinderella's glass slipper shaped thimble holders; 17-30: Clear glass; 17-31: Amber; 17-32: Blue; 17-33: Green.

17-34, 17-35: Silver thimble holders; 17-34: Roses in relief; 17-35: Melon shaped.

17-36, 17-37: Egg shaped silver
thimble holders.

17-38: Silver. Miniature charcoal
stove thimble holder and matching thimble. Dutch. Nineteenth
century.

17-39, 17-40: Leather covered
miniature trunk thimble holders.

17-41, 17-42: Velvet covered
book thimble holders with gilted
clasp; 17-41: Amber; 17-42:
Blue.

17-43: Seashell ship thimble
holder with bisque sailor boy on
deck. Souvenir of the Colombian
Exposition, 1893.

17-44: Silver. Combination thimble holder and needle case. Russian. Eighteenth century. Photo courtesy of the City Museum, Moscow, U.S.S.R.

17-45, 17-46: Tortoise shell knife box shaped thimble holders. Nineteenth century.

17-47, 17-48: Silver thimble holders with applied enamel disks on lid. American. Early twentieth century; 17-47: Army; 17-48: Navy.

17-49, 17-50, 17-51: Mauchline transfer ware wooden thimble holders. Scotland. Nineteenth century.

17-52: Assorted thimble holders. Bottom row, Left: Hand woven sweet grass. Right: Metal walnut shaped. Top row, Left: miniature leather covered trunk. Center: Silver with post to hold thimble. Right: Hand crocheted sun hat. Photo courtesy of the American Home Sewing Museum, West Warren, MA.

126

17-53, 17-54, 17-55, 17-56: Silver thimble holders with applied university emblems enamel disks on lids. American. Early twentieth century.

17-57, 17-58, 17-59: Silver thimble holders with post inside. American. Late nineteenth century, early twentieth century.

17-60, 17-61: Barrel shaped wooden thimble holders. Scotland. Nineteenth century; 17-60: Mauchline transfer ware; 17-61: Tartan ware.

17-62, 17-63: Mauchline transfer ware. Bottle shaped thimble holders. Scotland. Nineteenth century.

17-64, 17-65, 17-66, 17-67: Egg shaped wooden thimble holders. Left to right: Two fern ware, tartan, and mauchline. Scotland. Nineteenth century.

PART III

SEWING TOOLS

The Traditional Approach

CHAPTER 18

Art Needlework Tools
Implements of Loving Labor

The name "Art Needlework" is passé. The telephone company has deleted this classification from the yellow pages. Department stores have phased out their departments. The needleworker must turn to specialty shops to purchase her supplies and fulfill her other needs.

Art needlework is a labor of love. Fancy needlework, as opposed to general sewing and mending, always has been a hobby for people who enjoyed doing fine work with their hands. Needlework fads come and go, but fine needlework lives on.

Throughout much of the nineteenth century, every school girl was required to complete a sampler. This introduction to art needlework was part of her early education. Samplers were originally called "examplers" or "samp-cloths." Examples of decorative needlework stitches and patterns were practiced and preserved on the sampler. The school girl learned to use a thimble and other sewing tools while preparing her sampler.

INDIAN ART NEEDLEWORK

Early American sewing tools were those used by the native North American Indians. They were not made in a factory or imported. They were made with native material readily available from natural resources. The method of making and using these tools was passed down from one generation to another.

Indian women used imagination and taste when incorporating porcupine quills in their work. The colors of the quills varied. Dyeing them was a practiced art. Quill work decorated a variety of garments and accessories, e.g., shirts, hoods, moccasins, leggings, knife sheaths, and medicine bags.

There were four general methods of working with quills: sewing, weaving,

129

wrapping, and applied to birch bark. A bone bodkin was used for the sewing. It was later replaced by steel needles obtained from the white traders.

Women made sewing threads from sinew taken from the legs of deer. Lower Yukon women found a species of tough grass which could be made into thread after being beaten, dried, and frayed with little ivory combs. The stitching resembles what is known today as "back stitch," "couching stitch," and "chain stitch." The work was fine, considering the crudity of the tools used.

Bead work was a highly developed craft among the Plains tribes. A primitive guild was formed and only the most skilled beadworkers were accepted as members. European glass and porcelain beads brought by the white traders were used, as well as native material such as abalone, clam, and oyster shells. In the north and central plains, Indians carved beads from deer, goat, and sheep horns.

Eskimo women depended upon crude implements made from bones. The thimbles which they used varied according to locality and the accessible materials. Small oval pieces of tough sealskin were generally used for this purpose. These pieces had a slit extending across one edge which formed a loop-like strap through which the forefinger was thrust. The strap rested across the nail and the pad of the skin on the inner side of the finger. This type of thimble is made today and sold in Alaskan tourist shops. When the traders brought metal thimbles, the natives used them for garment ornaments rather than sewing. Holes were drilled into the cap of the thimble and a leather thong was drawn through the hole.

Needle cases were made of walrus ivory inlaid with sections of beads. Often a hollow animal marrow bone served as a needle case.

COLLECTIBLE FANCY NEEDLEWORK TOOLS

Many unusual art needlework tools appear in the antiques market, including tatting shuttles, lace bobbins, lucets, netting pins, tambour and crochet hooks, knitting needle point protectors and sheaths, and knitting spools. When each of these art needlework crafts were popular, ornate and unusual tools were made.

Tatting Shuttles

No particular skill and little concentration was needed to do tatting since it is mainly a simple rhythmic action. The motion gives grace and elegance to the tatter's hand and the illusion of great industry on her part. The tatter had the opportunity for conversation without being distracted.

Tatting, a method of making lace edgings and trimmings, reputedly originated in Italy during the sixteenth century. Interest in tatting fluctuated over the years, but its golden age was during the mid-nineteenth century.

Early tatting shuttles were made of abalone shell, brass, bone, wood, German silver (nickel), mother-of-pearl, steel, Sterling silver, gold, ivory, and tortoise shell. Modern ones are made of steel or plastic.

There was a time when tatting shuttles could be found on the counter of every variety store. Today you have to search for one in a specialty needlework shop. There is only one manufacturer in the United States and two in England still making tatting shuttles.

The tatting shuttle found in a Chinese export workbox frequently is ornate but often not functional. The carver had no idea how the shuttle was used. He

130

worked from drawings so his products looked like a tatting shuttle, but the blades were carved so close together that no room was left for the thread.

Early eighteenth century shuttles were much larger than the ones we know today, sometimes up to five inches long with larger spaces at the ends.

Lace Bobbins

The era of lace making reached its height in England during the eighteenth century. It was a cottage industry in many English villages. In some villages up to eighty percent of the men, women, and children were employed in the lace industry. Most English lace bobbins are slim and lightweight and depend on a cluster of beads wired on the lower end to give them weight.

Lacemakers used between twelve and several hundred bobbins, according to the size and fineness of the lace being worked. Some early bobbins were short and thick, and thus nicknamed "dumps" or "bobtails".

Many antique lace bobbins are marked to commemorate events, which helps date them. Scripture sayings and love messages appear on bobbins. Decorations were created by dots drilled into the bone or ivory. Colored inks were applied to the surface and wiped off immediately. The ink adhered only to the drilled dots. Bobbins were also made of wood, horn, pewter, brass, silver and gold. Modern bobbins are made of glass or plastic.

Lucet

The lucet is sometimes called a chain fork. It may be made of ivory, bone, wood, mother-of-pearl or tortoise shell, with or without a handle. It was used to make square rather than round cording. By the mid-nineteenth century, machine made cording made the lucet obsolete, but it remained in the workbox for many years.

Netting Needles (or Pins)

Netting is an ancient craft. Primitive people used nets for fishing and hunting, so the art of netting dates back to the earlier days. Hand made netting was used for curtains and bed coverings. Frilly collars and cuffs were fashioned with netting needles.

Netting needles are basically in the shape of a needle, long and slender with a divided fork-like prong. They were made of bone, ivory, horn, or tortoise shell.

Oriental ivory netting needles are stored in an ornately carved ivory tube. Chinese export workboxes from the late eighteenth and nineteenth centuries often had a roller and ratchet fitted into a compartment. This served to hold the foundation loop of the netting work to keep it taut.

Crochet And Tambour Hooks

The word "crochet" is French meaning hook. The French had written instructions for this craft as early as the sixteenth century. Crocheting is a form of knitting that is worked with the aid of a hook.

Tambour work and crochet require similar tools with hooks. One hook may be mistaken for the other. Tambour work is a chain stitch on fabric and requires a sharper point at the bottom of the hook than a crochet hook.

Both tambour and crochet hooks were made in graduated sizes. Tambour hooks were made in sets, with the steel hooks fitting into a removable handle. The handles often were ornate and made of bone, ivory, or silver. Steel hooks range from size one, the largest, to size twelve being the smallest and sharpest.

Older crochet hooks have cylindrical handles. A sheath slipped over the hook end to prevent damage to the hook and the slim shank. Twentieth century crochet hooks have a flattened section on the handle. The name of the manufacturer and size number are stamped on this flat section.

Crochet hooks are useful tools while doing other needlework. They are used to make loops in hairpin lace and in fringe work.

KNITTING ACCESSORIES

Knitting Needle Sheaths.

Knitting needle sheaths are figural disks with a tube soldered on to the back to hold one knitting needle. They were called "Knitting Pinns" during the eighteenth and early nineteenth centuries, the height of their popularity in England and Europe. Some were hand carved wood. Sheaths were designed in many novelty shapes such as fish, hearts, and urns.

A knitting sheath was a working aid rather than a storage place for knitting needles. The sheath was attached to the knitters waist band and acted as a third hand. While the right knitting needle was held firmly into the hole of the sheath, the knitter's right hand was free to manipulate the yarn.

It is difficult to recognize the purpose of these novelty shaped figures unless you had the opportunity to watch someone use one. If one appears in the antiques market it often is mislabeled and not offered as a knitting or needlework accessory.

Knitting Needle Point Protectors.

When not in use, a knitting needle is a sharp weapon. Point protectors were designed to protect a person from being stabbed. Corks often were used to cover the points, but fancy protectors also were designed for this purpose. Knitting needle point protectors were made of silver, ivory, and mother-of-pearl. They were made in pairs to cover the sharp points of the two needles when they were not in use.

Knitting Spools

A child's first experience with knitting is usually by using a knitting spool. An empty wooden thread spool with four nails partially hammered into one end is the home made version. Yarn is wrapped around the nails and lifted over the previous strand with a hair pin. This produces a tubular shaped rein and is the same principal used to manufacture stockings. Manufactured knitting spools may have more than four pins. The pins are often looped shape, similar to bell staples that are used to fasten electric wire. Modern knitting spools are molded from plastic.

ART NEEDLEWORK TOOLS OF TOMORROW

The machine age is here, but hand made art needlework will continue to be practiced. Modern textiles, yarns, and tools make the work easier. While older tools from the horse and buggy days are fun to examine and collect, modern tools are more functional.

Modern art needlework reflect our life style, but the modern tools will themselves someday become obsolete. Our heirs will be amazed to find the tools we used to make such fine needlework pieces. They will be tomorrow's collectibles.

Georgiana Brown Haberson wrote in *American Needlework* (Coward-McCann, New York, 1938) that spun glass would be the art needlework yarn of tomorrow. She was wrong. We do have man-made yarns such as nylon, orlon, and polyester. The colors are more vibrant and long lasting.

18-1, 18-2: Tatting shuttles; 18-1 top: Mother-of-pearl, 3″ long; 18-2 bottom: Carved ivory from Chinese export workbox, 2 ½″ long.

18-3, 18-4, 18-5, 18-6, 18-7, 18-8: Assorted tatting shuttles. Clockwise from top: Bakelite, carved ivory, Sterling silver, souvenir of the Pan Pacific International Exposition, San Francisco, 1915, tortoise shell, German silver (nickel).

18-9: Lucet, sometimes called a lyre or chain fork. Wood, 5″ long.

18-10: Graduated sized scissors in leather case; 18-11: Wood sock darner with silver handle; 18-12: Three embroidery punches; 18-13: Silver thread winder; 18-14: Silver needle case; 18-15: Silver handled embroidery scissors. Photo courtesy of the American Home Sewing Museum, West Warren, MA.

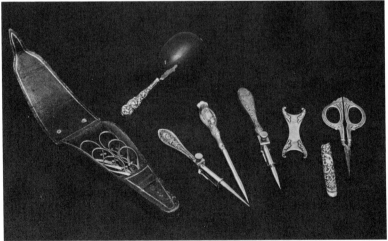

18-16: Tambour hook set in original wooden case. Tambour work is a method of chain stitching on fabric, which was held taut on a drum-like frame. The hooks were in graduated sizes that fastened into a removable handle. Tambour hook sets are often mistaken for crochet hooks.

18-17: Tambour hook set in mauchline transfer ware case.

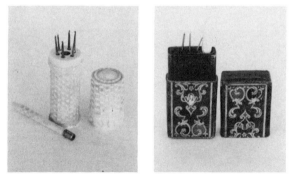

18-18: Tambour hook set, carved ivory case. The removable handle is made of ivory; 18-19: Tambour hook set in gold tooled leather case.

18-20: Sterling silver crochet hooks and silver sleeve. Three graduated hooks pivot into handle. American, Simons Brothers, Philadelphia, PA. Nineteenth century.

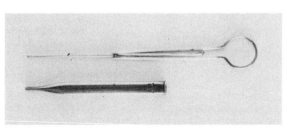

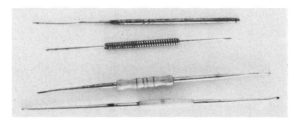

18-21: Early crochet hooks. Top, steel. Three double pointed hooks with holding bar in center.

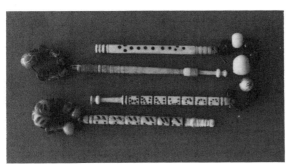

18-22, 18-23: Knitting needle point protectors; 18-22: Ivory; 18-23: Enamel on Sterling silver.

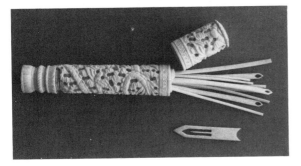

18-24: Decorated lace bobbins with beads.

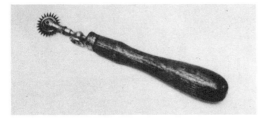

18-25: Netting needle set in original carved ivory case. Bottom: Gage. China, nineteenth century.

18-26: Embroidery pattern marking wheel. Photo courtesy of The American Home Sewing Museum, West Warren, MA.

18-27: Silver court plaster case. Court plasters were the forerunner of today's adhesive bandages. These were kept on hand in the sewing basket to bandage a finger that was bruised while sewing; 18-28: Silver needle case. Photo courtesy of The American Home Sewing Museum, West Warren, MA.

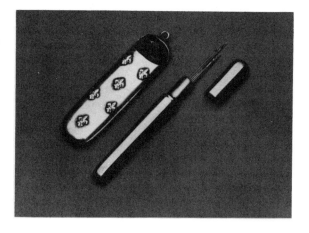

18-29: Assorted early crochet hooks.

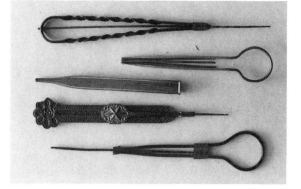

18-30: Assorted early crochet hooks.

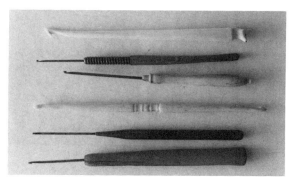

18-31: Nine pin knitting spool with spring tension. Patented by Averill and Company, NY, December 23, 1879.

18-32: Eskimo sewing case.
Drawstring and fringed leather
case. Attached hollow bone
needle holder. Bone needle.

CHAPTER 19

Chatelaines
The Charm Holders of Yesteryear

The name "Chatelaine" is French, and literally translates as "Lady of the Castle (or Chateau)." Chatelaines existed during Roman times, being worn by both men and women. Pockets in garments were non-existent. Necessary personal items were held on chains that fell from an ornate plate or medallion that clipped to the waistband of a garment.

Chatelaines increased in ornateness during the nineteenth century. It was the Victorian's version of keeping up with the Joneses. Silver and gold, as well as steel, were used to make chatelaines. Decorations included enamel, semi-precious stones, and cameos.

A chatelaine was a favorite wedding gift. It served a status symbol indicating the bride's new position as mistress of the household. A chatelaine was presented to Princess May of Teck on her wedding day. She later became Queen Mary. Her chatelaine was made of gold and bloodstone, set with diamonds and rubies. The stones on the medallion formed the letters of her name.

Between three and nine chains usually hung from the medallion. Occasionally up to twelve chains were found. Chatelaines were considered "day time" jewelry.

Sewing chatelaines usually contained a thimble bucket or case, sandwich-type pin cushion, scissor case or sheath, needle and bodkin case, and a tape measure. Additional accessories might include a memo pad made of slivers of ivory, scent bottle, or button hook. When a lady wore a watch, its winding key might be found on a chatelaine chain. Some of the chains were made of links of pierced metal that gave the illusion of being made of lace. Lucky charms also were attached to chatelaines.

Early chatelaines were sold with matching pieces attached to the chains. Later, the medallion with chains was sold without attachments. The customer attached whatever she wanted. When this occurred, the decoration of the pieces would not necessarily match. Sterling silver sewing gadgets and tools were status symbols for the professional milliner, dressmaker, or quilt maker. Specific tools to hang on chatelaines were made for each craft. A grateful customer gave her dressmaker a gift of a silver tool for her chatelaine. There is no way of telling if a chatelaine with mismatched pieces was assembled during the late nineteenth century or recently by an antiques dealer.

Chatelaines were made in the United States, England, and Continental Europe. Gorham, Tiffany, and Whiting made silver chatelaines. The medallion and the individual pieces will have the makers' mark. Missing chains or pieces bring down the value. The best examples are obtained from dealers who specialize in estate jewelry.

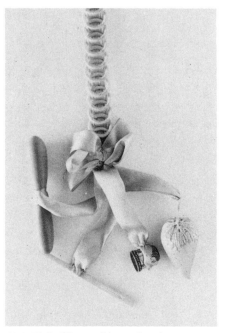

19-1: Lady working at embroidery stand wearing chatelaine. Nineteenth century.

19-2: Pink ribbon and bone ring chatelaine. Left to right: Glove darner, bodkin, thimble, strawberry emery. Shaker. American. Nineteenth century.

19-3: Silver plated steel chatelaine with lacy cut chains. Left to right: Disk pin cushion, scissors sheath, and thimble bucket; 19-4: Silver plated steel chatelaine. Lacy cut chains. Imitation Roman coins on clip. Left to right: Notebook or "aide memoire," needle case, thimble bucket, scissor sheath, and oblong pin cushion.

19-5: Silver plated on steel chatelaine. Lacy cut chains. Left to right: Scissors sheath, thimble bucket, needle case, and diamond shaped pin cushion; 19-6: Silver plated on steel chatelaine. Roman warrior's head on clip. Left to right: Scissor sheath, thimble bucket, oblong pin cushion, and tape measure.

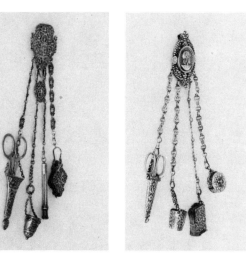

19-7: Steel chatelaine. Left to right: Thread bobbin case, disk pin cushion, tape measure, note book or "aide memoire" with ivory erasable leaves, scissor sheath, and thimble bucket.

19-8: Fob chatelaine. Gilted metal. Left: Enameled scent bottle. Crossed anchor and cross on one side. "Mitzpah" on reverse. Center: Thimble bucket. Right: Pencil holder; 19-9: Fob chatelaine. Left to right: Pin disk, scissor sheath, note pad or "aide memoire" with erasable ivory leaves, and thimble bucket.

19-10, 19-11: Thimble cases from chatelaines; 19-10: Silver. English. Nineteenth century; 19-11: Brass filigree thimble bucket.

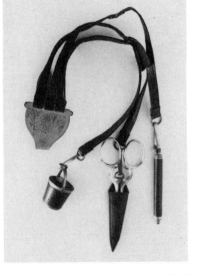

19-12: Leather chatelaine with brass clip. Left to right: Thimble bucket, scissor case, needle case.

CHAPTER 20

Darners

Many people do not "give a darn" today, but our great grandmothers did. Her much worn and needle-pricked darning egg was proof of the many hours she spent mending the family's socks. "A stitch in time" was not a superficial saying to her. It was her motto and way of life.

The darning stitch was a fancy embroidery stitch, as well as a mending stitch. A century ago little girls practiced the darning stitch on their samplers. There are four kinds of darning stitches: linen darning, twill darning, damask or fancy darning, and invisible darning (sometimes called fine drawing).

A multi-stranded soft cotton floss is used for darning socks. The darning needle with a long eye to keep the floss flat is used for this work. The simple in-and-out "linen darning" weaving stitch was used for mending socks.

Darning eggs or balls were made in a variety of materials: wood, glass, celluloid or porcelain. Potatoes and small gourds served as substitutes. A small hole, the size of a needle hole, was drilled into the gourd to permit the interior to dry. The dried seeds inside rattled. The outer skin of the gourd was varnished to preserve it and give it a warm glow.

A polished dried small coconut shell also was used for darning. A coconut has three "eyes" that can be punched to drain the coconut milk and permit the nut meat to air dry. The polished coconut shell made a durable and light weight darner.

WOOD

Most wooden darning eggs were made of solid wood. Some were hollow for the purpose of storing mending floss, a thimble, or the bee's wax used to strengthen yarn. Hollow handles stored needles.

Darners were made in shapes and designs unique to various countries. Tartan and Mauchline transfer ware darners came from Scotland. Gnarled olive wood eggs were made in the Middle East. The mushroom shaped darner was popular in Germany. Unless a darner was a souvenir, it usually is not marked with a manufacturer's trade mark or country of origin.

An unusual wooden darner was introduced at the Women's Pavilion at the 1876 Centennial Exposition in Philadelphia. This darner, invented by a Mrs. Harely of Philadelphia, was shaped like a small gourd, but with a concave top. It was hollow, to hold a ball of mending floss inside and had a hole for the thread to come through. The slender handle served as a glove darner and also was hollow to store needles.

GLASS

Blown glass darners were made in egg, ball, or foot shape. Because most glass darners were not made commercially, no two are alike. Glass blowers would use the glass that was left over at the end of a day's work to make darners

143

to take home as gifts for wives or friends. End-of-day glass or rainbow speckled glass darners that cost $15.00 in 1928 command ten times that price today.

Frederick Carder of Steuben Glass registered a trademark for Aurene glass in 1904. This iridescent glass is similar to Tiffany glass. The Aurene glass darners became very popular and were made commercially through the 1930s. Their current market value is in the $75 to $100 range.

STONE, IVORY, AND CELLULOID

Stone eggs could be used for darning, but were meant to be used as "hand coolers." A marble, known as blue-john and mined only in Derbyshire, England, was often used to make hand coolers. Since moisture would stain fine needlework, the needleworker had to keep her hands cool and dry at all times. If a stone egg was used for darning, its weight would tire the hands of the seamstress, thus darning tools that were used for mending were made with light materials.

The celluloid darner was patented in 1870. It was light weight and decorated with dainty floral decals. They disappeared from the market during the 1940s because celluloid was such a flammable material.

Ivory darning eggs with intricate etched decorations and silver handles were the toys of more affluent ladies. A fancy ivory darner was not used for such mundane mending as darning socks.

GLOVE DARNERS

Glove darners are slender tubes with finger size balls on either end. Some of the silver or wooden glove darners are hollow and serve as a needle case.

WHITE "EGGS"

White "eggs" made of any material were actually synthetic chicken eggs that farmers used to induce their chickens to lay. Many of these found their way into the sewing basket for use with a torn sock that needed mending.

DISPLAYING A DARNER COLLECTION

Egg or ball shaped darners can rest in an egg cup for display. Wooden darners with handles can be displayed on an old fashioned wall-type men's tie rack. The bar that was meant to hold the ties is far enough from the wall to hold the egg of the darner upright.

20-1, 20-2: Silver handled darners; 20-1: White ceramic; 20-2:
Painted black wood.

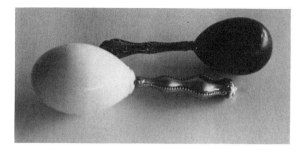

20-3, 20-4, 20-5: Silver glove
darners.

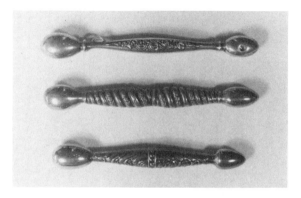

20-6, 20-7: Wooden stickware
darners; 20-6: Mushroom
shaped; 20-7: Concave shaped.

20-8: Celluloid darner with decaled floral decoration.

20-9, 20-10: Glass darners; 20-9: Blue foot shaped; 20-10: Ball shaped iridescent green Aurene glass. Patented by Frederick Carder of Steuben Glass in 1904.

20-11, 20-12: "End of Day" multicolored glass darners.

20-13, 20-14: Wooden darners. Hollow ball opens for storage of needle, thread, and thimble.

20-15: Thread and scissors are stored inside the ball of the wooden darner. A thimble is stored in the handle.

CHAPTER 21

Pin Cushions

Fish and animal bone fragments and sharp thorns served as the first pins. They were delicate and required a safe protected storage place when not in use. The North American Indians used soft animal skin folded into a case to hold their pins.

Pinpillows, pinlows, and pin poppets were among the early names given to pin storage devices. Today, "pin cushion" is the term most commonly used.

Pin cushions make a unique and colorful collection. Pin cushions were found in almost every household. In the nineteenth century it was not uncommon to find one in almost every room. Pin cushion design changed with the popular taste, hence pin cushions are an excellent barometer to measure the popularization of period styles. Each novel shape or design reflects the taste and needs of a specific bygone era.

MATERIALS AND STUFFING

Many older cloth pin cushions were made from scraps of material, often left over remnants. The "Crazy Quilt" pattern cushion is one example. Small pieces of fabric were joined together with embroidery stitches to create a piece large enough to make a cushion. Some cushions had removable covers made of netting, embroidered fabric, or crochet. They were attached with stitches or pinned to the muslin base cover that contained the stuffing material.

A variety of material was used to stuff pin cushions. Early cushions were stuffed with bran or sawdust, but bran tended to attract moths and other insects. Although wool was the best stuffing material as it safeguards pins from rust, it also served as a delicacy for moths. Many wool and bran stuffed cushions deteriorated, and those that survive often are in poor condition.

Wool stuffing, whether clippings from a sheep, unraveled knitted yarn, or scraps from a woolen blanket, was snipped into small pieces before stuffing. This made a smooth, rather than a lumpy cushion.

SHAPES

Ball-shaped pin cushions featuring an attached cord or ribbon were fashionable as early as the seventeenth century. They were hung from a lady's waist band, much like a chatelaine. Early ball-shaped cushions often were made of fine silk, with a motto, initials, and date knitted into the fabric.

During the nineteenth century, ornate and decorative pin cushions often doubled as wall or table decorations. Favorite shapes include fans, butterflies, or hearts. Another early shape involved embroidering the cushion so that it resembled a sampler (or exampler). Children were taught to mark household linens with cross stitched letters. It was a simple task to apply the same skills to decorating a pin cushion.

Shaker pin cushions usually are made of smooth silk in the shape of a heart or triangle. Two corners of a triangle shaped cushion are often brought together, forming a loop to hang the cushion.

A pattern and instructions for a pin ball appeared in *Godey's Lady's Book* in 1885. This harlequin patchwork pinball was made of velvet, silk, or satin, "... in as many bright and varied colors as possible. Five sided patches placed edge to edge, then side to side or base to base, around the ball, alternate with bands of four-pointed stars, whose points fill the space left by the tip to tip formation. When finished, the ball should be stuffed with ends of wool and joinings stuck with dummy pins."

Pin cushions took many new shapes as the nineteenth century ended. The tomato shape is the most common, often with a strawberry shaped emery attached. Women continued to make home made cushions, but "store bought" cushions quickly became more common. Novelty shapes such as animals, birds, fruits, wheelbarrows, coaches, jockey caps, books, etc., were popular. All were made to catch the eye.

China figurines of a boy or girl holding a basket shaped pin cushion were made in Germany and Japan during the early twentieth century. The tall round hat on the figure served as a thimble holder. Occasionally a tape measure was included in the base of the figure.

A Dressmaker's Companion is often mistaken for a peddler's doll. This was a table top pin cushion and sewing tool holder, popular during the 1850s and 1860s. A small doll, perhaps seven or eight inches tall, with a cloth or wooden body and a china head, hands, and feet was selected. It was mounted on a stand and dressed. A basket "hat" became the pin cushion. The doll figure, dressed in a full skirted gown, wore a skirt with many pockets. Sewing aids, e.g., a packet of needles or a thimble, was stored in the pockets.

Another style of dressmaker's pin cushion rests on the arm of a chair or the seamstress' knee. It was either round or rectangular and has straps extending from two sides. The ends of the straps are weighted with covered lead weights to hold the cushion steady while resting on a chair's arm. It is an easy transition to a model that attaches to the dressmaker's wrist

PIN STUCK DESIGNS

Pin stuck cushions, popular from the seventeen to nineteenth century, had decorations made entirely of pins which could not be removed without spoiling the pattern. These were not for every day use, for there was no room left on the cushion for more pins.

No baby's layette was considered complete without a maternity pin cushion. A pin stuck saying on a layette cushion would read, "Welcome Little Stranger," or "Sweet Babe." Existing examples have only a year date. Pin stuck and beaded cushions with sentimental sayings included in the design were love token gifts from tongue-tied swains. Heart shaped was the most common.

Round, flat sandwich cookie shaped pin holders were made for the purse or pocket. Some were part of the original fittings of a workbox. The outer layers were made of ivory, mother-of-pearl, wood, silver, or other metals.

SOUVENIR CUSHIONS

Souvenir cushions were made in every imaginable shape and material. The American Indians made beaded cushions for the tourist trade. Some souvenir cushions were manufactured abroad even though they were marked as a souvenir of an American mountain or seaside resort.

Sea shell cushions were popular souvenirs of seaside vacations. Cushions encrusted with a multitude of small sea shells glued in a decorative pattern around the base are sometime called "Sailor's Valentines." These were made by the natives of the Caribbean and purchased by the seaman as gifts for loved ones back home. They were not made by the sailors, per se, but many collectors consider them "nautical" collectibles.

CLAMPS

A sewing clamp or vise topped with a pin cushion was a useful needlework adjunct. It stayed in place during sewing, holding the necessary pins and needles for the needlework project. The pin cushion clamp was used as a substitute for a sewing bird. Unlike the bird clamp, which held the fabric by means of a spring devise, the pin cushion clamp held fabric that was pinned to the cushion.

Wooden clamp pin cushions were made of turned wood that was stained with lacquer or painted. Souvenir wooden clamp pin cushions contained decaled or painted pictures of tourist attractions. Other pin cushion clamps were made of metal, bone, or ivory. The small ivory clamps topped with a silk pincushion were originally part of a Chinese export workbox.

Spool stands topped with pin cushion were popular sewing table decorations. The multicolors of the spools of thread made an attractive "tree" decoration. A cup shaped holder on top of the spool stand held the pin cushion. It was often removable. In many cases, the pin cushion may be missing, a result of deterioration or discarding. Spool stands were made of iron, brass, wood, or silver plated base metal. They were popular during the last quarter of the nineteenth century. Some were on a revolving base; others were stationary. Some originally came with a glass dome to protect the thread from dust.

EMERIES

An emery, sometimes mistaken for a pin cushion, is stuffed with a powder that is a combination of mica and alumina with traces of metallic oxides. Emery powder was stuffed firmly into small cushions that were made of coarse, sturdy fabric.

Needles were poked into an emery several times to remove dirt, rust, or oil that clung to them. Modern needles should not be stored in an emery cushion for the emery powder will destroy the plating on the needles.

The most common shape for an emery is a strawberry, often covered with bright red fabric, usually silk. Another late nineteenth century emery shape was a black "mammy's" face with a red checkered bandanna twisted on her head.

Emeries were found in fitted workboxes. The emery cushion was located in a decorative case, usually in the shape of a bucket or basket.

21-1: Embroidered pin cushion commemorating the coronation of Queen Victoria, circa 1844. Photo courtesy of the American Home Sewing Museum, West Warren, MA.

21-2, 21-3: Carved bog wood pin cushions. Ireland. Nineteenth century; 21-2: Bowl shaped; 21-3: Cooking pot shaped with legs and handles.

21-4: Assorted pin cushions and emeries. Left to right: Boot shaped cushion with satin drawstring storage bag on top. Wooden slipper with pin cushion on heel and thimble holder in toe. Sea shell sandwich pin cushion. Satchel shaped cushion with gilted handle and closure for storage pocket. Two silver capped strawberry emeries. Cushion on knitted base. Cushion on vegetable ivory pedestal. Photo courtesy of the American Home Sewing Museum, West Warren, MA.

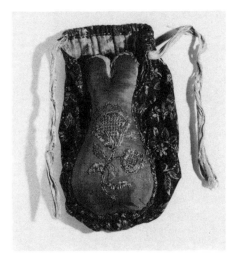

21-5: Pocket pin cushion. Eighteenth century. Photo courtesy of the Smithsonian Institution. Photo #67611.

21-6: Souvenir of Niagara Falls beaded pin cushion. American Indian craft. Nineteenth century.

21-7: Assorted emeries in shapes of strawberries, tomato, and carrot. Left: Two strawberry emeries with silver caps.

21-8: "Sailor's Valentine" pin cushion. Made by Caribbean Island natives and sold to sailors. Nineteenth century.

21-9: Silver chickadee bird cushion. Nineteenth century. Photo courtesy of the American Home Sewing Museum, West Warren, MA.

21-10: Sea shell pin cushion.

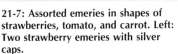

21-11: Sea shell pin cushion.

21-12: Sea shell pin cushion.

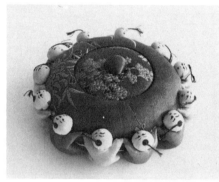

21-13: Chinese dolls hold hands around silk covered pin cushion. Center compartment stores a thimble or other small items. China. Modern.

21-14: Sea shell pin cushion.

21-15: Patchwork pin cushion with dummy pins on seams. English. Nineteenth century.

21-16: Carved wooden bear holds spool of thread between its paws and pin cushion on its back. Germany. Nineteenth century.

21-17: Wooden painted doll pushes barrel pin cushion. Tape measure is in the barrel.

21-18: Metal spool stand with pin cushion in center. Knob on top holds a thimble. Unmarked. Early twentieth century.

21-19: Silver plated shoe pin cushion. Continental. Late nineteenth, early twentieth centuries.

21-20: Silver pin cushion.

21-21: Tooled red leather boot holds pin cushion. Japan. Modern.

153

21-22: Hand made knitted pin cushion with thimble holder in center.

21-23: Hand knitted pin ball has silver band with ring to hold a ribbon or chain. Knitted into the outer cover, "The Gift is Small. Respect is all." Note that the letter "F" replaces the letter "S." American. Late eighteenth, early nineteenth centuries.

21-24: Tomato shaped pin cushion sits in an oversized pewter thimble. Modern.

21-25: Teakwood barrel cushion. Brass plate states it was made from wood taken from the sailing ship *H.M.S. Ganges*, built in Bombay, India, 1821 and broken up in Plymouth, England, in 1930. This was the last sailing ship to serve as a sea-going flagship for the British navy.

21-26: China boy figurine holds basket pin cushion. Tape measure inside base. A knob on top of his head holds a thimble. Germany. Early twentieth century.

21-27: Carved ivory pin cushions from Chinese export work boxes. China. Nineteenth century.

21-28: Blue velvet pin cushion on Tunbridge stick ware base; 21-29: Emery, tape measure and thread waxer on Tunbridge stick ware base. English. Nineteenth century.

21-30, 21-31: Colored prints under glass on sandwich pin cushions. Mirror on reverse. English. Nineteenth century.

21-32, 21-33, 21-34: Hand made pin balls that hung from the belt of a dress or apron. American. Circa eighteenth century; 21-32: Embroidered satin; 21-33: Knitted with silver band, marked "The Gift is Small, Respect is All." The letter "F" replaced the letter "S," as the custom of the era. The reverse has initials of the maker and the date; 21-34: Checkerboard knitted pin ball with satin ribbon band and loop.

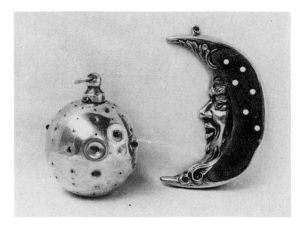

21-35: Sterling pin ball 3″ diameter; 21-36: 3 ¼″ high man-in-the-moon pin cushion, by William B. Kerr & Co. Photo courtesy of *Silver Magazine*, Whittier, CA.

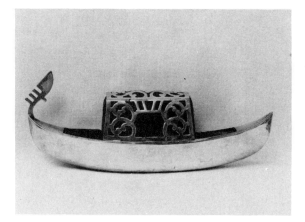

21-37: Sterling pin cushion in shape of an Egyptian river boat. 6 ¼″ long, 2″ high. Made by Dominick & Haff. Photo courtesy of *Silver Magazine*, Whittier, CA.

21-38, 21-39: Chatelaine pin cushions; 21-38: Sterling with applied copper flying fish; 21-39: Silverplated Japanese fan, 3 ⅜″ long, marked "Pat'd Nov. 2, 1880." Photo courtesy of *Silver Magazine*, Whittier, CA.

21-40, 21-41, 21-42, 21-43: Silver plated pin cushions from A. J. Hall, San Francisco, CA., catalog, 1895–1896. "...finished with fine cotton plush...$1.25 per dozen wholesale." 21-40: Frog with cushion in its mouth; 21-41: Fat man squatting with pin cushion "hair." 21-42: Bowl; 21- ?: "Knitted" bootie cushion. Photo courtesy of *Silver Magazine*, Whittier, CA.

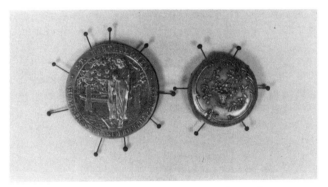

21-44, 21-45: Flat "sandwich cookie" shaped pin cushions for pocket or purse; 21-44: Religious "medal": St. Bartholomew; 21-45: Raised floral design. Continental. Nineteenth century.

CHAPTER 22

Scissors

A pair of scissors is essentially two knives, crossed in the middle, and held together with a pin. Sydney Smith, an English clergyman, said that "Marriage resembles a pair of shears, so joined that they cannot be separated; often moving in opposite directions, yet always punishing anyone who comes between them."

Some cultures have a superstition about giving scissors as a gift. It is feared that a sharp edge might cut the friendship. A small coin is included with the gift of a scissors or a knife. The coin is then returned to the giver to symbolize the "purchase" of the gift.

During the eighteenth century, small dainty embroidery scissors, ranging in length from two and one-half to three and one-half inches, housed in decorative cases were given as engagement gifts. Verses praising the virtues of fidelity and love were included with the gift.

Scissors are made in a wide variety of sizes, from the tiniest working scissors, measuring under two inches, to a tinsmith's shears. Before the 1850s, scissors were made entirely by hand. It took over one hundred and fifty different steps to make a pair of scissors, beginning with the raw steel and ending with the finished product.

The art of making fine handmade scissors was lost during the nineteenth century. Hand made scissor making was slow and required patience and accuracy. As the price of labor increased, the craft was not commercially profitable.

PARTS OF A SCISSOR

BOWS: Holes through which the thumb and first finger are thrust.

SHANK: The part connecting the bows and the blades. A rivet or screw on the shank holds the two pieces of the scissors together. The manufacturer's name appears on the shank.

BLADES: The part that does the cutting. The blades touch each other only at the tip and at the base near the rivet or screw. There is a gap between these two points.

Scissors are made for either right handed or left handed people.

DESIGNS AND DECORATIONS

Scissors were made in a wide variety of designs. In France, a popular design for embroidery scissors was called "Jambes des Princesses," legs of the princess. The shanks were shaped like the legs of a woman with fancy boots. This design is being reproduced today.

During the mid-nineteenth century, the Rogers Company of England produced scissors with dolphin, fish, and scrolls on the handles. Often four graduated sized pairs were sold as a set in a leather case. Rogers also made scissors with a name cut into the metal.

The Persians developed the bird form scissors, with the beak serving as the blades. The Dutch originated the stork shaped scissors. They often had a matching sheath or case. Stork design scissors are also being reproduced.

158

Scissors with mother-of-pearl bows were originally part of a fitted workbox of mother-of-pearl tools. The other tools were a thimble, needle case, bodkin, and snowflake shaped thread winder. Mother-of-pearl sewing tools were made in the early nineteenth century in a group of work shops located near the Royal Palace, Paris, France. The shell work is known as Palais Royal. The blades were imported from England or Germany.

Spain contributed the damascene decorations on scissors. The black and golden color decorations is called Toledo work.

One of the most elaborately decorated pair of scissors ever made was presented to Queen Victoria on her coronation. James Atherton, the maker, was employed by Wilkinson and held the official title of "Scissor Filer." It is reported that it took four months to make the scissors.

The scissor pattern books of Peter Atherton, a nineteenth century scissor filer and brother of James, are in the archives of the R. and J. Ragg Scissor Company, Sheffield, England. The Athertons were considered some of the cleverest scissor makers of their time.

Probably the finest display of fancy scissors ever shown at one time and in one place was the Wilkinson's exhibit at the 1851 Crystal Palace Exposition in London. There were six pairs less than two inches long; the smallest, according to the official catalog, were only 1/16th inch long and weighed 1/24th of a gram. At the other end of the scale was a pair twenty-four inches long, weighing eight pounds. The Athertons probably made some of these scissors. James Atherton was 70 in 1851 and nearly 80 when he retired.

Scissors were made in the United States as early as the nineteenth century, often with blades imported from Germany. The most common American shank design is the rococo style with "C" or "S" scrolls and flowers.

Chinese scissors are distinctive. The bows are bent metal and are large in proportion to the size of the blade. Small embroidery Chinese scissors are usually enclosed in a embroidered silk case.

Souvenir Scissors

Scissors that commemorated people and events were made in Germany during the nineteenth and early twentieth centuries. Portraits of King Franz Josef and Queen Elizabeth of Austria appear on medallions below the bows of one such pair.

Souvenir scissors for American events were also made in Germany. One commemorated the Columbian Exposition in Chicago, 1893, another the Louisiana Purchase Exposition, St. Louis, Missouri, 1904.

A scissors made in Italy honors Pope Pius XII. It is marked "ANNUS SANCTUS 1950" and "Angesa, Italy."

Lace Scissors

The "Lace Scissors" has a small ball of metal at the end of one blade. The name is not entirely accurate, as they were not intended for use when making bobbin or needlepoint lace. These lace scissors were used during the making of simulated laces called Carrickmacross, in which layers of fabric were placed over net. After working the design, the surplus was cut away. The knob on the end of one blade stopped the sharp point of the scissors from cutting through both layers of fabric. Lace scissors were introduced in the nineteenth century.

Universal Scissors

One of the most unusual scissors came from Germany in the nineteenth and early twentieth centuries. It was the veritable Swiss Army knife of scissors. Besides cutting, the scissors was designed to serve seventeen other functions, some of which are out-dated today. This scissors can cut buttonholes, a metal tube, cigars, and wire. It also can serve as a ruler, measure, nail file, screw driver, cigar box opener, cartridge extractor, tapping hammer, pen knife, glass cutter, glass breaker, marking wheel, and ink scratcher or eraser. Finally, it also had a peep-hole stereoscope or Stanhope, often featuring a picture of a church or some tourist attraction.

Button Hole Scissors

The button hole scissors has an adjustable screw and ratchet, which can be set to start the cut for a hand bound buttonhole any distance up to a half inch from the edge of the cloth. Before this scissors was invented, button holes were cut with a button hole knife, which had to be hit with a mallet.

Another early button hole gadget was made of brass. Thomas B. Doolittle of Bridgeport, Connecticut, patented it on September 3, 1892. It had a sliding sharp-pointed knife that was used to rip seams, as well as cut button holes.

A clamp with a guillotine devise also cut buttonholes. A bird and asp were included in the decoration on this button hole cutting device, but they had no function in the operation.

Pinking Shears

The name "pinking" has nothing to do with color. The pinking shears cut raw edges of fabric in a zig-zag or scallop shape to prevent raveling. The earliest use for pinking was for decorative purposes during the sixteenth century. Various shaped eyelets and slashes were cut into fabric to reveal the different colors and textures of the fabric underneath.

Pinking shears as we know them today were first introduced during the 1920s. Earlier a pinking knife or wheel was used to make decorative cuttings on fabric. The pinking knife was struck with a mallet to cut the fabric.

By the nineteenth century, a hand turned pinking machine replaced the pinking knife. Cutting wheels with various designs were used in this machine.

When oil cloth was sold by the yard as a table covering, a machine with a decorative cutting wheel was used to cut a piece from the bolt of fabric. These commercial pinking machines were manufactured under the name "Columbus Coated Fabric." The fabric company was eventually purchased by Bordens, the milk company.

Pinking machines, hand turned and electric, are made today, mainly for men's trousers manufacturers. Men's trousers are sold unhemmed to stores.

Doll collectors are constantly searching for pinking shears and machines with unusual decorative cutters. Antique dolls are frequently costumed with petticoats and ruffles finished in fancy pinked edges.

Pinking shears and wheel machines with fancy cutting patterns have more value than those that make a simple zigzag cut. Test a pinker on fabric, not paper, before buying it. Paper is a natural enemy of scissors and shears and quickly dulls their cutting blades. Avoid any pinker that does not cut fabric easily. Sharpening and repairing an old fancy blade pinker may cost more than the piece itself.

Drizzling

The practice of drizzling is also known as parflage or raveling. Fine and unusual sets of tools were created for this task. A complete set consists of a pointed awl or stiletto for picking the thread, a fancy scissors, and a knife shaped tool, all enclosed in a decorative case. It is rare to find a drizzling set. If a set does surface, it usually is not recognized. Fine examples can be viewed in museum collections.

The craze of drizzling started in France in the court of Marie Antonette during the eighteenth century and continued through the early nineteenth century. This strange fad consisted of unpicking gold and silver threads from garments and tapestries and selling the metal. The original object of this work was to salvage the precious metal from old and tarnished articles. When old pieces were no longer available,the craft was practiced on new, usable garments. Gentlemen wore gold braids, laces, and bands on their garments. It was not unusual for their lady friends to demand these adornments when they outlived their usefulness so they could pick out the precious metal threads.

Much old and valuable needlework was destroyed by the practice of drizzling. The craze of drizzling did not extend downward to the common or ordinary people. They did not have access to fabrics that were decorated with precious metals. The craft faded away over time.

22-1: Reproduction of scissors in the Museum of London, England. The original has been authenticated to be a 1692 design. Photo courtesy of Gingher, Inc.

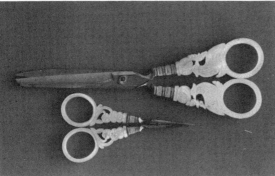

22-2, 22-3: Mother-of-pearl handled scissors, gilted shank. These delicate scissors are from French fitted workboxes, circa 1800. The blades were made in either Germany or England.

22-4, 22-5: Mother-of-pearl handled scissors, gilted shank. French. Circa 1800.

22-6: Mother-of-pearl handled scissors, gilted shank. French. Circa 1800.

22-7, 22-8: Mother-of-pearl handled scissors, gilted shank. French. Circa 1800.

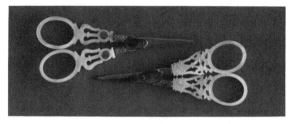

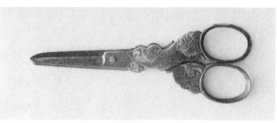

22-9: Steel scissors. Cupid in flight on the shank. Germany. Nineteenth century.

22-10: Lacy cut steel scissors marked "Ricoido." Continental. Eighteenth century.

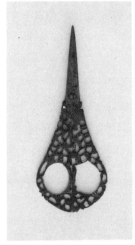

22-11: Knife edge applique scissors. Six inches long. Photo courtesy of Gingher, Inc.

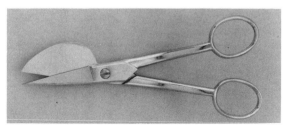

163

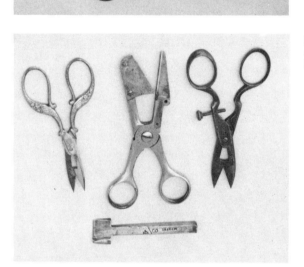

22-12: Chinese steel scissors. Nineteenth century.

22-13, 22-14, 22-15: Buttonhole cutting scissors; 22-16: (bottom): buttonhole cutting knife.

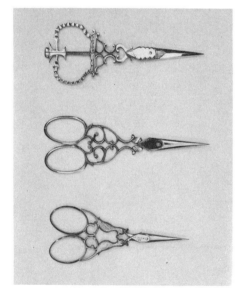

22-17, 22-18, 22-18a: Embroidery scissors made in Sheffield, England, for the Great Exposition, London, 1851. Photo courtesy of the Sheffield City Museum, Sheffield, England.

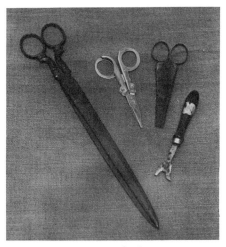

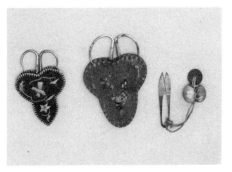

22-21, 22-22: Chinese embroidery scissors in hand embroidered felt cases; 22-23: Chinese spring snips with bells and coin attached.

22-19, 22-20: Assorted scissors. 22-19: Eighteenth century iron. 22-20: Seam ripper. Photo courtesy of the American Home Sewing Museum, West Warren, MA.

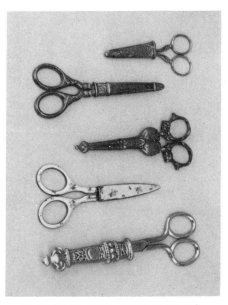

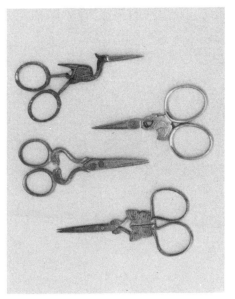

22-24, 22-25, 22-26, 22-27, 22-28: Scissors in protective sheaths. 22-24 (top): Silver, American. Simons Brothers, Philadelphia, PA; 22-25: Silver, Dutch. Engraved "Wilhelma"; 22-26: Brass, unmarked; 22-27: Green enamel with flowers, Germany. Nineteenth century; 22-28: Brass, unmarked.

22-29, 22-30, 22-31, 22-32: Figural embroidery scissors; 22-29 (bottom): Butterfly; 22-30: Asp; 22-31: Swan; 22-32 (top): Stork.

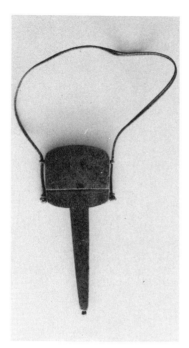

22-33, 22-34: Presentation scissors; 22-33: Royal Coat of Arms and initials VR underneath. Made by Edwin Hunter, Sheffield, England, 1851; 22-34: Scissors with Royal Coat of Arms. Made by John Gibbins & Sons, Sheffield, England, 1851; Photo courtesy of the City of Sheffield Museum, Sheffield, England.

22-35: Steel scissor case, marked "Je Meur Pour Less Mein." (I [the pelican] die for my loved ones.) French. Eighteenth century.

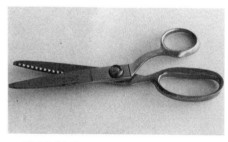

22-36: Modern pinking shears.

22-37: Silver filigree scissor case. Russian. Second half of the eighteenth century. Photo courtesy of the City Museum, Moscow, U.S.S.R.

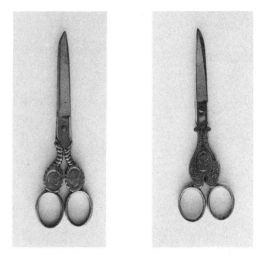

22-38: Portraits in medallions on shank of steel scissors. King Franz Josef and Queen Elizabeth of Austria. Nineteenth century; 22-39: Portrait of the Pope appears in a medallion on the shank of this steel scissors. It is marked "Annus Sanctus 1950" and "Angesa, Italy."

22-40, 22-41: Scissor cases; 22-40 (top): Embossed silver, unmarked; 22-41: Silver. English. Nineteenth century.

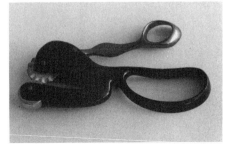

22-42: Buttonhole cutting clamp. Note the figures of a bird and asp incorporated in the design. Steel. Nineteenth century.

22-43: Scissor operated pinking wheel. Black enamel on steel. Early twentieth century.

167

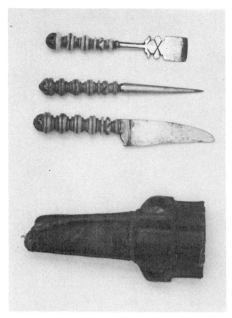

22-45: Commercial pinking machine. Used to cut oil cloth that was sold by the yard as table covering.

22-44: Drizzling set. Incomplete. Scissor missing. Photo courtesy of the Sheffield City Museum, Sheffield, England.

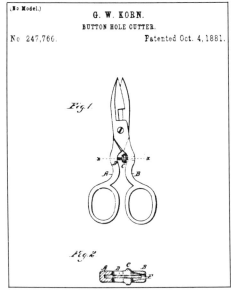

(No Model.)

G. W. KORN.
BUTTON HOLE CUTTER.

No 247,766.   Patented Oct. 4, 1881.

Fig. 1

Fig. 2

22-46: Clamp pinking machine, marked "Hannum Pinking Machine, Patented Nov. 2, 1897."

22-47: Patent drawing for the button hole cutter patented by George W. Korn, October 4, 1881.

The Universal Scissors

22-48: The Universal scissors made by E. V. Klever, Jr. in Solingen, Germany. It has seventeen functions besides cutting. It measures 4 ½″ from bow to point.

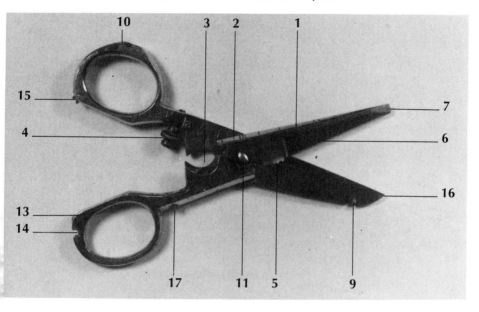

1. The flat side of the upper blade has a straight edge marked as a ruler.

2. Toward the bow end, near the joint, when the blades are open, appears a tiny crotch which catches and cuts wire.

3. Next to it is a larger circular one to clip cigars.

4. A screw between the handles adjusts a buttonholer.

5. The saw-teeth can hold and sever a small tube.

6. One edge of the upper blade serves as a nail file.

7. The square flattened end or butt of the upper blade forms a screw driver.

8. This blade can also be used to pry open a box lid.

9. A tiny notch near the bevel of the under blade can withdraw cartridges from a firearm.

10. A flattened part of the outer rim of one bow may be used as a tack hammer.

11. The lower blade, at its center, has a projecting cylindrical pivot. This permits one to take the scissor apart, like modern poultry shears.

12. When apart, one blade may be used as a pen knife.

13. The base of one bow contains a tiny revolving steel wheel for cutting glass.

14. Glass may also be cracked or split apart by means of a small notch next to the wheel.

15. The other bow has a small toothed wheel (like a pastry jagger) for marking paper or perforating dress patterns.

16. The tip of one blade can be used as an ink scratcher or eraser.

17. The last use of the multi-purpose scissors is a Stanhope or "peep." This one has a picture of the U.S. Capitol, Washington, D.C.

CHAPTER 23

Sewing Birds and Clamps
The Bird That Flew into Oblivion

The most common sewing bird is one with a bird, resembling a cross between a barn swallow and a canary perched upon a clamp. A emery or pin cushion is on its back, and another cushion is attached to the clamp. This "bird" was patented by Charles Waterman in 1853, the patent date appearing on the rounded edge of the bird's wing. This sewing bird nested in many sewing baskets. The company ledgers for 1854 show that 52,000 birds were sold, producing $25,000 in income.

A little ditty, included in the original box, is a nineteenth century version of advertising salesmanship. It reads:

> BEHOLD A WILLING WARBLER
> CONTRIVED SO CUNNINGLY.
> THE HEMS YOU TURN
> WE'LL HOLD QUITE FIRM
> NOT PINNED UPON YOUR KNEE.

The sewing bird became the seamstress' third hand. Its beak held an end of a long bed sheet or wide skirt edge while the woman was hemming.

Actually, "sewing bird" is a misnomer. Clamp tops came in many forms, among which were butterflies, dogs, or fish. It is hard to call these "sewing butterflies" or "sewing dogs", so the name "sewing bird" refers to all of the novelty shapes.

The sewing bird was attached to a clamp that fastened to the work table. Manufacturers argued that the clamps had a health benefit because they eliminated rounded shoulders and stooped back while sewing.

Charles Waterman sold his new invention to Elihu Geer, a shop keeper in Hartford, Connecticut. Geer placed an ad in the *Hartford Times* on June 5, 1852 that read:

> "THE LATEST INVENTION AND MOST USEFUL ARTICLE FOR THE USE OF THE LADIES THAT CAN BE FOUND. THE ABOVE ENGRAVING TELLS THE WHOLE STORY OF ITS USE AND USEFULNESS, AND HEALTH PRESERVING PROPERTIES. LOOK AT THE CONTRAST OF THE HUMAN FORM WHERE IT IS USED AND WHERE IT IS NOT, (THE USER IS SITTING GRACEFULLY ERECT, AND THE NON-USER IS PAINFULLY HUNCHED OVER THE WORK), THEN COME OR SEND YOUR ORDERS FOR ONE OR MORE AT THE STATIONERY AND FANCY GOODS SALON OF ELIHU GEER, 10 STATE STREET."

The Yankee Peddlers, the brothers Horace and Dennis Wilcox, bought thousands of Waterman's "birds" and sold them from their traveling "stores" as they drove their horses and wagons through New England and the "new frontiers" as far west as Ohio. The wholesale price was four, five, or six dollars per dozen, depending on whether the bird had on its back a plain, fancy, or ultra-fancy cushion, or whether it was made of brass, silver plated, or solid silver.

The sewing bird was made and offered for sale into the first quarter of the twentieth century. The 1914 catalogue of the Baird-North Company, Providence, Rhode Island, offered a silver plated sewing bird for eighty-five cents.

The Waterman style "bird" was reproduced during the 1950s and again during the 1980s. Each time the patent date was eliminated from the wing. Some of the 1950s "species" have the word "Japan" stamped on the inside of the clamp with faded red corduroy covering the pin cushion.

The 1980s reproduction is a better looking bird, but not marked at all. It comes in a box stating that it is a reproduction of the antique "bird." Once it is removed from its "nest" in the box and the paper destroyed, it often is offered as a genuine antique. Close examination and extreme caution must be exerted when buying a sewing bird.

OTHER SEWING CLAMPS

Sewing clamps were made of various materials, including brass, iron, bronze, wood, ivory, or silver. Some were commercially manufactured; others were home made or made individually by a craftsman.

Wood Clamps

Cylindrical wooden clamps were sometimes topped with removable pin cushions under which was a compartment to store alum or French chalk. These powders kept the seamstress' hand cool and dry during long hours of sewing. Perspiration could stain the fabric or rust the needle. The compartment also served as a place to store bees wax to strengthen thread or a safe place to store a thimble.

Some wooden clamps had thread winders attached to them. Thread and yarn was sold in hanks or skeins during the early nineteenth century and had to be rewound. Thread on wooden spools did not become common until the 1850s. Today, wooden spools are a thing of the past. They have been replaced with plastic spools. When the American Thread Company closed its spool plant in Milo, Maine, in 1975, the last factory making wooden spools in the United States vanished.

An example of a sophisticated form is a painted wooden clamp, English, circa 1800. It is a complete sewing aid. A pin cushion, two thread winders, thimble case, and tape measure are incorporated into the design of this clamp. The markings on the yellow silk tape were hand inked in "nails" instead of inches. This clamp is similar to one in the archives of the London Museum that is catalogued as a "Brighton Trifle."

Early nineteenth century painted Tunbridge clamps are identified by the painted bands of colored stripes on the light wooden clamp. Some were marked with sentimental sayings, such as "The Absent Not Forgotten." "A Present From Tunbridge" denotes a souvenir piece.

The familiar Tunbridge stickware clamps with the mosaic patterns were made later. James Burrows perfected this technique in the late 1820s. Tunbridge stickware production reached its peak during the 1850s; its decline started during the 1880s. By the 1920s production all but ceased, although there was a short-lived revival of the craft during the 1930s.

Souvenir clamps were made in Germany. A transfer picture of a spa or other tourist attraction identifies these.

Steel and Iron Clamps

Joseph Rogers and Sons of Sheffield, England, made steel netting vices. Clamps stamped with the company name and "Cutlers to His Majesty" date between 1821 and 1837. The clamps stamped "Cutlers to Her Majesty" were made after 1837.

Rogers' clamps were elaborately decorated with steel studs and cut steel decorations. The plating process used by Rogers was called "Rogersine" and was stamped on many of the plated steel clamps. This plating gave the metal a mirror finish. Rogers used a maltese cross as a trademark on their cutlery. The Rogers Company is still in existence, but no longer manufactures sewing clamps.

Another English example, circa 1800, is a gilded iron clamp topped with a cowry sea shell pin cushion. It is a stationary pin cushion clamp on which fabric could be pinned to the cushion with a straight pin.

Many iron clamps were custom made by a blacksmith. Although they were well constructed and functional, little attempt was made to make these beautiful or decorative.

Bone and Ivory

Small clamps made of ivory were part of Chinese Export workboxes that were made in China for American and European trade. They were beautifully carved and almost too delicate to be used for sewing.

Carved scrimshaw whalebone clamps were made by seamen during the whaling era of the nineteenth century. Many of the scrimshaw clamps are exact copies of the metal clamps that were marketed at that time.

Netting Clamps

Clamps were used to create the netting that was fashioned into curtains, bed coverings, frilly collars, and cuffs for milady's garments. Netting clamps have a hook instead of a spring type holder. The foundation loop of the netting work was attached to this hook. Netting clamps date from the late eighteenth to mid-nineteenth century. The art of netting went out of fashion when crochet work became popular.

By the end of the nineteenth century clamps became plainer and simpler, though baroque style clamps appeared from time to time. The invention of the sewing machine marked the downfall of the sewing bird. The bird was a protected specie for a while, but eventually was discarded when the sewing machine became a permanent member of the household.

In 1950 Professor Mayton Copeland of Bowdoin College, Brunswick, Maine, published an article about sewing birds in *Old-Time New England,* the bulletin of The Society for the Preservation of New England Antiquities. "Sewing Birds

Viewed by a Naturalist" classifies sewing birds into orders, families, genera, species and varieties. Professor Copeland identified five orders:

1. Bill Grasper (Bird grasps cloth in bill. It opens bill.)
2. Sub-Bill Grasper (Bird grasps cloth beneath bill. It does not open bill.)
3. Body Graspers (Known from one example.)
4. Pin Birds. (Bird holds cloth by pin on back. Small. Fastens to dress.)
5. Superior Bird. (Cloth not held by bird, only by clamp.)

Professor Copeland collected bird figural clamps. He stated that "Connecticut is the birthplace of most if not all ordinary American birds" and "No, sewing birds do *not* lay eggs."

COLLECTIONS

The Smithsonian Institution in Washington, D.C. has some of the finest examples of antique sewing clamps. The most impressive collection can be seen at the Monmouth Museum, Lincroft, New Jersey. This is the collection of the late Eugenie Bijur, who started to collect sewing birds during the 1930s. The collection consists of over 300 clamps of all types: rug braiders, hemming clamps, yarn winders, and netting hooks. Material used for their manufacture includes wood, iron, ivory, brass, silver plated, britannia, tin, and steel.

Sewing Clamps were also made in England and Continental Europe. The London Museum has a fine collection.

23-1: Detail from painting "In the Old Time Sewing Room" by Anna Whelan Betts. A manufacturer of sewing birds claimed a health advantage for sewing birds. They promoted good posture.

23-2: Drawings showing the function and purpose of the sewing bird. Photo courtesy of the National Gallery of Art, Washington, DC. Index of American Design. Va-Mscl-33.

23-3: Gilted brass cast sewing bird with pin cushion below its beak.

23-4: Detail drawing of the sewing bird. Photo courtesy of the National Gallery of Art, Washington, DC. Index of American design. Ill-Me-75.

23-5: Bronze sewing bird perched in ring topped with pin cushion (missing.) Eugenie Bijur collection. Photo courtesy of the Monmouth Museum, Lincroft, NJ.

23-6: Gilted brass sewing bird perched on clamp. Pin cushion missing.

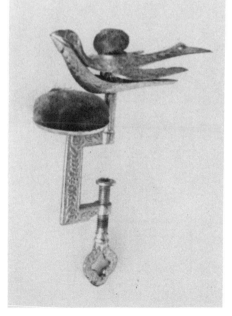

23-7: Gilted brass sewing bird with emery on back and pin cushion on clamp. Patent date February 15, 1853, appears on the shoulder of the wing. Note: A reproduction of this model sewing bird has currently surfaced on the antiques market. The patent date has been deleted from the wing of the reproduction.

23-8: Brass sewing birds on iron clamp. Pin cushion missing.

23-9: Iron sewing bird with heart shaped thumb screw.

23-10: Cross hatched iron sewing bird perched on round pin cushion.

23-11: Butterfly clamp. Silver plated brass. Variation of clamp patented by John Lane, 1853.

23-12: Sewing clamp in the shape of a dog. Silver plated brass. Second half of nineteenth century.

23-13: Silver plated sewing bird in flight. Pin cushion rests on twisted metal post. Needle case attached to clamp. English. Early nineteenth century.

23-14: Sturdy iron clamp in the shape of a worm.

23-15: Fish shaped sewing clamp. Gilted metal.

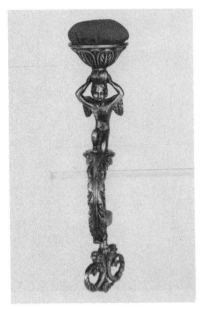

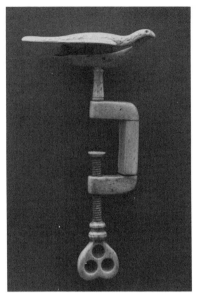

23-17: Hand carved bone sewing bird. Copy of the 1853 Waterman's brass bird.

23-16: Cupid clamp holding pin cushion above its head. The foot of cupid raises when wing is pressed.

23-19: Brass dolphin clamp, topped with pin cushion. Turn screw is an angel's head with wings. The mouth opens when the tail is depressed. Early nineteenth century.

23-18: Chrome plated baroque sewing clamp with pin cushion.

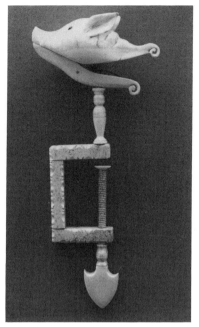

23-21: Hand carved bone clamp in the shape of a dog's head.

23-20: Scrimshaw ivory and bone clamp in shape of a pig's head.

23-23: Chrome plated clamp with pin cushion and spool holder. Fabric is held by ball on top of clamp. Thumb lever on clamp over concealed spring.

23-22: Heavy brass clamp. Engraved in script "A. Grofs 1851."

179

23-24: Metal clamp with pin cushion.

23-25: Early painted Tunbridge clamp. The black, green and red strips are plainly visible. Circa 1800.

23-26: The label of this clamp states "A Present from Tonbridge," which is the early spelling.

23-27: Tunbridge ware clamp with pin cushion. Mid nineteenth century.

23-28: Early painted Tunbridge clamp with pin cushion on top. 1790-1830.

23-29: Turned rosewood clamp with pin cushion top.

23-30: Tunbridge "C" clamp with removable pin cushion top. A mirror and storage for a thimble under the cushion. Mid nineteenth century.

23-31: Rosewood clamps topped with yarn winding cage and pin cushion (missing.) This model was always made in matched pairs.

181

23-33: Sycamore clamp with ivory and ebony pin cushion top.

23-32: Wooden clamp painted white with blue decorations. A round mirror is inserted in the front of the clamp, and pin cushion on top.

23-34: Sycamore clamp topped with ivory and ebony pin cushion. The removable cushion covers compartment to hold a thimble or bee's wax to strengthen thread.

23-35: Sycamore "C" clamp with
rosewood pin cushion. This
model tends to split when clamp
is tightened to a table. Reverse
side of this one has a brass plate
to repair the split.

23-36: Wooden clamp painted
white, with blue decorations. A
round mirror inserted in front of
clamp, and pin cushion on top.

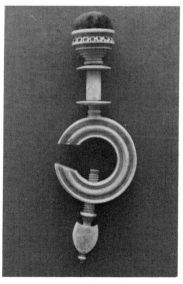

23-37: The label on this states
fondly "The Absent Not Forgotten."

23-38: Ivory "C" clamp with pin
cushion top.

183

23-39: Ivory clamps from Chinese export work boxes.

23-40: Button hole cutting clamp. Note bird and asp worked into design. Black enamel on iron. Nineteenth century.

23-41, 23-42: Two blue and white painted wood clamps; 23-41: Mirror in front and pin cushion on top; 23-42: Painted "C" clamp with pin cushion. Photo courtesy of The American Home Sewing Museum, West Warren, MA.

CHAPTER 24

Tapes and Measures
"Rule of Thumb"

The expression "Rule of Thumb" dates from the time when an inch was measured by the length of a lady's shortest thumb joint - from the knuckle to the tip of the thumb. This was not a consistent method of measuring, but the thumb was always "at hand" to do the job.

Tape measures made during the early nineteenth century were marked in "NAILS" rather than inches. A "NAIL" is equal to 2 1/4th inches, or 5.6 centimeters. There were no numbers on the tape. Tapes were marked N, HQ, Q, H, and Y. These letters represented:

> N - Nail or 2 1/4th inches
> HQ - Half Quarter or 4 1/2 inches
> Q - Quarter or 9 inches
> H - Half or 18 inches
> Y - Yard or 36 inches

An inch equalled three barleycorns or 1/12th of a foot.

Measuring tapes were often sold without any markings. The seamstress marked the tape with letters or numbers. This often created problems as the measurements were not consistent from one lady's tape to another.

WOODEN MEASURES

The traveling peddler and small town dry goods store used wooden yardsticks. Even these measures were not accurate. The peddler's yardstick was deliberately calibrated to be short of a yard. When he gave the customer a few extra inches of fabric, she thought that she was getting a bargain.

CLOTH TAPE MEASURES

Cloth tape measures were enclosed in decorative cases that were made from a variety of materials: brass, bone, ivory, mother-of-pearl, sea shells, and silver. A small knob projected from the case that could be turned to rewind the tape. Modern tapes have a spring devise to rewind them.

Many old tape measures originally were part of a workbox. The case matched the other pieces in the box. As such, most were made of either silver, ivory, or mother-of-pearl.

Modern, twentieth century, spring wind-up or hand turned tapes would make a fascinating collection. They were made in a variety of novelty shapes. Catchy sayings were printed to give them a little humor. "Pull my head, not my leg" appears on a turtle-shaped tape measure. A straw hat says, "Most Hats Cover the Head. This One Covers the Feet." Another play on words appears on a high button shoe measure that says, "Three Feet In One Shoe."

Celluloid and bakelite tapes in various novelty shapes were made during the first half of the twentieth century. A pig, with its curly tail that acts as a winder, was a symbol of good luck. A realistic looking white hen's egg has a fake house fly on it that acts as the pull-end of the tape.

Tapes enclosed in sea shells were sold as souvenirs of seaside resorts such as Cape Cod, Massachusetts. The natural sea shell was a constant reminder of the vacation.

Vegetable ivory tape cases with Stanhope microfilm peep hole pictures were sold as souvenirs. The Stanhope was named for Lord Charles Stanhope, a nineteenth century English scientist who invented the tiny glass rod lens on which a picture could be applied. Sir David Brewster developed a similar product called a "Coddington Magnifier." The name Stanhope has been used for a long time to describe all these novelty "peeps".

A tiny glass rod approximately 1/4th inch long, and 1/10th an inch in diameter, was inserted into ivory and vegetable ivory tape measures and needlecases. The tiny black dot on the rod was an early version of microfilm photography. The photograph might be a view of a resort tourist attraction, or a cathedral. Text examples included the Lord's Prayer and the Ten Commandments.

Sometimes the Stanhope is missing from an antique piece. The empty hole is not for hanging the piece on a chatelaine as some dealers assert. The missing Stanhope greatly lowers the value.

William Purcell patented a brass thimble with a peep inserted into the cap in 1880. It was not a practical invention as the picture and the glass might: (1) interfere with the sewing or (2) be damaged by the needle.

A modern version of the peep hole thimble is made today. The photos look old. The clue to spotting this modern example is that the glass tube in the cap is much longer than the nineteenth century version. It can hit the tip of the finger when the thimble is worn.

Prices for tape measures vary. The condition of the tape and the case is an important consideration. A broken spring mechanism is almost impossible to repair and lessens the value.

24-1: House fly perched on white celluloid egg. The fly serves as the pull for the tape.

24-2: Celluloid flower seller with a basketful of flowers. The ladybug is the pull for the tape.

24-3: The duck is a complete purse size mending kit. The "hat" is a thimble. The bill is a combination thread winder and needle case, and the sharp point is a punch or seam ripper. The tape is housed in the round body.

24-4: Celluloid sailing ship tape. The pull is on the base of the aft of the ship.

24-5: Brass mill house tape. The waterwheel turns the tape. English. Nineteenth century.

24-6: Reverse side of mill house tape has a veranda.

24-7: Brass turtle tape. "Pull my head and not my leg" is on the back of the turtle.

24-8: The "Golden Rule" tape.

24-9: Silver plated pig tape. The curly tail is the winder.

24-10: Plastic cottage measure with the pull in the chimney. Modern.

24-11, 24-12: Silver tape measures; 24-12: Thimble shaped.

24-13: The 1930s style bakelite radio.

24-14: Vegetable ivory tape with emery cushion on top. English. Nineteenth century.

24-15: Combination multicolored thread braid and tape measure. A convenient length of colored thread could be pulled from the braid without destroying it.

24-16: Gutta Percha, a material similar to hard rubber. Marked "Patd July 13, 1869, reissued June 13, 1871." The patent was issued for the mechanical spring inside the tape.

24-17: Novelty shaped silver tapes from fitted work boxes. English. Nineteenth century.

24-18: Mother-of-pearl rulers from fitted work boxes. Early nineteenth century.

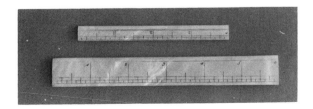

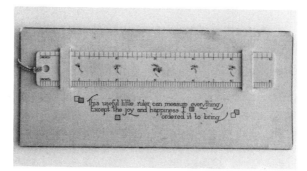

24-19: A 1920s greeting card with celluloid ruler.

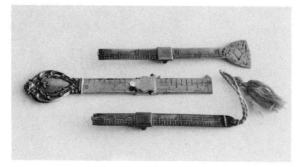

24-20: Silver and silver plated hem
measures.

CHAPTER 25

Work Tables, Workboxes, and Sewing Cases

Martha Washington was a most enthusiastic needleworker. The mahogany work table with rounded saddle bag storage compartments on each end was named in her honor. Most models had three drawers in the center and flip top lids on the rounded ends. Several American furniture and cabinet manufacturers made versions of this cabinet. The form was popular from the middle of the nineteenth century to the middle of the twentieth century.

Black lacquered sewing stands and workboxes were imported from the Orient. The stands were fitted with carved ivory implements including a thimble, thread winder, bobbins, thread barrel, clamp, bodkin, etc. The Chinese artisans modeled the implements they made after pictures. The Orientals had no idea how the implements were to be used. As a result, many of the implements are lovely to look at, but not usable as working tools.

Often art needlework tools, such as tatting shuttle, clamp, and netting pins, were included in sewing stands. Each tool had its special compartment in a removable tray.

Many of the carved ivory tools that are offered for sale individually at antiques shows today were once part of a matching set in a fitted sewing work box. A Chinese lacquered workbox complete with the original matching carved ivory tools is more valuable than a collection of individual tools. Empty Chinese lacquered workboxes loose their value as sewing collectibles.

The Sheraton or Hepplewhite style ladies work table, with a fabric bag or pouch suspended from the bottom of the table, originated about 1800. Later, a trough-shaped wooden drawer replaced the fabric pouch. The Sheraton style work table is oval in shape and has bronze fittings on the base of the legs. Some tables were equipped with chess boards and used as game tables. Early hand made Victorian tables, usually minus the original sewing tools, sell for about $900 to $1,200, depending on condition, design, and workmanship.

PORTABLE WORKBOXES

The popularity of portable fitted workboxes began in the eighteenth century and extended through the nineteenth century. They were made of wood or leather and fitted with gold, silver, or mother-of-pearl tools. Smaller boxes include basic tools such as a thimble, needle case, scissors, and thread winders. The larger ones added a measuring tape, bodkin, emery, waxer, and other sewing related implements.

A bottom drawer of larger boxes served as a writing desk, the hinged writing surface lifted for storage of writing implements and paper. Sometimes it contained a secret compartment that could be opened by pressing a hidden spring lock. This is where a young lady could hide love letters from snooping eyes.

It is not unusual to find a scent bottle in a fitted sewing box. The bottle may have held some pungent substance, a whiff of which helped ladies recover from fainting spells. It has not been determined if this was necessary because women were frailer in those years, or because it was fashionable to wear their garments and corsets tightly. Whatever the reason, smelling salts were always kept close at hand.

The table top fitted sewing box in the shape of a baby grand piano originated in France about 1800. A music box that played one or two tunes was included in the design. Gold, silver, or mother-of-pearl tools were the original fittings. A piano work box, fitted with the original tools and a music box in working condition, is a rare find today and commands a four figure price when offered at auction.

LADY'S COMPANION

Contrary to popular belief, a Lady's Companion was not always a gentleman. It was a small, portable sewing case usually with the name "LADY'S COMPAN-ION" stamped in gold letters on the outside of the box. The box was made of leather, painted wood or tortoise shell. The fittings included the basic tools needed for sewing circle sessions: thimble, scissors and bodkin. Often a mechanical pencil and a note book were included; occasionally a scent bottle was found. The Lady's Companion was popular during the late eighteenth and nineteenth centuries.

ETUI

The ornamental cased etui was first used during the seventeenth century. It was used by both men and women. Pockets were non-existent during that period, and personal necessities such as a comb, keys, and sewing tools were carried in these cases. Many were not fitted with sewing tools. Etui are elaborately decorated with fruits and foliage or classical scenes. Some are enameled or inlaid with semi-precious stones. Etui measure from four to five inches long and have a chain that can be attached to the waist band of a garment. They store the necessary tools that sometimes hung loosely from the chains on a chatelaine.

TWENTIETH CENTURY POCKET SEWING KITS

Charming purse-size celluloid sewing kits for emergency mending were popular during the early 1900s. Shaped like animals or people, with a thimble serving as the hat, the case held needle and thread. Occasionally, a spring scissors and manicure tools were included in the kit.

Plain tube or egg shaped purse size sewing kits were used as advertising giveaways. The thimble was either stored inside or served as the cap of the kit. A common version is the German made egg or bullet shaped metal kit with swirls of colored paint. Coca Cola distributed millions of aluminum sewing kits with their advertising message printed on the case.

In 1912 the Whiting Manufacturing Company made a Sterling silver kit that was complete and compact. Though it was only 2 1/2 inches tall, excluding the protruding thimble, it contained everything needed for emergency mending: needle, pins, thread, and thimble. When the United States mobilized for World War I, this same patented sewing kit was made of steel, painted olive drab, and used as the official sewing kit of the doughboys. The instructions included in the Army's kit explains how to use the self-threading needles. This is proof that this type of needle is not a new invention. After the war, sewing kits were painted forest green, had a decal of the Girl Scouts logo applied, and became part of the Girl Scout's camping equipment.

Whiting type kits made of common metal sell for about $15. Modern spools do not fit the kit, so buy one with the original spools.

25-1: Black and gold lacquered Chinese export workbox. Nineteenth century; 25-2: Black lacquered Chinese workbox label states it was from Canton, China.

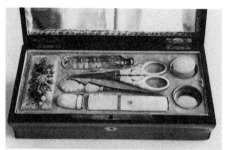

25-3: Fitted Chinese export lacquered workbox.

25-4: Sandalwood box fitted with mother-of-pearl tools. French. Circa 1800.

25-5, 25-6: Mahogany baby grand piano shaped workbox. Ivory "keys." Mother-of-pearl tools inside the piano. Mirror under lid and music box under pin cushion.

194

25-7: Wooden sewing case. Mirror inside lid. Fitted with silver sewing tools.

25-8: Painted wood sewing kit fitted with silver tools. French. Nineteenth century.

25-9: Wood sewing case fitted with silver tools.

25-10: Black leather box with silver topped emery, thimble, scissors, embroidery punch, and glove darner. American. Circa 1900.

25-11: Small leather box holds silver thimble, thread waxer, and emery. English. Nineteenth century.

25-12: Small leather box holds emery, thimble, thread waxer, and tape measure. Inside lid has scissors, bodkin, and embroidery punch. English. Nineteenth century.

25-13, 25-14: Brown leather oval sewing case with gilted medallion on cover. Interior fitted with gilted silver tools. French. Nineteenth century.

25-15: Leather sewing cases fitted with gilted silver tools. French. Nineteenth century.

25-16: Leather oval sewing case fitted with silver tools. French. Nineteenth century.

25-18: Leather covered case with gilted silver tools. French. Late nineteenth century.

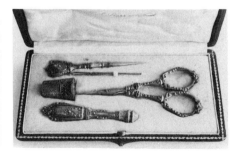

25-19: Leather covered case with silver gilt tools. French. Nineteenth century.

25-20: Oval leather covered kit fitted with gilted silver thimble and scissors. French. Twentieth century.

25-21: Heart shaped sewing box with thimble, scissors, and silver topped emery. This was offered in the 1900 Sears Roebuck catalog for $1.40.

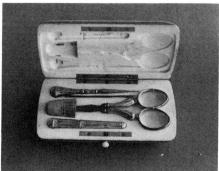

25-22: Carved ivory sewing case fitted with silver tools. French. Early nineteenth century.

25-23: Tortoise shell case, inlaid with silver. French. Nineteenth century.

25-24: Leather sewing box, fitted with silver tools. English. Nineteenth century.

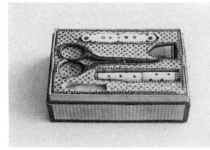

25-25: Paper covered sewing kit. Ivory thimble, needle case, and seam ripper.

25-26: Reverse painting on glass oval inserted on the cover of a wood case.

25-27: Hand painted lid of a French nineteenth century sewing box.

25-29: Silver table top sewing stand. Needle case rests on blue velvet pin cushion. It has top to hold thimble and serves as post for a spool of thread. A silver tube holds scissors. English. Nineteenth century.

25-28: Mahogany and silver table top sewing stand. Gorham. Circa 1895.

25-30: Spanish walnut shell. Gilt metal tray holds scent bottle, embroidery punch, thimble, and scissors. The blades of the scissors are ½" long. Early nineteenth century.

25-31: Spanish walnut with velvet tray, holding embroidery punch, needle case, thimble, and scissors. Early nineteenth century.

25-32: Goose egg shell, holding ivory thimble, metal embroidery punch, needle case, and bodkin. Glass scent bottle has metal cap. A tiny leather covered book printed in French is included in this egg shell. French. Circa 1800.

25-33: Meissen porcelain egg fitted with gold sewing tools. German. Nineteenth century.

25-34: Lady's Companion. Lid and front opens. Fitted with scent bottle, bodkin, embroidery punch, thimble, and pink silk pin cushion. Paper packets of needles are stored in the pockets in front and inside doors.

25-35: Sewing box, painted wood, hinged, decorated on top with spread eagle, flag and "UNION FOREVER." Inscribed "LADY'S COMPANION." Circa 1860-65. Photo courtesy of the Museum of the City of New York.

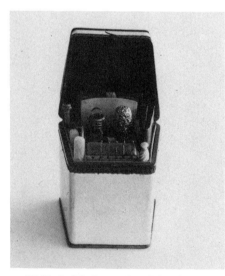

25-36: Lady's Companion. Painted wood. Fitted with tambour hook set, scent bottle, thimble, needle case, bodkin, pencil holder, and ivory note book. English. Nineteenth century.

25-37: Lady's Companion. Leather covered. Fitted with thimble, needle case, embroidery punch, scent bottle, and scissors. Mirror inside lid.

25-38: Enamel etui. Enamel on brass.
English. Nineteenth century.

25-39: Silver etui.

25-40: South Staffordshire enamel etui.
Enamel on brass. English. Nineteenth
century.

25-41: Gilted etui.

25-43: Fish shaped silver bodkins. Simons Brothers Company, Philadelphia, PA. American. Nineteenth century.

25-42: Gilted etui with blue enamel.

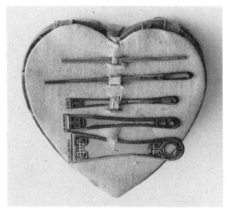

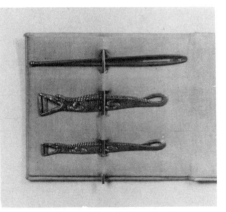

25-45: Alligator shaped silver bodkins. Simons Brothers Company, Philadelphia, PA. Nineteenth century.

25-44: Silver bodkin set with geometric design. Heart shaped silk case. No maker's mark. American. Nineteenth century.

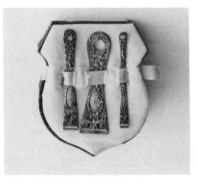

25-46: Ornate silver bodkins in green shield shaped silk case. No maker's mark. American. Nineteenth century.

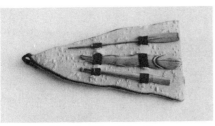

25-47: Silver bodkin set in silk case. Sporting theme: Oar, football, and baseball bat.

25-48: Folding paper needle and pin box. Paper packets of needles are held under the ribbons. Glass head pins inserted into center cube. English. Nineteenth century.

25-49: Silver anchor shaped needle case with chain.

25-50, 25-51: Silver key shaped needle cases with chatelaine clips and chains.

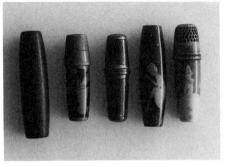

25-52: Velvet covered volume shaped needle case. Paper packets are held under ribbons on leaves. English. Nineteenth century.

25-53: Celluloid and wood mending tubes with thimble caps.

25-55: The World War I sewing kit opened. The instructions, which are packed inside the kit, describe the method of opening the kit! Olive drab and white thread spools fit over the needle tube. The thimble rests on the needle tube, and the open top cap holds the thimble in place. The thimble acts as a pull to open the kit.

25-54: Ivory and celluloid mending tubes with thimble caps. Bottom: Spring operated miniature scissors screws into bottom of tube.

25-56: Thimble topped silver sewing kit. Patented by Whiting and Co., Providence, RI, 1912; 25-57: The same patented kit made of steel and painted olive drab. Used as the official sewing kit for the military during the first World War; 25-58: The same patented kit made of steel and painted forest green. Used as the official Girl Scout camping mending kit, circa 1920.

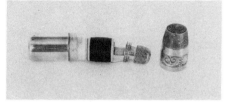

25-60: Silver sewing kit. The cap is in the shape of a large thimble. Thread, needle tube, and thimble are inside. Webster and Co., New York. Early twentieth century.

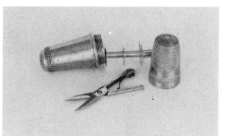

25-59: Silver mending kit. Spools of thread fit on a needle tube. The combination punch and glove darner acts as holder for the thimble. S. Cottle, New York. Late nineteenth century.

25-61: Silver gilt sewing kit appears to be two thimbles when closed. Only one is an actual thimble. Combination thread winder and needle tube and spring scissors store inside. French. Nineteenth century.

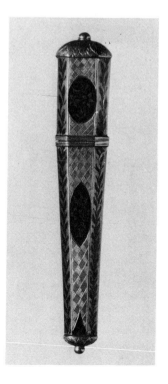

25-62: Needle case. Silver gilt and niello. Russian. Circa 1800. Photo courtesy of the City Museum, Moscow, U.S.S.R.

205

25-63: Silver needle cases from fitted work boxes.

25-64: Silver needle case. Russian. First half of the nineteenth century. Photo courtesy of the City Museum, Moscow, U.S.S.R.

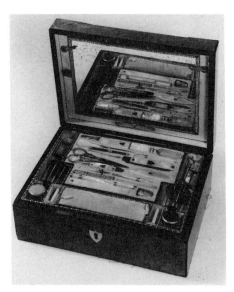

25-65: Sewing box. Fitted with mother-of-pearl, gold and steel implements. Circa 1790-1800. Initialed on top CVR for Catherine Livingston Van Renselaer, 1745-1810. Wife of Stephen Van Renselaer. Photo courtesy of Museum of the City of New York.

25-66: Bisque porcelain egg. Gilted basket inside hold silver gilted sewing tools. French.

25-67: Gold tooled leather portable sewing cases stamped "Lady's Companion." Nineteenth century.

25-68: Lady's Companion holds necessary sewing tools for a sewing circle meeting. Nineteenth century.

25-69: Black lacquered sewing table. China. Nineteenth century. Photo courtesy of the American Home Sewing Museum, West Warren, MA.

207

PART IV

SEWING TOOLS

New Approaches

CHAPTER 26

Black Memorabilia in the Sewing Basket

Sewing items picturing or depicting Black people predate the Civil War. Today, it is difficult to look at them without seeing racial overtones. Many show Black people in a degrading manner. Often, the more stereotyped the presentation, the more desirable the object is as a collectible.

Blacks were a favorite subject on advertising trade cards. A Clark's O.N.T. (Our New Thread) Spool Cotton trade card depicts a Black woman picking cotton in the field and a white woman sewing. The caption on the trade card reads, "The Thread That Binds the Union - North to South." Clark's intention at that time was to sell cotton thread, not to make a social or political statement. Other thread trade cards pictured Black people to demonstrate that their brand of cotton thread was color fast. It would not run or fade during washing.

Manufacturers, as well as other pursuits, mocked and mimicked the English spoken by the poorly educated Blacks. For example, the instruction card for a 1913 emery in the shape of a Black woman reads:

> "Neber you be frightened, honey.
> I ain't axin' fo yo money.
> Law, I jes despise to wheedle!
> Ain't you got a squeaky needle?
> Fetch it to Aunt Dinah, chile.
> Let her shine it up awhile."

Emery powder in the bag removed perspiration and rust from the needle, making it easier to glide through fabric. The familiar "Mammy" figure was part of the pin cushion design. Many homemade examples had an embroidered face with a red bandana kerchief on the head.

Celluloid, tube-shaped, purse-size mending kits were made in the shape of a Black person. A thimble served as the hat. Thread and needles were stored inside the "body" of the figure. These kits were normally made in the form of a Black man rather than a "Mammy." One marked "Souvenir of Havana, Cuba" was made for the tourist trade.

A painted wooden needle holder in the form of a Black man in a full dress suit, complete with tie and cummerbund, is a departure from the normal stereotype of the Black as a farm hand. When the hat is removed from the needlecase, the needles pop up. When a string near the feet is pulled, the needles recede and the hat returns to position on top of the head.

In another item, a Black "Frozen Charlotte" miniature china doll sits waist deep in a thimble shape block of white bee's wax. Thread was drawn across the wax to give it strength and smoothness.

Sewing items and other pieces depicting Black people are now classified, perhaps inaccurately, as American folk art or country art. Sewing tools collectors have to compete with Black memorabilia collectors for these pieces. Figural and novelty pieces depicting Blacks are no longer produced. Most pieces found at flea and antiques markets dated from the 1930s and earlier.

26-1: Singer sewing Machine Trade Card: "Rhodesia."

26-2: Singer Sewing Machine Trade Card: "Zululand."

26-3: Black frozen Charlotte sits waist deep in thimble shaped block of bee's wax used to strengthen thread; 26-4: "Mammy" head with red bandanna emery to remove rust and dirt from needles; 26-5: Cigarette is the pull for a tape measure.

26-6: Black purse size mending kits hold thimble, needle, and thread; 26-7: Needle cases. Remove the hat and needles extend. Pull the string on base and needles recede and hat goes back to top of head.

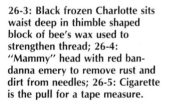

CHAPTER 27

Gadgets
"Build a better mouse trap...."

Year after year imaginative inventors patent gadgets meant to make needlework easier. Many are never produced commercially, or are distributed in small quantities within a small geographic area.

When one of these oddities is found in the bottom of a sewing basket, collectors often have difficulty determining the function of the piece. If the original instructions accompany the gadget, the mystery is solved. A patent number on the piece means a trip to the library to locate the description and drawings of the patent. For items without a patent, your guess is best.

Many large libraries have copies of patent records, either in book form or on microfilm. Photo copies of patents can be obtained from the U. S. Patent and Trademark Office, Washington, D. C. 20231. When ordering a copy of a patent from the U.S. Patent Office, include the patent number, date of patent (if known), name of the patentee, and a brief description of the piece. There is a charge of $1.50 for each patent ordered. If you want more information regarding patent searches, write for the *Obtaining Information from Patents, Patent Classification and Search Services* available from the U.S. Patent and Trademark Office.

The library of Thimble Collectors International has an extensive file of thimble patent papers. Members may obtain copies for the cost of the photocopying plus postage.

Many patented sewing gadgets have a patent date included somewhere in the design. A patent date alone may not be enough information to obtain a copy of the patent from the U.S. Patent and Trademark Office. The more information you supply, the greater the chance your request will be answered. If production started before a patent was granted, "Pat appl'd For" or "Pat Pending" often appears on the piece. Your research chore is increased considerably

BUTTON HOLE CUTTING KNIFE

A brass gadget with a sharp wedge-shaped sliding knife is a commonly found sewing gadget. It is a button hole cutter. One example is an "Improvement in Button-Hole Cutter" patented by Thomas B. Doolittle of Bridgeport, Connecticut, Patent No. 131,085, dated September 3, 1872. In his specifications, Doolittle states, "My invention has for its object the production of shielded or covered wedge-shaped button-hole cutter, provided with a novel means of securing the covering plates together and forming at the same time suitable thumb and finger plates for moving the knife or cutter, and having the shield so shaped at the 'grasp' end as to facilitate the handling of the instrument and preventing liability of cutting the fingers."

SEAM RIPPERS

A seam ripper, scissors-like in appearance, has non-cutting short blades, one of which is pointed and the other blunt at the end. It is marked "Pat. May 6,

1900." It may have been a handy contraption when it was invented, but it is clumsy compared to today's seam ripper.

EMBROIDERY PUNCHES

A swordfish shaped embroidery punch, touted as the "King of all Embroidery Needles," was manufactured by the H. W. Curtis Company, Chicago, Illinois. This nineteenth century device was especially intended for "zephyr and silk raised embroidery work, desirable for table and chair scarfs, lambriquins for mantels, windows and pianos, sofa cushions, toilet sets, wall banners, lamp mats, baby carriage robes, stove polishing mittens, etc." Curtis, the inventor, solicited agents to sell his new product.

Another embroidery device was the Princess Embroidery Machine, manufactured and distributed by the Princess Embroidery Supplies Company, Philadelphia, Pennsylvania. The instructions for this machine were to work on the back of the fabric, rather than on the front side as required by the Curtis embroiderer. The user is instructed to work slowly at first, and begin "as though you were leaning to operate a typewriter or sewing machine." The manufacturer wanted to associate his new embroidery punch with a long list of new labor saving devices that were developed in the late nineteenth century.

FASTENERS

The Yeiser Hook and Eye Company of Philadelphia, Pennsylvania, patented a new "barred and invisible" hook and eye on June 11, 1909. Garments from this era were secured by buttons, snaps, lacing, or hooks-and-eyes. Yeiser's hook-and-eye sets were guaranteed not to slip, turn, buckle or wobble. They would stay firm and remain so as long as the garment lasted. A package of two dozen hooks, two dozen invisible eyes, and two dozen standard eyes cost ten cents in 1909.

NEEDLE THREADERS

The "Magic Thimble," with its thread cutting knife and wire needle threader, was patented in the 1920s. The two devices are enclosed in a protective channel on the side of the thimble. Each can be slid out of the channel independently. When extended above the cap of the thimble, the wire threader would thread needles, and the cutting knife would clip threads. This thimble was marketed extensively. Many surface in today's antiques market. It can be recognized by the protective channel on the side, and the marking "M.T. Patented" on the band.

Two patented needle threaders were produced by the Threadmaster Company, Elizabeth, New Jersey, in the 1950s. Model 100, Patent #2,281,180, is an automatic needle threader for individual needles. Model 500, marked "Patent Pending," is for automatic sewing machine needles. In Model 100 a needle is inserted into a hole on the threader. A shaft is fed through the eye of the needle by pressing a plunger. The end of the shaft has a hook to which thread is attached. When the plunger is released, the shaft is drawn back through the needle, pulling the thread with it.

The Threadall sewing machine needle threader, made by Threadmaster, works on a different principle. Thread is inserted across a slot on the threader. The threader is placed on the sewing machine needle, a button is pushed to release a shaft, and the threader withdrawn. The needle is threaded.

PATTERN DRAFTING MACHINES

Patents for apparatus capable of measuring and marking, drafting patterns, and garment cutting were issued as early as 1821. Allan Ward of Huntsville, Alabama, patented a method for cutting garments on June 16, 1821. Aaron A. Tentler of Philadelphia, Pennsylvania, 1841 (Patent #1,944) was the earliest system designed specifically for cutting women's garments.

Nineteenth century pattern drafting systems were praised as "magical devices," but are seldom recognized when encountered today. Early garment drafting systems represented a technological and economic breakthrough. Home sewers could make a better garment, and dressmakers with little training could create fashionable garments. The early garment drafting systems provided the basis for the sizing system used for paper patterns and factory made clothing.

A garment drafting system is almost useless unless you have a copy of the original instructions. This does not mean that you should pass up the opportunity to buy an antique drafting system if the instructions are missing. If the system appears to be complete except for the instructions, a "wanted" advertisement in THIMBLETTER or Thimble Collectors International's BULLETIN, might produce a copy of the original instruction book from another collector.

It is worth noting that some early drafting systems did not include skirt or sleeve pieces. The makers assumed that these parts could be drafted from the armhole and waist measurements. Instruction books often include unusual names for the parts and style of a garment. These include waists, polonaise, redingote, mother hubbard, wrapper, basque, and bodice.

One of the more popular and extensively marketed pattern drafting systems was invented by Albert McDowell during the late nineteenth century. McDowell patented and made at least five different versions of his machine. He was granted patents in 1879, 1885, and 1886. The different patents reflect McDowell's response to changes in fashion.

Body measurements were made with a tape measure. A sliding pointer on the brass tool was placed at this number. When all the measurements were transferred to the pattern drafting machine, a paper pattern could be drawn.

A dressmaker had a major problem if a customer wore a tight corset when being measured and a looser corset when she tried on the finished garment. The fashion of the day was tight fitting clothes; no "ease" was allowed.

During the last quarter of the nineteenth century, hundreds of drafting systems were patented. These systems became obsolete in the early twentieth century, when looser dress styles, printed paper dress patterns, and ready-made clothes achieved popularity.

IN SUMMARY

Collecting these gadgets provides an interesting insight to bygone eras. If possible, buy any of these patented gadget items in their original packaging and with the original instructions.

27-1: Brass needle threaders patented by the Threadmaster Co., Newark, NJ, 1951. One model, The Threadmaster, is designed to thread hand sewing needles. The other, Threadall, is for machine needles.

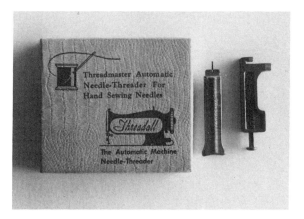

27-2: Instructions for the operation of the Threadall sewing machine needle threader has line drawings showing the operation of the gadget.

Operating Instructions for *Threadall*

The Automatic Machine Needle-Threader

1. THREADALL, as illustrated, before operating.

2. Withdraw shaft into body by retracting button.

3. Insert thread across slot, as illustrated, hold taut.

4. Place THREADALL against needle and slide downward until click is audible.

5. Push button. This will release shaft, inserting thread through needle.

6. Withdraw THREADALL from threaded needle.

27-3: Brass buttonhole cutter with steel blade knife was patented and manufactured by Thomas B. Doolittle, Bridgeport, CT, September 3, 1872. Wedge-shaped cutting knife is shielded to protect the fingers from being cut. The blade could be set firmly at any position to insure that each buttonhole would be the same size.

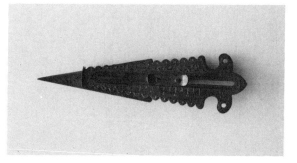

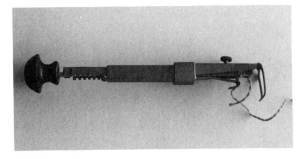

27-4: The Princess Embroidery Machine. American. Late nineteenth century.

27-5: The instructions for the Princess Embroidery Machine show a line drawing of its operation. It was patented and manufactured by the Princess Embroidery Supplies Co., Philadelphia, PA. The machine could make beautiful things for the home, including embroidered waists, tea aprons, piano scarfs, and library table covers.

A

E

F

Needle when set properly should be about 1¼ inch from bridge to point of needle.

BRIDGE

1¼ INCHES

NEEDLE POINT

H

G

I

C

D

B

IMPORTANT   (Patented)

Before using machine examine it thoroughly, note EXACT position of needle, so that when changing needles you will make no mistake in getting them the right length. It is VERY IMPORTANT that the needle be set according to directions.

The machine is mechanically perfect, and if it fails to do perfect work, you have not set your needle correctly or you are trying to use too heavy thread, as it is ESSENTIAL that threads used, must pass FREELY through eye of needle.

27-6: The swordfish shaped embroidery gadget was invented and made by H. W. Curtis Art Co., Chicago, IL. Circa 1900.

27-7: This seam ripper gadget has one wooden handle and one bow handle. One blade is pointed and the other is blunt. The blade is stamped "Pat'd May 22, 1900." No maker's name is on this seam ripper.

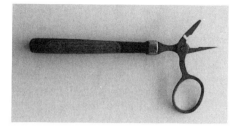

27-8: Patent drawing for the bodice of the McDowell Pattern Drafting Machine. In 1853, the complete pattern drafting system cost $17.50 in brass, or $20.00 for nickel plated. The complete system consisted of the brass or nickel plated drafting tool, instruction book, measure book, square measure, diagram for setting the machine, toothed tracing wheel, and tape measure.

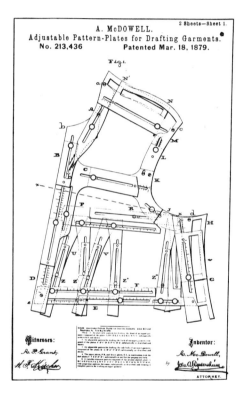

27-9: An advertisement for the Mc-Dowell pattern drafting machine showing the interior of a dressmaker's shop. Customers are viewing the new machine. Left: Slopers of the New Princess design, to be made without darts. Photo courtesy of the Smithsonian Institution, Washington, DC. #73-3646.

CHAPTER 28

Paper Memorabilia

Sewing tools collectors keep scrapbooks of photographs, prints, drawings, and reproductions of paintings that show people doing needlework, especially if an antique sewing tool is included. This spin-off collectible can be found in many forms.

PAPER

Pictures with a needlework theme are found on trade cards, old postcards, and reproductions of paintings. If you do not find an actual sewing implement at an antiques show or flea market, you probably will find one or more of these paper products. A picture of a woman doing needlework often shows her in a relaxed and pleasing position. Several tools relating to the craft are usually seen on a work table.

TRADE CARDS

Trade cards were a nineteenth century method of advertising products. The colorful lithographed cards were distributed free, packaged with products, or given out by the retailer. They were collected and preserved.

Many antiques dealers who specialize in selling trade cards appear at indoor antiques shows. It is rare to find them at outdoor markets since the perils of wind and rain can ruin their stock. Their trade cards are often stored in plastic pocket pages bound in loose leaf binders.

Take a clue from the dealers. This is the safest way to store and display your trade card collection. Also make certain to get a pocket size large enough to fit the biggest example in your collections.

Trade cards advertising thread often do not show women doing needlework. The themes focus on the strength or fast color nature of the thread. Over twenty different thread manufacturers distributed cards promoting their products. Clark's Mile-End, Clark's O.N.T., and J. and P. Coats Thread Companies distributed their cards in huge quantities.

Sewing machine trade cards usually show a woman working at a machine. At least twenty-five different sewing machine manufacturers distributed cards touting the benefits of their machines. The Singer Sewing Machine Co. produced more than one hundred twenty-five different cards.

The Singer "Native Costume" series cards were among the most popular. A boxed set of thirty-six cards was given free to visitors of the Singer exhibit at the 1893 Columbian Exposition in Chicago. Photographers went to far away places to photograph people wearing their native costumes while sitting at a Singer sewing machine. Some of the operators were men.

A description of the country and history of its people was printed on the back of each picture card, thus making it a mini geography lesson. The Singer motto, "The machine that sews everywhere," was highlighted. Some of the countries no longer exist, others have changed their name. For example, Ceylon

218

is now Sri Lanka, and Bosnia and Servia are part of Yugoslavia. The cards were so popular that Singer published a second series in the 1920s.

Singer's red "S" girl trademark made its debut in 1870 and became one of the best known advertising symbols in the world. Singer spent over one million dollars in promotion. Other promotional items include: pocket mirrors, tape measures, thimbles, face powder tissue, fans, and calendars. Singer became a household word. When a woman spoke with pride in her voice about her "Singer," she was not talking about her pet canary, but about her sewing machine.

Trade cards that are in perfect condition command the highest prices. Cards with damage, such as a bent or missing corner, tears, or stains are priced lower. Cards that have been trimmed to eliminate minor edge tears also diminish in value.

POSTCARDS

Old postcards picturing people doing needlework can be found at paper dealers' booths. Dealers usually sort their stock by category. "Needlework" picture cards are found in several categories, e.g., Advertising, Foreign, Museums, Occupations, or Women. "Advertising" cards may have a message and picture of a sewing machine. "Museum" cards often feature a reproduction of a painting that shows a woman doing needlework. These also will be filed under "foreign" if the museum that published the card is from overseas.

Prices for old picture postcards vary from dealer to dealer. Cards published before 1930 tend to cost more than those printed after that date. Learn to differentiate the early from the more recent cards. Again, check for damage. Bent, torn, or stained cards are worth less than examples in perfect condition. Used postcards with messages and canceled stamps do not add or detract from the value of the card.

MAGAZINE COVERS

Old needlework magazine covers with beautiful pictures of people doing needlework are very collectible. Magazine covers are usually larger than the 8 1/2" X 11" plastic ring binder protector pages. Trimming the cover to fit the page can lessen the value. Keep them in large, flat archival storage boxes. Consider framing some for wall decoration. A few of Norman Rockwell's *Saturday Evening Post* covers portray needlework activities.

PHOTOGRAPHS

Search the old photograph inventories of paper dealers for pictures of people doing needlework. Women were so proud of their sewing machines, they were often photographed working at their machine. Photographers often posed their subjects doing hand needlework. Sewing tools on the table next to the subject or a chatelaine hanging from chains clipped to the waistband of a woman's skirt are other possibilities. The famous early photographer, Wallace Nutting, photographed many of his models doing needlework.

Old photographs can also be found at postcard dealers. Photographers offered postcard size prints of pictures, complete with the postcard markings on the reverse side.

POSTAGE STAMPS

Many nations, including the United States, have issued postage stamps with needlework related pictures on them. These miniature engravings are works of art. Stamp dealers are not surprised when you ask for these stamps. They classify this as a "topical" collection in the stamp trade.

Portraits of men and women doing needlework have appeared on stamps issued by over twenty-five different countries. Included are the crafts of spinning, weaving, lace making, hand printing textiles, knitting, crocheting, rug making, embroidering, and quilting. Sewing tool collectors who have done research on this "topical" postage stamp area have combined their research. The information is in the library of Thimble Collectors International and available to members for the cost of copying and postage.

Postage stamps are cataloged by the *Scott Catalog* number. Stamp dealers use this number to find the stamp you want.

The United States Postal Service has issued several postage stamps with needlework themes. These include:

Betsy Ross Sewing the Flag	1952	Scott #1004-A451
American Homemaker Sampler	1964	Scott #1253-A685
Needlepoint Christmas Tree	1973	Scott #1508-A922
Seamstress	1977	Scott #1717-A1106
American Quilts (4 stamps)	1978	Scott #1745-A1134
		Scott #1746-A1135
		Scott #1747-A1136
		Scott #1748-A1137

The stamp commemorating the 200th anniversary of the birth of Betsy Ross was issued in Philadelphia, Pennsylvania, on January 2, 1952. The stamp shows Betsy Ross sewing the first American Flag.

The Homemaker's five-cents stamp, issued in honor of the fiftieth anniversary of the passage of the Smith-Laver Act by Congress, has a design of a cross stitch sampler. It was released on October 28, 1964 at Honolulu, Hawaii.

The Skilled Hands for Independence stamp series was issued on July 4, 1977, in Cincinnati, Ohio. "The Seamstress," one of the stamps in the series, pictures a colonial woman sewing.

The four stamps in the "American Quilt" series were issued in Charleston, West Virginia, on March 8, 1978. The series honored American Folk Art.

FIRST DAY COVERS

A "First Day Cover" is a commemorative postage stamp on an envelope, canceled in the city where the stamp was first issued. Most first day covers are American in origin. A colorful "cachet," or picture, is printed on the envelope to illustrate the theme of the stamp. Several commercial companies print cachet envelopes, including Colorano "Silk," Artmaster, Elete, Postal Commemorative Society, and Postmasters of America Philatelic. Each company produces a different cachet. The Colorano "Silk" cachet is printed on a textured silk-like fabric that is mounted on the envelope. Others have the cachet printed directly on the envelope.

First Day covers are more expensive than the stamp value alone, and the stamps should never be removed. They make an interesting and colorful collection.

NEW PAPER COLLECTIBLES

Newly published postcard reproductions picturing old paintings can be found at museum gift shops. The museums may not have the original paintings in their collections, but sell the cards to raise funds. Collectors often buy cards with needlework pictures to use as gifts or for trade with other collectors.

ART REPRODUCTION CATALOGS

Art reproduction catalogs offer new prints of old pictures. Small size prints will fit into your scrap book. Larger ones are meant for framing. More reproductions of old pictures are being offered as their original copyrights expire. Look through these catalogs for needlework related pictures.

NOTE PAPER AND GREETING CARDS

Your local card shop is a good source for needlework related pictures. Sewing and needlework related pictures are used on note paper and greeting cards. Mother's Day cards and birthday cards for a mother or grandmother often carry sewing theme pictures.

STORING YOUR PAPER COLLECTION

The new self-sticking scrap book pages that are popular today are dangerous to use. Paper tends to stick permanently to these pages. If you do use the self sticking pages, back your collectibles with a piece of paper cut one quarter inch smaller than the piece. The backing sheet should be loose, not glued to your card or picture. Leave enough room between your cards for the overlay plastic sheet to stick to the backing on the page.

The safest method of storing paper collectibles is in plastic pocket pages that fit into a three ring binder. This is the method used by postcard dealers to store their most expensive and valuable cards.

Vinyl pocket pages, made with various size pockets, are available at photo supply stores or by mail. One mail order source is R. D. Eisele, 1717 Prairie St., Grinnell, Iowa 50112. Other sources are listed in the postcard section in antiques publications.

28-1: Post card, The New Home Sewing Machine Company. 1909.

28-2: Post card, woman making pillow lace. Italy. 1900.

Three Patriots

28-3: Post card, The 1918 cover picture, Successful Farmer Pub. Co. © 1918. "Three Patriots." A Blue Star mother stitching her window banner.

28-4: A Valentine post card postmarked 1912.

28-5: A World War I era post card shows a doughboy mending, but dreaming of his mother doing it for him.

28-6: Early twentieth century photo post card of a girl working at a sewing machine, circa 1905.

28-7: Sewing machine manufacturers produced lithographed trade cards in huge quantities. Wheeler & Wilson Sewing Machine.

28-8: Trade card. New Davis Sewing Machine Co.

28-9: Trade card for New Home Sewing Machine Co., circa 1892.

28-10, 28-11: Trade cards for the Singer Sewing Machine Co., © 1899.

28-12: Trade card. The Wilson Shuttle Sewing Machine.

28-13: Old lithographed trade cards for thread make a colorful paper collection. Willimantic Thread Co.

28-14: Trade card. Household Sewing Machine Co.

28-15: Trade card. Florence Spool Silk.

28-17: Trade card. J. & P. Coats Spool Cotton.

28-16: Trade card. Clark's O.N.T. Spool Cotton.

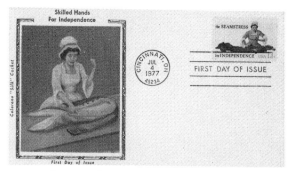

28-18: "First Day of Issue" postage stamp covers with needlework theme stamps. "The Seamstress," July 4, 1977. Picture is applied fabric.

28-20: Postage stamps with needlework theme are issued by postal services around the world.

28-19: First Day Cover. The American Homemaker, Feb. 2, 1976.

28-21: Nineteenth century painting show women doing needlework. From the painting *At the Embroidery Frame* by A. V. Ramberg.

28-22: From *Alice in Wonderland,* by Lewis Caroll. The Dodo bird presented Alice with a thimble as a prize at the end of a race.

28-23: Woman tatting. Mrs. Seymour Fort (?), by Singleton Copley, 1737–1815. Wadsworth Atheneum, Hartford, CT.

28-24: *The Sewing School,* Constant Artz, 1837–1890. Rijks Museum, Amsterdam, The Netherlands.

CHAPTER 29

"Twenty Pocket" Collectibles
Paper Sewing Kits, Needle Books, and Needle Threaders

"Twenty Pocket" collectibles are small paper matchbook-size sewing kits, needle books, and needle threaders that fit into the modern twenty pocket pages made to store 35mm photo slides. The pages are kept in a ring binder for safe and easy storage.

Paper sewing kits have been used as advertising giveaways for years. Three or four digit telephone numbers in the advertising provide a clue to the age of the kit. Occasionally a calendar will be printed inside the kit cover.

Some of the needles may be rusty or long-lost. When a list of the original contents is present, it provides a glimpse into the past. A Stephens Coal and Wood (established 1853) advertising needle book contains a 1909 calendar inside the cover and lists the names of the needles and their use: Glove or Fur Needle, Straw or Milliners Needle, Tape Needle, Worsted Needle, Motto or Chenille, Double Long Cotton Darners, Yarn Darner, Wool Darner, Fine Darner, Extra Fine Silk Darner, Carpet Needle, and Shoe Button Needle. This list gives you a clue to the items that were kept in repair years ago. The names of many of these special needles are no longer part of our vocabulary.

A surviving Aug. Thomas catalog for advertising needle books is marked "Effective Oct. 2nd 1933." The least expensive needle book cost $25.70 per thousand, F.O.B. New York. The cost also included printing the advertising. The catalog states, "We usually have sufficient stock to make up from 1 to 1 1/4 million books, and expert employees to average 40,000 books daily." The sales message continues: "(needle books) last a long time, are used daily, advertisement is read frequently, they work constantly and faithfully, spreading good will for the donor's business or product. If money is to be spent for advertising, make that advertisement effective!"

The 1933 Thomas catalog contains many sample needle book covers. Among the businesses represented are: a bank, ice cream shop, bakery, clothing store, laundry, fur shop, and a newspaper. The laundry needle book includes a self addressed detachable postcard, intended for use by a customer who wanted pick-up service but did not have a telephone.

Hotels provide matchbook mending kits for their guests. Generally, the kits are never used, but taken home. A mini-collection can be acquired rapidly by having your friends save mending kits from their travels.

Match book mending kits contain several colors of thread wound around cardboard, needles, safety pins, and some shirt buttons. Some also include an emery to file a broken fingernail and a *Band-Aid* plastic strip. Some older kits contain tabs with a glob of glue at the tip that resemble matches. The glue, when moistened, will stop a run in a silk stocking.

Larger needle books can be stored in postcard-size pocket pages. The lithograph art work on the covers gives a clue to the period when they were made and their country of origin. Many needles were manufactured in Germany, England, and Japan. The needle books frequently were printed in the United States and then filled with needles imported from abroad. The "Army and Navy Needle Book" series was made during the 1920s. One needle book cover shows the battleship *Iowa* sailing at full steam. Another needle book illustrates an unnamed battleship over which a bi-wing World War I airplane flies. Both have black paper packets of different size needles glued inside the book.

The wire needle threader is also classified as a Twenty-Pocket collectible. An aluminum threader with an embossed cameo profile is the most common. Others have advertising logos. The aluminum disk threader is made in Japan. Needle threaders with steel disks are made in the United States. Advertising information also appears on many of the steel disk needle threaders.

29-1: Paper mending kit. The cover is diecut in the shape of a woman's legs, to reveal the mending floss inside the kit.

29-2: Matchbook mending kit.

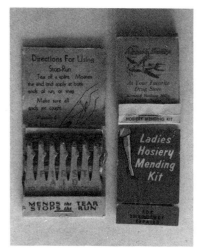

29-4: Matchbook mending kits.

29-3: Matchbook mending kits.

29-5: Matchbook mending kits.

29-6: Paper packets of needles.

230

29-7: Paper packets of needles.

29-8: Lithographed paper needle book.

29-9: Lithographed paper needle book.

29-10: Lithographed paper needle book.

29-11: Lithographed paper needle book.

29-12: Lithographed paper needle book.

29-13: Aluminum packets of needles.

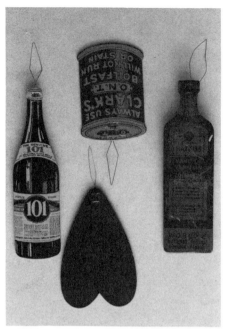

29-15: Store counter display card of wire needle threaders.

29-14: Unusual shaped wire needle threaders.

29-16: The Prudential Insurance Company's paper pin holder.

CHAPTER 30

Sewing Machines

Antique sewing machines are not as popular among collectors as other sewing implements. Yet, they deserve attention.

The earliest known foreign patent for a sewing machine was granted in 1830 to Barthelemy Thermonnier, a French tailor. He installed eight of his new machines in a workshop to fill a uniform contract for the French army. A mob of angry tailors attacked his shop. They feared that the new labor saving device was a threat to their trade.

Elias Howe, Jr. of Spencer, Massachusetts, was awarded the first United States patent for a sewing machine on September 10, 1846. Howe's machine was an improvement over Thermonnier's machine—it used two threads instead of one, thus making a stronger, locking stitch. The Howe machine was crude. Cloth was sewed in a vertical position rather than horizontally. Tension could not be applied to the cloth except by hand. The needle and thread were advanced by a hand crank.

Howe demonstrated a model of his machine at a Boston clothing factory. The machine sewed a seam five times faster than any seamstress in the factory. Nevertheless, the factory owner was reluctant to buy it. The machine could not do a complete job on a garment, much hand sewing was still required. The fear remained that the mechanical sewer would cause unemployment. Finally, the thought of purchasing thirty to forty machines was overwhelming.

Sewing machines were displayed in the Crystal Palace at the 1851 Great Universal Exhibition in London. The British press ignored this new invention, but an Italian newspaper reporter for *Giornale di Roma* wrote, "..a small brass machine, about the size of a quart pot, you fancy it is a meat roaster; not at all. It's a tailor. Yes, a veritable stitcher. Present a piece of cloth to it; suddenly it becomes agitated, it twists about, screams audibly. A needle sets to work, and lo and behold, the process of sewing goes on with a feverish activity."

In 1851 Isaac Merritt Singer founded the I.M. Singer Company in Boston, Massachusetts. His first machine, patented August, 1851, was called Singer's Perpendicular Action Sewing Machine. The fabric was supported horizontally on a table instead of being suspended vertically. When Howe learned that Singer had produced and marketed a machine similar to his own, he demanded payment for infringement of his patent. When the court decided that Howe's claim was valid, Singer paid a lump sum settlement based on royalties on the machines he had already sold. In 1856, Singer offered a "hire purchase" plan to sell his machines, an early form of today's lease-purchase agreement.

Singer's early machines were designed for factory use. In 1858 he produced a domestic lightweight "family" model. He promoted and advertised them extensively along with hiring pretty girls to demonstrate them in luxurious showrooms. Increased sales and home usage of the sewing machine by the beginning of the Civil War led Ebenezer Butterick of Boston, Massachusetts, to start a paper dress pattern company in 1863.

By 1870 there were sixty-nine sewing machine manufacturers in the United States, producing 700,000 machines a year. By 1876 the number made by the more popular American manufacturers were: Singer, 1,700,000; Wheeler and Wilcox, 1,200,000; Howe, 700,000; Grover and Baker, 550,000; Weed "Family Favorite," 220,000; Florence, 150,000; Wilcox and Gibbs, 150,000; and American, 120,000.

The number of manufacturers increased to one hundred and twenty-four by 1880. Competition soon affected the industry, and the number of manufacturers decreased to sixty-six by 1890.

Machines were made in Europe and Great Britain. The sewing machine's popularity reached everywhere. In the late nineteenth century, Russia's Czar Alexander III ordered workers to use sewing machines to make 250,000 tents for the Imperial Army. In the 1930s, Admiral Richard Byrd carried six Singer machines with him on his expedition to Antarctica.

Solomon Jones patented an electric motor to run a sewing machine in 1871, but electric sewing machines were not accepted by the buying public until the early twentieth century.

A variety of attachments were patented and produced for early sewing machines, among which were binders, quilters, braiders, markers, guides, gatherers, and button hole makers. All helped make the frilly Victorian fashions. Many of these attachments, still packed in their original box, can be found at antiques markets.

CHILDREN'S TOY SEWING MACHINES

Toy sewing machines were made for the "little seamstress." Singer made miniature copies of their full size machines in the early 1900s. A brass toy sewing machine was sold in England during the nineteenth century under the trade name TABITHA, but the maker's name does not appear on the machine. "Tabitha" is the Greek translation of Dorcas, the teen-ager in the Bible who sewed for the poor. The 1912 Sears Roebuck and Company catalog offered four models of toy sewing machines, ranging in price from 45 cents to $2.98. Many early twentieth century toy sewing machines were made in Germany.

Early toy machines were made of metal and hand cranked. Plastic models arrived in the 1940s and 1950s. Today, toy sewing machines powered by batteries or household current, using an adapter, are available.

COLLECTING SEWING MACHINES

Many old sewing machines were relegated to the scrap heap when they were no longer useful. Others were used as a trade-in when purchasing a newer model. A surprising number have survived.

Machines appear in forgotten storage places such as attics and barns. Flea markets, country auctions, and antiques shops are the best places to find old machines. Junk shops and thrift shops, such as the Salvation Army and Goodwill, are other possible sources.

Collectors should contact local museums and ask them to direct offers of old sewing machines to them. Museums do not accept old sewing machines for several reasons, e.g., limited space, the machine is not considered historically important, or the machine is not appropriate to the museum's collection.

An old sewing machine is incomplete without an instruction book. An original book is preferred, but a photocopy serves the purpose. The printing date provides a clue to the machine's age. The ornamental decorations also help date a machine. Scroll designs were popular decorative motifs at the turn of the century. Machines made during the 1920s had geometric motifs.

Dealers tend to price old sewing machines based on how ornate or interesting they look, hoping someone will buy them as a decorative object. Rarer machines, usually unattractive, are often mispriced.

Many old machines have been dismantled. The ornate ironwork stand becomes the base for a table. The oak drawers with fancy brass pulls are hung in bathrooms or sewing rooms to store small objects. The machine "head" is mounted on a wood plank and serves as a base for a lamp.

The creative reuse craze has destroyed many antique sewing machines. If you have a machine for sale, do not attempt to alter or restore it. Sewing machine collectors seek complete original machines in "as is" condition. Any attempt to clean a machine with harsh abrasive cleaners will destroy the decorations on the machine and ruin its value.

MUSEUMS

Several museums have antique sewing machines in their collections. These include the American Home Sewing Museum, West Warren, Massachusetts; Deutsches Museum, Munich, West Germany; Science Museum, South Kensington, London, England; Sheldon Art Museum, Middlebury, Vermont; and, the Smithsonian Institution, Washington, D. C.

The Smithsonian Institution collection includes many novelty-shaped, hand-turned sewing machines among which are: "Cherub" (circa 1858), "Serpent" (patented in 1859), and "Horse" (patented in 1858). The oldest figural machine was made in the shape of a gray squirrel. The needle traveled through the head, the foot was the thread guide, and the tail held the thread.

30-1: Typical paw-foot hand operated machine, 1862-1867. Common, but sought by collectors because of the novelty design. Several varieties of this machine were made. Photo courtesy of Carter Bays, Columbia, SC.

30-2: The American, 1870-1875. Head only. Common. Photo courtesy of Carter Bays.

30-3: Florence (machine head), 1860-1885. Common. Frequently mounted on fancy stand. Photo courtesy of Carter Bays.

30-4: Grover & Baker treadle machine, 1860-1870. Common. Photo courtesy of Carter Bays.

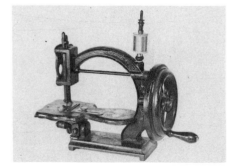

30-5: Grant Brothers, 1865-1870. Common hand operated machine. Photo courtesy of Carter Bays.

30-6: The Jones, 1880-1900. Common British hand operated machine. Photo courtesy of Carter Bays.

30-7: The Ladd & Webster machine, 1857-1865. Rare. Photo courtesy of Carter Bays.

30-8: The Lathrop machine, 1875. Rare. This one is serial #12. It is believed that less than 100 were made. Photo courtesy of Carter Bays.

30-9: The Leavitt, 1860-1869. Rare. Prized by collectors. Photo courtesy of Carter Bays.

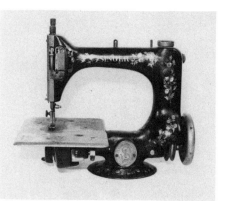

30-11: Singer chainstitch machine, circa 1920. Of little value to advanced sewing machine collectors. Photo courtesy of Carter Bays.

30-10: The Quaker City, 1858-1861. Rare. Photo courtesy of Carter Bays.

30-12: Sloat's Elliptic, 1860, with mirror and pin cushion. Scarce. Photo courtesy of Carter Bays.

30-13: Watson, 1860. A scarce hand operated variety. Photo courtesy of Carter Bays.

30-14: Typical machine, 1890-1930. Usually mounted on an oak treadle stand. Very common. Millions were made and thousands still exist. Of little value to a true sewing machine collector. Photo courtesy of Carter Bays.

30-15: Wheeler & Wilcox lockstitch machine, 1872. Note glass pressure foot to allow seamstress to observe stitches. Photo courtesy of American Home Sewing Museum.

30-16: Gibbs Patent model, 1857. Smithsonian Institution. #45504-E.

30-17: Wheeler & Wilson, 1861-1877. Common. Made in large quantities. Sewing machine collectors starts his collection with this one. Photo courtesy of Carter Bays.

30-18: Grover & Baker patent model, 1851. Smithsonian Institution. #23003-G.

30-19: Morey & Johnson patent model, 1849. Smithsonian Institution. #48440.

30-20: Grover & Baker patent, 1855. Smithsonian Institution. #45572-F.

30-21: "Horse" machine, patented by James Perry, 1858. Smithsonian Institution. #45505-C.

30-22: Elias Howe, patent model, 1846. Smithsonian Institution. #25525-B.

240

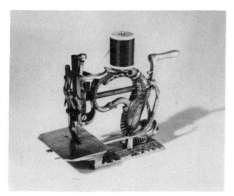

30-23: Dolphin machine, patented by T. J. W. Robinson, 1855. Built by D. W. Clark, Bridgeport, CT. Smithsonian Institution. #45505.

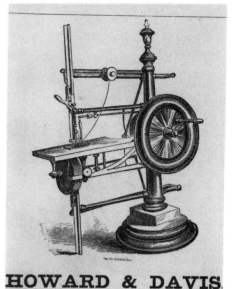

HOWARD & DAVIS

30-24: Robinson Patent, #13064, 1855. Smithsonian Institution. #48091-F.

30-25: Isaac Singer patent model, 1851. Smithsonian Institution. #45572-D.

30-26: A. B. Wilson patent model, 1851. Smithsonian Institution. #45504-B.

PART V

ADDITIONAL INFORMATION

CHAPTER 31

Reproductions and Fakes
An Educated Collector is a Wise Collector

Antique reproductions are here to stay. "Repros" are openly advertised in antiques publications. It is up to the collector to become aware of what is being reproduced and how to recognize a "repro" or a fake.

Reproductions of antique thimbles and sewing tools are part of the "repro" trend. It is not uncommon to find museum gift shops selling reproductions of thimbles in their collection.

The Metropolitan Museum of Art in New York City has reproduced an early nineteenth century French gold thimble in a gold plate over silver format. This "repro" is marked "MMA." Its silver quality is 925. A card describing the history of the original is included with the reproduction. Once this thimble reaches the secondary market, i.e., antique shows or shops, and the descriptive card is removed, collectors think it is a genuine antique.

The Smithsonian Institution gift shop offered a "second strike" of the Washington, D.C., souvenir thimble. This thimble, made for the Smithsonian Institution by the Simons Brothers Company of Philadelphia, used the same dies as the original nineteenth century issue. The new issue is marked "S.I." inside the cap. The cardinal rule is that a reissue of an older thimble is worth less than the original issue.

The design for the Simons Liberty Bell thimble was patented September 6, 1892 (Design Patent #21,844). The original issue has 13 stars stamped on the thimble. The Liberty Bell thimble was reissued for the Bicentennial, but the stars were deleted and "76" was substituted. It is important for the collector to be alert for any slight design variations that distinguish a "reissue" from the original.

A reproduction brass sewing bird has appeared on the antique market. The original has the 1853 patent date on the rounded edge of the wings, while the "repro" does not. The reproduction comes with a card describing the history of

243

the sewing bird. Again, once this card is separated from the bird, the piece is often offered as the genuine antique in the secondary market.

The most menacing fraud that a thimble collector will encounter today is fake Russian enamel thimbles. Poorly made, cast thimbles are being offered as genuine pre-revolution Russian-made objects. No dealer will admit that this is a fake, probably because he does not wish to be humiliated by admitting he was "taken". The fakes have the Russian "84" mark on the rim along with another mark that is deliberately indistinct.

A recast of a lovely old Gabler German thimble has recently surfaced in the antiques markets in Europe. It will not be long before this scalloped rim, banded clover leaf pattern thimble finds its way to the United States market. Collectors should be cautious when a thimble looks like it has been cast, is not smooth inside, and has shallow indentations on the outside.

RECOGNIZING REPRODUCTIONS

It is getting harder and harder to find quality antique thimbles and sewing tools. Whenever there is a ready market, reproduction artists enter. Additional reproductions most assuredly will surface in the antique market in the years ahead.

One protection against being fooled is to join a collectors' club or subscribe to a collectors' publication. Newsletters constantly alert collectors to what is happening in the market.

A "repro" may surface anywhere, gradually drifting across the entire country as dealers travel from show to show. It is almost impossible to trace the basement workshop where the newly made "antique" fakes originated.

A collector should buy from a reliable dealer who guarantees his piece as old and is willing to give a full refund if it is not. A written receipt with the dealer's name and address is a necessity.

Collectors often buy reproductions of antique thimbles and sewing tools because they cannot afford the three figure price of a genuine antique. Reproductions should always be cataloged as such in your personal record. If necessary, start a separate numbering system for reproduced pieces, prefixing the numbers with the letter "R" to indicate it is a "repro." Do not pollute your collection by mixing genuine antiques with "repros."

31-1: Fake Russian enamel thimble with "84" silver quality mark and a smeared maker's mark. The indentations are shallow and the wire work is part of the casting. The reproduction is rough inside and thick at the rim, 31-2: Genuine post revolution Russian enamel thimble. The "84" silver quality mark was replaced with a three digit mark after the revolution. The maker's mark and silver quality mark are sharp and readable. The wire work that enclosed the enamel is applied to the band of the thimble. The interior of the thimble is smooth.

31-3: A Kate Greenaway-style girl holds the thimble between her hands. Cast in pewter.

31-4: Boy leaning on pole holding thimble above his head. Cast in bronze color metal.

31-5: Reproduction of French gold thimble issued by the Metropolitan Museum of Art, New York, NY, 1980. The mark, M M A, is plainly visable. Wording on card that came with the reproduction of the French gold thimble: "The original rose and yellow gold engraved thimble may have belonged to a set of needlework implements, contained in a carefully fitted case. Although the original thimble is unmarked, the decoration in two tones of gold is a technique especially favored by French goldsmiths. The Museum's reproduction is electroformed in silver, gold plated and antiqued. Proceeds from the sale of all publications and reproductions are used to support the Museum." The photograph of the original thimble in the museum's collection appears in the Gold Thimble chapter.

31-6: Liberty Bell, early twentieth century issue. Note stars stamped on band; 31-6a: Liberty Bell, 1976 issue. Note "*76*" on band.

31-7: Fake recast of the Ketcham and McDougall "Louis XV" pattern. It can be recognized by the script monogram on the band, "F.J.L.," which is part of the casting; 31-7a: Genuine Ketcham and McDougall "Louis XV" pattern thimble. Circa 1924.

246

31-8, 31-9, 31-10: Three bronze color reproductions of antique thimbles. Unmarked, reproduced in Israel. They originally were packaged in cellophane with a card stating they were reproductions of early thimbles. When removed from the package, they could be offered as genuine antiques.

31-11: Patent date, Feb. 15, 1853, appears on the shoulder of the wing of the genuine antique brass sewing bird. The date has been deleted from the reproduction of this model bird.

31-12: The cat thimble and spool holder is cast in pewter. The reverse side of the base has part of a Pairpoint mark. This was picked up during the casting of the base. The mark is not complete.

CHAPTER 32

Marks

The following marks are frequently found on thimbles and sewing tools. They are the ones that you are most likely to encounter. Information about unidentified marks, often supplemented with drawings, appear in the "Question and Answer" columns of *THIMBLETTER* and *THE BULLETIN* of Thimble Collectors International.

Lora Lee Cordes did the artwork for these drawings. Her efforts are greatly appreciated.

PATTERN AND TRADEMARK NAMES

American

Priscilla	Simons Brothers Company
Quaker	Simons Brothers Company
S.B.C. (enclosed in a keystone)	Simons Brothers Company

English

Steel Lined Silver

Dorcas	Charles Horner
Dreema	Henry Griffith
Dura	Walker and Hall
Doris	Abel Morral

Composition or Celluloid

Halex	Charles Iles
Ivorine	Charles Iles

Aluminum Alloy

Alurine	Charles Iles
Stratnoid	Laughton & Son

Silver

The Spa	Henry Griffith

MODERN BRITISH THIMBLE MAKERS INITIALS

S.F.	Samuel Foskett
H.G. & S.	Henry Griffith
C.H.	Charles Horner
J.S. & S.	Joseph Swan & Son
J.W. Ltd., Made by Griffith for:	James Walker. Jeweler

 A.L.&Co.

32-1: Aiken Lambert & Co., New York, NY, c1890.

32-2: E. & J. Bass, New York, NY, 1890-1930.

32-3: Thomas Brogan, New York, NY, 1896-1930.

32-4: Carter, Gough & Co., Newark, NJ, 1890-1920.

32-5: S. Cottle Co., New York, NY, 1865-1920.

32-6: Foster & Bailey, Providence, RI, 1898-1951.

32-7: Goldsmith Stern Co., New York, NY, 1912-1916.

 KEENE 925/1000

32-8: A. T. Gunner Mfg. Co., Attleboro, MA, 1920 to present.

32-9: Charles A. Keene, New York, NY.

32-10: C. Klank & Sons, Baltimore, MD, 1892-1911.

32-11: Charles Iles, Sr., Birmingham, England, ninteenth century to present. Nickel and plated thimbles.

 MMA J MIX

32-12: Ketcham & McDougall, New York, NY and Elizabeth, NJ, 1875-1932.

32-13: La Pierre Mfg. Co., Newark, NJ and N.Y., NY, 1888-1929. (Bought by International Silver 1929).

32-14: Metropolitan Museum of Art, New York, NY, 1980 to present.

J. Mix, Albany, NY, 1817-1850.

32-16: H. Muhr's Sons, Philadelphia, PA, 1885-c1900.

32-17: H. Muhr's Sons. (Gold filled mark)

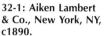

249

32-18: Paye and
Baker Mfg. Co.,
North Attleboro, MA,
1891-1935.

32-19: D. C. Percival
& Co., Boston, MA,
c1900. (Made by
Waite Thresher Co.)

32-20: Smithsonian
Institution, Washington, DC, 1981 to
present.

32-21: Simons Brothers Co., Philadelphia,
PA, 1840 to present.

32-22: Simons Brothers Co., Philadelphia,
PA, 1919-1952. (Industrial Alloy mark).

32-23: Simons Brothers Co., Philadelphia,
PA, 1840 to present.
(Gold filled mark).

32-24: Stern Brothers
Co., New York, NY,
1890-1912.

32-25: Stern Brothers
Co., New York, NY,
1890-1912. (Gold
filled mark).

32-26: Towle Silversmiths, Newburyport,
MA, 1890 to present.

32-27: Unger Brothers Co., Newark, NJ,
1896-1915.

32-28: Untermeyer-
Robbins & Co., Inc.,
New York, NY, 1900-
1915.

32-29: John von
Hoelle, Philadelphia,
PA, c1980 to present.

32-30: Waite
Thresher Co., Providence, RI, 1860-
1927. (Thimble dies
sold to Simons).

32-31: Webster Company, North Attleboro, MA, 1896-
1950. (Sold to Reed
& Barton).

32-32: Gabler Bros.,
West Germany, 1824-
1963. (Similar mark
used in England, Portugal, Italy, and Germany).

32-33: Helmut &
Thorvald Greif, Creglingen, West Germany, twentieth century.

32-34: J. A. Henkels,
Solingen, West Germany.

250

32-35: Lotthammer-Eber, Pforzheim, West Germany.

32-36: David-Andersen, Olso, Norway.

32-37: P. Lenain, Paris, France.

32-38: Soergel & Stollmeyer, Schwabisch, Gmund, West Germany.

32-39: Charles Horner, Birmingham, England, 1906-1940. (Steel lined).

32-40: Frank Kursch & Son Co., Newark, NJ, 1904-1915.

32-41: Coalport porcelain. England.

32-42: Swedish Hallmark.

32-43: French Assay Mark.

32-44: Gorham Corporation, Providence, RI, 1818 to present.

32-45: Shepard Manufacturing Co., Melrose Highlands, MA.

32-46: Franklin porcelain, Franklin Center, PA, (Current Mark).

32-47: Hemmessly porcelain, England, (Current Mark).

32-48: Meissen porcelain, East Germany, (Current Mark).

32-49: Royal Doulton, England, (Current Mark).

32-50: Royal Crown Derby, England, nineteenth century to present.

32-51: Bayreuth porcelain, West Germany.

CHAPTER 33

Catalogs

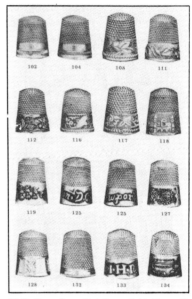

33-2: Page from Ketcham & McDougall wholesale catalog, circa 1915.

SELL TWO THIMBLES
WHERE YOU SOLD ONE BEFORE

A pair of thimbles in a most pleasing gift case. The one on the left (No. 266) of heavy silver overlaid with 14Kt. gold, beautifully hand chased, made especially for embroidery and fancy work. The one on the right (No. 137) is a general utility thimble of quality,

The set makes an attractive gift or price. The price is $3.00 the set. Of course, other styles may also be combined.

KETCHAM & MCDOUGALL, Inc.
15 MAIDEN LANE, NEW YORK
Thimble Makers for 94 Years

33-1: Ketcham & McDougall wholesale promotional sheet.

PRICE LIST *of*

Gold and Silver Thimbles

In Effect March 1st, 1926

098G

See Catalog for Illustrations
Sizes 5 to 12

KETCHAM & McDOUGALL
Incorporated
Thimble Makers Since 1832
Our Name is Your Complete Guarantee

Our AUTOMATIC EYE GLASS HOLDERS are of same High Class. ¶ Millions depend on them to keep their glasses handy. ¶ Made in one quality. with a style to fit every individual and every pocket-book - 75c. to $20.

Catalogs Sent Upon Request

STERLING 925/1000 SILVER THIMBLES

Style No.	Description		Weight	Per Dozen
101	Plain	. . . . .	Light	$2.60
103	Plain	. . . . .	Medium	3.75
105	Plain	. . . . .	Heavy	5.00
106	Plain	. . . . .	Extra heavy	6.00
107	Chased	. . . .	Medium	5.00
108	Chased	. . . .	Heavy	6.00
109	Chased edge	. . .	Heavy	5.80
110	Faceted	. . . .	Heavy	7.00
113	Plain band	. . .	Heavy	5.80
114	Engraved band	. .	Heavy	6.60
116	Queen Teie	. . .	Heavy	8.00
117	Cleopatra	. . . .	Heavy	8.00
126	Embroidery, bead rim		Heavy	8.00
129	Fluted band	. . .	Heavy	7.30
132	Knurled to rim	. .	Heavy	5.00
136	Louis XV rim	. .	Heavy	7.30
137	Chased scroll	. .	Extra heavy	8.00
139	Paneled	. . . .	Heavy	7.30
140	Chased rim	. . .	Heavy	5.40
143	Chased scroll	. .	Heavy	6.60
144	Embroidery, Louis XV rim	.	Extra heavy	15.75
146	Chased rim	. . .	Light	3.20
151	Damask	. . . .	Heavy	5.00
163	Wild Rose, French gray	. .	Heavy	8.00
167	Renaissance	. . .	Medium	4.10
173	Plain, fancy rim	. .	Medium	3.75
176	Plain, fancy rim, French gray	. .	Heavy	5.40
178	Greek border, French gray	. .	Medium	4.10
179	Daisy border, French gray	. .	Medium	4.10
186	Engine turned	. .	Heavy	10.50

---

14 KARAT GOLD THIMBLES

Style No.	Description		Weight	Each
40X	Chased edge	. . .	Medium	$3.90
41X	Chased	. . .	Medium	4.15
44	Engraved band	. .	Extra heavy	5.75
47	Faceted band	. .	Extra heavy	6.00
63	Fluted band	. . .	Extra heavy	6.00
67	Paneled band	. .	Extra heavy	6.00
68	Louis XV edge	. .	Extra heavy	5.75
70	Chased rim	. . .	Heavy	4.15
71	Chased scroll	. .	Heavy	4.90
75	Square panels	. .	Extra heavy	6.00
76	Bead rim	. . .	Heavy	4.15
78	Plain rim	. . .	Heavy	4.15
84	Plain, lined edge	.	Heavy	4.15
86	Plain, double rim	.	Heavy	4.15
89	Wild Rose, rose finish	Extra heavy	5.75

14 KARAT GREEN GOLD THIMBLES

Style No.	Description		Weight	Each
42G	Chased edge	. .	Medium	$4.25
43G	Plain band	. . .	Extra heavy	5.50
46G	Engraved band, lines	Medium	4.50
48G	Greek border	. .	Medium	4.40
49G	Cleopatra	. . .	Extra heavy	6.25
52G	Plain faceted	. .	Extra heavy	6.25
66G	Embroidery, plain band	. .	Extra heavy	7.75
88G	Embroidery, Louis XV edge	. .	Extra heavy	7.75
91G	Engine turned	. .	Extra heavy	6.25
91AG	Engine turned	. .	Extra heavy	6.25
93G	Engine turned, lines	Extra heavy	6.25
97G	Renaissance	. .	Heavy	4.40

33-3: Ketcham & McDougall wholesale price list: March 1, 1926. Prices for silver thimbles are per dozen. Prices for gold thimbles are per thimble.

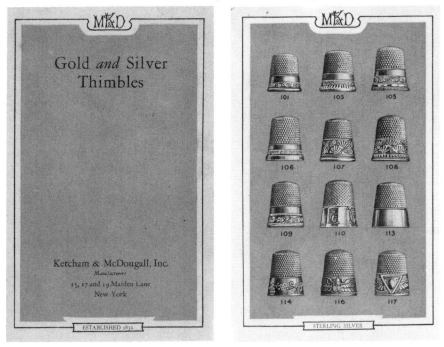

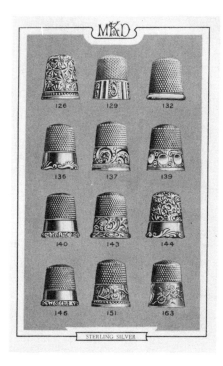

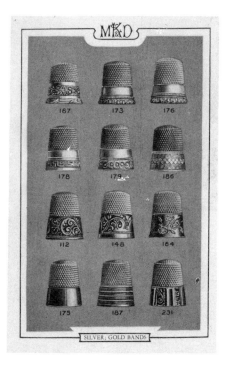

Ketcham & McDougall wholesale catalog, 1924.

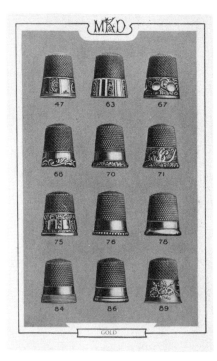

254

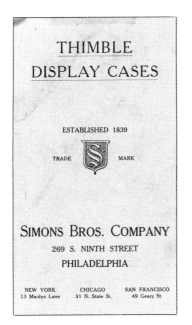

THIMBLE
DISPLAY CASES

ESTABLISHED 1839

TRADE MARK

SIMONS BROS. COMPANY

269 S. NINTH STREET

PHILADELPHIA

| NEW YORK | CHICAGO | SAN FRANCISCO |
| 13 Maiden Lane | 31 N. State St. | 49 Geary St. |

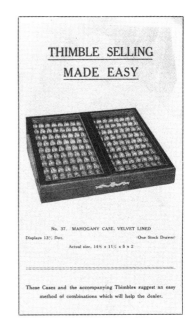

THIMBLE SELLING
MADE EASY

No. 37. MAHOGANY CASE, VELVET LINED
Displays 13½ Doz. (One Stock Drawer)
Actual size, 14½ x 11½ x 5 x 2

These Cases and the accompanying Thimbles suggest an easy
method of combinations which will help the dealer.

No. 13. MAHOGANY CASE, VELVET LINED
Displays 6 Doz. (One Stock Drawer)
Actual size, 10 x 9 x 4½ x 2½

No. 23½. MAHOGANY CASE, VELVET LINED
Displays 3 Doz. Actual size, 9½ x 6 x 1⅞

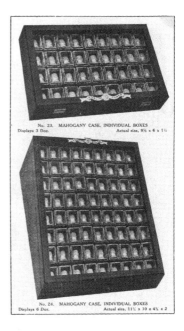

No. 23. MAHOGANY CASE, INDIVIDUAL BOXES
Displays 3 Doz. Actual size, 9½ x 6 x 1⅞

No. 24. MAHOGANY CASE, INDIVIDUAL BOXES
Displays 6 Doz. Actual size, 11½ x 10 x 4½ x 2

Simons Brothers Co., Philadelphia, PA, thimble display cases catalog, circa 1923.

No. 26. PAPER TRANSPARENT TOP, INDIVIDUAL BOXES
Displays 1 Doz.   Actual size. 4½ x 4 x 1½

No. 39.   PAPER BOX
Displays 1 Doz.   Actual size, 5 x 3½ x ¾

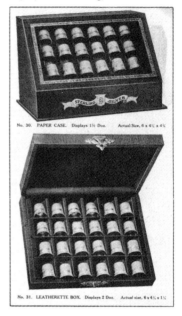

No. 30.   PAPER CASE.   Displays 1½ Doz.   Actual Size, 6 x 4½ x 4½

No. 31.   LEATHERETTE BOX.   Displays 2 Doz.   Actual size, 6 x 4½ x 1½

No. 32.   PAPER CASE
Displays 6 Doz.   Actual size, 6 x 3½ x 1½

STERLING
SILVER THIMBLES
MADE IN U.S.A.

No. 34.   PAPER BOX
Displays 1 Doz.   Actual size, 4½ x 2½ x ¾

No. 44.   PAPER NOVELTY BOX
Individual Boxes, Displays 1 Doz.   Actual size, 4½ x 4 x 1½

256

Simons Brothers Co., Philadelphia, PA, thimble display cases catalog, circa 1923.

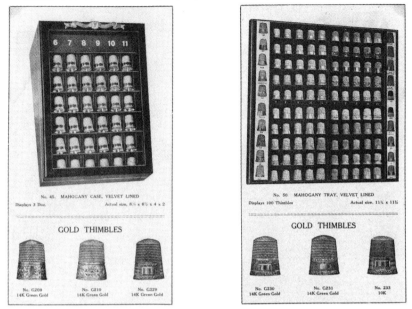

33-6: Simons Brothers Co., Philadelphia, PA, supplement wholesale catalog, May 1, 1928.

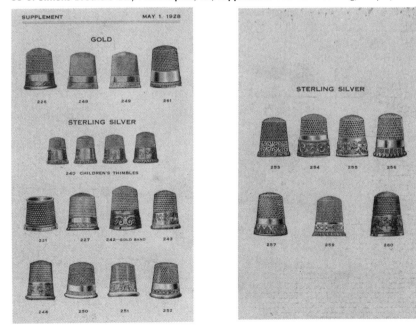

257

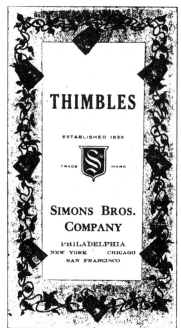

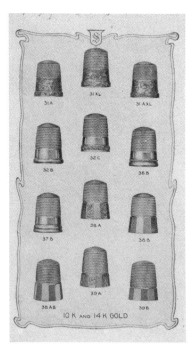

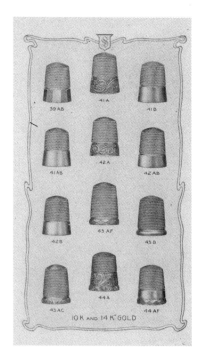

Simons Brothers Co., Philadelphia, PA, wholesale catalog, circa 1925.

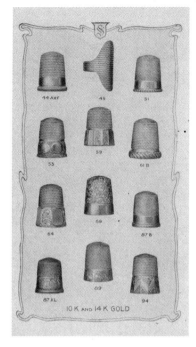

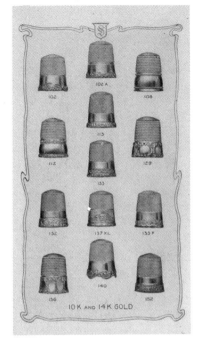

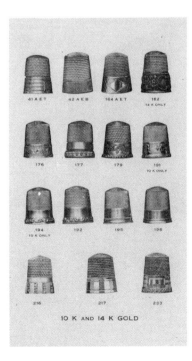

259

Simons Brothers Co, Philadelphia, PA, wholesale catalog, circa 1925.

Simons Brothers Co., Philadelphia, PA, wholesale catalog, circa 1925.

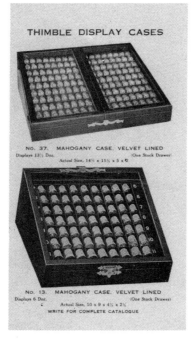

33-8: A page from Stern Brothers Co. wholesale catalog.

33-9: Webster Company, North Attleboro, MA, wholesale thimble catalog, circa 1920. Prices are per dozen.

Webster Company, North Attleboro, MA, wholesale thimble catalog, circa 1920. Prices are per dozen.

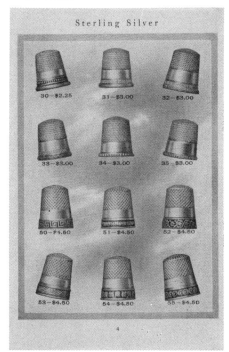

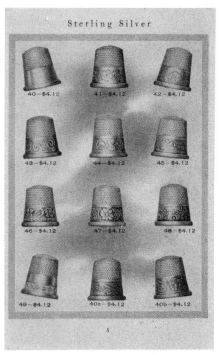

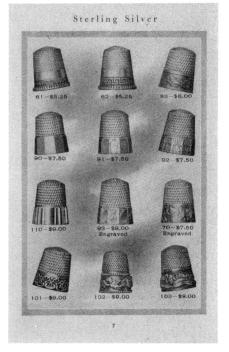

CHAPTER 34

Bibliography

BOOKS

Aldridge, Elizabeth, *Thoughts on Thimbles*, Des Moines, IA, Thimble Collectors International, 1983.

Andere, Mary, *Old Needlework Boxes and Tools*, Great Britian, David & Charles, 1971.

Clabburn, Pamela, *The Needleworker's Dictionary*, New York, NY, William Morrow & Co., Inc., 1976.

Colby, Averil, *Pincushions*, New York, NY, Scribner's Sons, 1975.

Dreesmann, Cecile, *A Thimble Full*, The Netherlands, Uitgeverij Cambium, 1983.

Greif, Helmut, *Talks About Thimbles*, Creglingen, West Germany, Fingerhutmuseum, 1983.

Groves, Sylvia, *Needlework Tools and Accessories*, New York, NY, Arco Publishing, 1966.

Holmes, Edwin F., *Thimbles*, Dublin, Ireland, Gill and Macmillan, 1976.

—, *A History of Thimbles*, Cranbury, NJ, Cornwall Books, 1985.

Houart, Victor, *Sewing Accessories, An Illustrated History*, London, England, Souvenir Press, 1984.

Jewell, Brian, *Veteran Sewing Machines*, Cranbury, NJ, A. S. Barnes, 1975.

Kidwell, Claudia B., *Cutting A Fashionable Fit*, Washington, DC, Smithsonian Institution Press, 1979.

Lundquist, Myrtle, *The Book of a Thousand Thimbles*, Lombard, IL, Wallace-Homestead, 1970.

—, *Thimble Treasury*, Lombard, IL, Wallace-Homestead, 1975.

—, *Thimble Americana*, Lombard, IL, Wallace-Homestead, 1981.

Mathis, Averil, *Antique and Collectible Thimbles and Accessories*, Paducah, KY, Collector Books, 1986.

Rath, Jo Anne, *Antique and Unusual Thimbles*, Cranbury, NJ, A. S. Barnes and Company, 1979.

Rogers, Gay Ann, *An Illustrated History of Needlework Tools*, London, England, John Murry, 1983.

von Hoelle, John, *Thimble Collectors Encyclopedia*, International Edition, Lombard, IL, Wallace-Homestead, 1986.

Whiting, Gertrude, *Tools and Toys of Stitchery*, New York, NY, Columbia University Press, 1928.

—, *Old-Time Tools and Toys of Needlework*, New York, NY, Dover Publications, 1971.

BOOKLETS

Bertrand, Christina, *Brass Thimbles*, Des Moines, IA, Thimble Collectors International, 1986. 76 pages.

Betensley, Bertha, *52 Thimble Patents,* Westville, IN, privately printed; 1980/56 pages.
Channing, Marion L., *The Textile Tools of Colonial Homes,* Marion, MA, privately printed, 1971, 64 pages.
Gilbert, K. R., *Sewing Machines,* London, England, Science Museum, 1970, 24 pages.
Greif, Helmut, *Nurenberg Thimblemakers,* Des Moines, IA, Thimble Collectors International, 1986, (English translation by Gertrude Kiebler) 30 pages.
Head, Carol, *Old Sewing Machines,* Bucks, England, Shires Publications, 1982, 32 pages.
Holmes, Edwin F., *John Lofting, an Early Thimble-Maker,* Des Moines, IA, Thimble Collectors International, 1984, 14 pages.
Jeffords, Mignon S., *Sharing Sewing Sets,* Spartansburg, SC, privately printed, 1984, 36 pages.
Johnson, Eleanor, *Needlework Tools,* Bucks, England, Shires Publications, 1980, 32 pages.
—, *Thimbles,* Bucks, England, Shires Publications, 1982, 32 pages.
Mealings, Richard, and von Hoelle, John, *Charles Iles, Thimblers to the World,* Wilmington, DE, Dine-American, 1984, 8 pages.
Philadelphia Thimble Society, *Henry Muhr and Sons, Philadelphia Thimble Makers,* Philadelphia, PA, 1985, 24 pages.
von Hoelle, John, *Benjamin Halstead, America's First Thimble Manufacturer,* Wilmington, DE, Dine-American, 1985, 24 pages.
—, *The Family Simons,* Wilmington, DE, Dine-American, 1985, 24 pages.
—, *The Story of Stern Brothers & Company,* Wilmington, DE, Dine-American, 1985, 24 pages.

NEWSLETTERS

"Thimbletter," Lorraine Crosby, editor, 93 Walnut Hill Road, Newton Highlands, MA 02161.
"Thimble Collectors International," 6411 Montego Bay, Louisville, KY 40228.

Books can be purchased from many book shops or directly from the publishers. Book sellers who specialize in books about antiques and collectibles display at many major antiques shows. Others sell by mail. Generally, book stores and chains do not stock books on special subjects for any length of time, but you can always request a special order copy.

Index

Figure	Low	High	Figure	Low	High	Figure	Low	High
7-1	—	6,000	7-70	150	175	8-9	35	40
7-4	150	200	7-71	125	150	8-10	40	50
7-5	150	200	7-72	125	150	8-11	25	35
7-6	150	200	7-73	125	150	8-12	25	35
7-7	300	350	7-74	100	125	8-13	25	35
7-8	75	100	7-75	100	125	8-14	100	150
7-9	75	100	7-76	100	125	8-15	20	25
7-10	75	100	7-77	100	125	8-16	20	25
7-11	65	85	7-78	100	125	8-17	20	25
7-12	65	85	7-79	100	125	8-18	25	35
7-13	65	85	7-80	100	125	8-19	25	35
7-14	75	100	7-81	100	125	8-20	25	35
7-15	75	100	7-82	100	125	8-21	25	35
7-16	75	100	7-83	900	1,000	8-22	40	50
7-17	90	125	7-84	100	125	8-23	25	35
7-18	90	125	7-85	100	125	8-24	50	65
7-19	90	125	7-86	100	125	8-25	50	65
7-20	90	125	7-87	100	125	8-26	50	65
7-21	90	125	7-88	100	125	8-27	50	65
7-22	90	125	7-89	100	125	8-28	50	65
7-23	90	125	7-90	100	125	8-29	50	65
7-24	90	125	7-91	100	125	8-30	50	65
7-25	90	125	7-92	100	125	8-31	50	65
7-26	90	125	7-93	75	100	8-32	50	65
7-27	90	125	7-94	75	100	8-33	1,000	1,200
7-28	100	125	7-95	75	100	8-34	1,000	1,200
7-29	100	125	7-96	75	100	8-35	1,000	1,200
7-30	100	125	7-97	75	100	8-36	600	800
7-31	100	125	7-98	75	100	8-37	600	800
7-32	150	200	7-99	150	175	8-38	600	800
7-33	150	200	7-100	150	175	8-39	600	800
7-34	150	200	7-101	150	175	8-43	600	800
7-35	90	110	7-102	150	175	8-44	200	250
7-36	90	110	7-103	150	175	8-45	200	250
7-37	90	110	7-104	150	175	8-48	25	35
7-38	100	125	7-105	75	100	8-49	25	35
7-39	100	125	7-106	75	100	8-50	25	35
7-40	100	125	7-107	75	100	8-51	100	125
7-41	100	125	7-108	100	150	8-52	100	125
7-42	100	125	7-109	100	150	8-53	100	125
7-43	100	125	7-110	100	150	8-60	100	125
7-44	90	110	7-111	100	150	8-61	100	125
7-45	90	110	7-112	100	150	8-62	100	125
7-46	90	110	7-113	100	150	8-63	400	500
7-47	75	100	7-114	100	150	8-64	100	125
7-48	75	100	7-115	100	150	8-65	100	125
7-49	75	100	7-116	100	150	8-66	25	35
7-50	125	150	7-117	100	150	8-67	25	35
7-51	125	150	7-118	100	150	8-68	25	35
7-52	125	150	7-119	100	150	8-69	60	75
7-53	125	150	7-120	75	100	8-70	50	65
7-54	125	150	7-121	200	250	8-71	60	75
7-55	100	125	7-122	75	100	8-72	30	40
7-56	300	350	7-123	125	150	8-73	30	40
7-57	300	350	7-124	125	150	8-74	30	40
7-58	300	350	7-125	125	150	8-75	115	135
7-59	150	175	7-126	85	110	8-76	800	1,000
7-60	150	175	7-127	85	110	8-77	800	1,000
7-61	150	175	7-128	85	110	8-78	1,000	1,200
7-62	100	125				8-80	90	125
7-63	75	110	8-2	60	85	8-81	90	125
7-64	110	125	8-3	60	85	8-82	90	125
7-65	200	225	8-4	60	85	8-83	90	125
7-66	300	350	8-5	25	35	8-84	90	125
7-67	400	500	8-6	25	35	8-85	90	125
7-68	150	175	8-7	25	35	8-86	75	85
7-69	150	175	8-8	200	250	8-87	75	85

Figure	Low	High	Figure	Low	High	Figure	Low	High
8-88	75	85	8-158	25	35	10-2	500	600
8-89	75	85	8-159	25	35	10-3	500	600
8-90	75	85	8-160	25	35	10-6	250	300
8-91	75	85	8-161	25	35	10-7	300	350
8-92	75	85	8-162	25	35	10-9	100	125
8-93	75	85	8-163	25	35	10-10	100	125
8-94	75	85	8-164	25	35	10-11	100	125
8-96	40	60	8-165	25	35	10-12	250	300
8-97	40	60	8-166	25	35	10-13	250	300
8-98	40	60	8-167	25	30	10-14	250	300
8-99	50	65	8-168	25	30	10-15	75	100
8-100	50	65	8-169	25	30	10-16	75	100
8-101	50	65	8-170	25	35	10-17	15	25
8-102	35	50	8-171	75	100	10-18	75	100
8-103	35	50	8-172	25	35	10-19	200	225
8-104	25	35	8-173	18	25	10-20	200	225
8-105	25	35	8-174	18	25	10-21	35	40
8-106	25	35	8-175	18	25	10-22	35	40
8-107	25	35	8-176	15	20	10-23	35	40
8-108	25	35	8-177	15	20	10-24	15	20
8-109	25	35	8-178	15	20	10-25	15	20
8-110	25	35	8-179	8	15	10 26	15	20
8 111	25	35	8-180	8	15	10-27	15	20
8-112	25	35	8-181	8	15	10-28	15	20
8-113	25	35				10-29	15	20
8-114	25	35				10-30	75	100
8-115	25	35	9-1	300	350	10-31	250	300
8-116	100	150	9-6	45	55	10-32	75	100
8-117	100	150	9-7	45	55	10-34	35	40
8-118	100	125	9-8	45	55	10-35	100	150
8-119	35	50	9-9	45	55	10-36	250	300
8-120	35	50	9-10	45	55	10-37	75	100
8-121	35	50	9-11	45	55	10-38	75	100
8-122	50	60	9-12	50	60	10-39	75	100
8-123	50	60	9-13	50	60	10-40	50	60
8-124	50	60	9-14	50	60	10-41	75	100
8-125	50	75	9-15	50	60	10-42	75	100
8-126	50	75	9-16	50	60	10-43	50	75
8-127	50	75	9-17	50	60	10-44	50	65
8-128	35	40	9-18	45	55	10-45	75	100
8-129	35	40	9-19	45	55	10-46	25	35
8-130	35	40	9-20	45	55	10-47	15	20
8-131	75	100	9-21	45	55	10-48	100	150
8-132	75	100	9-22	45	55	10-49	75	100
8-133	75	100	9-23	45	55	10-50	75	100
8-134	75	100	9-24	275	300	10-51	45	50
8-135	75	100	9-25	275	300	10-52	45	50
8-136	75	100	9-26	275	300	10-53	75	100
8-137	35	40	9-27	100	150	10-54	75	100
8-138	35	40	9-28	100	150	10-55	75	100
8-139	35	40	9-29	125	150	10-56	75	100
8-140	75	100	9-30	125	150	10-57	75	100
8-141	75	100	9-31	125	150	10-58	75	100
8-142	75	100	9-32	75	85	10-59	75	100
8-143	35	40	9-33	75	85	10-60	50	60
8-144	35	40	9-34	75	85	10-61	50	60
8-145	35	40	9-35	125	150	10-62	50	60
8-146	30	40	9-36	125	150	10-66	75	100
8-147	30	40	9-37	125	150	10-67	75	100
8-148	30	40	9-38	125	150	10-68	75	100
8-149	30	40	9-39	125	150	10-69	75	100
8-150	30	40	9-40	125	150	10-70	75	100
8-151	30	40	9-41	125	150	10-71	75	100
8-152	60	75	9-42	125	150	10-72	75	100
8-153	30	40	9-43	125	150	10-73	75	100
8-154	30	40	9-44	45	55	10-74	75	100
8-155	30	40	9-45	45	55	10-75	75	100
8-156	30	40	9-50	25	35	10-76	75	100
8-157	60	75	10-1	250	300	10-77	75	100

Figure	Low	High	Figure	Low	High	Figure	Low	High
10-78	75	100	11-17	275	300	12-21	50	75
10-79	75	100	11-18	50	75	12-22	50	75
10-80	75	100	11-19	150	200	12-23	150	175
10-81	75	100	11-20	35	40	12-24	150	175
10-82	75	100	11-21	15	25	12-25	150	175
10-83	75	100	11-22	15	25	12-26	75	85
10-84	75	100	11-23	15	25	12-27	75	85
10-85	75	100	11-24	25	35	12-28	75	85
10-86	75	100	11-25	25	35	12-29	1,000	1,200
10-87	75	100	11-26	25	35	12-30	1,000	1,200
10-88	75	100	11-27	25	35	12-31	200	300
10-89	75	100	11-28	25	35	12-32	1,000	1,200
10-90	75	100	11-29	25	35	12-33	1,000	1,200
10-91	75	100	11-30	25	35	12-34	1,000	1,200
10-92	75	100	11-31	25	35	12-35	1,000	1,200
10-93	75	100	11-32	25	35	12-36	1,000	1,200
10-94	75	100	11-33	25	35	12-37	1,000	1,200
10-95	75	100	11-34	25	35	12-39	150	175
10-96	75	100	11-35	25	35	12-40	150	175
10-97	75	100	11-36	15	25	12-41	150	175
10-98	75	100	11-37	15	25	12-42	150	175
10-99	75	100	11-38	15	25	12-43	150	175
10-100	75	100	11-39	15	25	12-44	150	175
10-101	75	100	11-40	15	25	12-45	1,200	1,500
10-102	75	100	11-41	15	25	12-46	1,200	1,500
10-103	75	100	11-42	25	30	12-47	1,200	1,500
10-104	75	100	11-43	25	30	12-48	40	60
10-105	50	60	11-44	25	30	12-49	40	60
10-106	50	60	11-45	10	15	12-50	40	60
10-107	50	60	11-46	10	15			
10-108	90	100	11-47	10	15	13-1	35	50
10-109	90	100	11-48	35	50	13-2	35	50
10-110	90	100	11-49	35	50	13-3	35	50
10-111	250	300	11-50	35	50	13-4	25	35
10-112	250	300	11-51	10	15	13-5	25	35
10-113	250	300	11-52	10	15	13-6	25	35
10-114	200	250	11-53	10	15	13-7	25	35
10-115	60	70	11-54	25	35	13-8	25	35
10-116	60	70	11-55	15	20	13-9	25	35
10-117	100	135	11-56	15	20	13-10	35	50
10-118	45	55	11-57	15	25	13-11	35	50
10-119	35	45	11-58	1	2	13-12	35	50
10-120	100	150	11-59	15	25	13-13	600	700
10-121	100	150	11-60	8	12	13-14	600	700
10-122	25	35	11-61	8	12	13-15	600	700
10-123	35	45	11-62	8	12	13-16	600	700
10-124	35	45	11-63	75	85	13-17	600	700
10-125	35	45	11-64	15	20	13-18	600	700
10-126	200	250	11-65	15	20	13-19	600	700
10-127	200	250	11-66	15	20	13-21	100	135
10-128	200	250	11-67	15	20	13-22	100	135
10-129	25	30				13-23	100	135
10-130	25	30	12-2	15	20	13-24	25	35
10-131	25	30	12-3	15	20	13-25	25	35
10-132	25	30	12-4	15	20	13-26	25	35
10-134	25	30	12-5	3,000	3,500	13-27	25	35
			12-8	65	75	13-28	25	35
11-2	8	10	12-9	65	75	13-29	25	35
11-3	8	10	12-10	65	75	13-30	200	250
11-4	8	10	12-11	65	75	13-31	200	250
11-5	60	75	12-12	65	75	13-32	200	250
11-6	60	75	12-13	65	75			
11-7	60	75	12-14	65	75	14-2	250	300
11-9	60	75	12-15	65	75	14-3	250	300
11-10	60	75	12-16	65	75	14-4	250	300
11-11	60	75	12-17	25	35	14-6	75	100
11-13	60	75	12-18	25	35	14-7	75	100
11-14	60	75	12-19	25	35	14-8	75	100
11-16	200	250	12-20	50	75	14-9	60	85

Figure	Low	High	Figure	Low	High	Figure	Low	High
14-10	60	85	16-26	25	35	17-13	35	40
14-11	60	85	16-27	25	35	17-14	35	40
14-12	300	350	16-28	25	35	17-15	25	35
14-13	300	350	16-29	25	35	17-16	25	35
14-14	350	400	16-30	25	35	17-17	25	35
14-15	250	300	16-31	1	3	17-18	40	50
14-16	250	300	16-32	1	3	17-19	40	50
14-17	250	300	16-33	1	3	17-20	40	50
14-18	250	300	16-34	1	3	17-21	1,800	2,200
14-19	250	300	16-35	1	3	17-23	1,800	2,200
14-20	250	300	16-36	1	3	17-25	100	125
14-21	1,200	1,500	16-37	1	3	17-26	100	125
14-22	1,200	1,500	16-38	1	3	17-27	35	50
14-23	100	150	16-39	1	3	17-28	35	50
14-24	50	75	16-40	1	3	17-29	35	50
14-25	50	75	16-41	1	3	17-30	75	90
14-26	50	75	16-42	1	3	17-31	75	90
			16-43	1	3	17-32	75	90
15-1	150	200	16-44	1	3	17-33	75	90
15-2	150	200	16-45	1	3	17-34	100	125
15-3	75	100	16-46	1	3	17-35	100	125
15-4	15	20	16-47	1	3	17-36	50	60
15-5	15	20	16-48	1	3	17-37	50	60
15-6	15	20	16-49	1	3	17-38	150	175
15-7	50	75	16-50	1	3	17-39	65	75
15-8	15	20	16-51	1	3	17-40	65	75
15-9	10	15	16-52	1	3	17-41	75	100
15-10	35	40	16-53	1	3	17-42	75	100
15-12	15	20	16-54	1	3	17-43	100	125
15-13	35	50	16-55	3	5	17-45	125	150
15-14	15	25	16-56	3	5	17-46	125	150
15-18	10	15	16-57	3	5	17-47	175	200
15-19	10	15	16-58	1	3	17-48	175	200
15-20	10	15	16-59	1	3	17-49	35	50
15-21	75	100	16-60	1	3	17-50	35	50
15-22	90	125	16-61	1	3	17-51	35	50
15-23	90	125	16-62	1	3	17-53	175	200
15-26	25	35	16-63	1	3	17-54	175	200
15-27	25	35	16-64	1	3	17-55	175	200
15-28	25	35	16-65	1	3	17-56	175	200
15-29	35	40	16-66	1	3	17-57	125	150
15-31	35	40	16-67	1	1.50	17-58	125	150
15-32	150	200	16-68	1	1.50	17-59	125	150
			16-69	1	1.50	17-60	50	60
16-1	3	5	16-70	40	55	17-61	75	100
16-2	20	25	16-71	40	55	17-62	25	35
16-3	20	25	16-72	40	55	17-63	25	35
16-4	20	25	16-73	40	55	17-64	75	100
16-5	1	3	16-74	40	55	17-65	75	100
16-6	1	3	16-75	40	55	17-66	75	100
16-7	1	3	16-76	40	60	17-67	50	60
16-8	5	8	17-77	40	60			
16-9	5	8	16-78	40	60	18-1	60	75
16-10	5	8	16-79	3	5	18-2	35	50
16-11	5	8	16-80	3	5	18-3	5	10
16-12	5	8	16-81	3	5	18-4	20	25
16-13	3	5				18-5	35	50
16-14	3	5	17-1	75	85	18-6	35	50
16-15	3	5	17-2	35	40	18-7	35	50
16-16	1	3	17-3	35	40	18-8	15	20
16-17	1	3	17-4	35	40	18-9	60	75
16-18	1	3	17-5	35	40	18-16	35	50
16-19	1	3	17-6	35	40	18-17	50	65
16-20	1	3	17-7	35	40	18-18	125	150
16-21	1	3	17-8	50	75	18-19	75	100
16-22	1	2	17-9	35	50	18-20	25	35
16-23	1	2	17-10	35	40	18-21	10	15
16-24	1	2	17-11	35	40	18-22	25	30
16-25	25	35	17-12	75	100	18-23	35	50

Figure	Low	High	Figure	Low	High	Figure	Low	High
18-24	15	25	22-2	75	100	23-41	75	100
18-25	60	75	22-3	75	100	23-42	75	100
18-26	5	8	22-4	75	100			
18-29	10	15	22-5	75	100	24-1	15	20
18-30	8	10	22-6	75	100	24-2	25	35
18-31	25	35	22-7	75	100	24-3	35	40
18-32	35	40	22-8	75	100	24-4	35	40
			22-9	25	30	24-5	60	70
19-2	25	35	22-10	75	90	24-7	35	40
19-3	250	275	22-12	15	20	24-8	5	8
19-4	250	275	22-13	15	20	24-9	60	75
19-5	250	275	22-14	15	20	24-10	5	8
19-6	250	275	22-15	15	20	24-11	25	35
19-7	225	275	22-16	8	10	24-12	25	35
19-8	85	100	22-24	25	35	24-13	35	40
19-9	60	75	22-25	25	35	24-14	35	40
19-10	100	125	22-26	35	40	24-15	15	20
19-11	35	40	22-27	40	50	24-16	20	25
19-12	125	150	22-28	25	30	24-17	25	35
			22-29	25	30	24-18	75	100
20-1	25	35	22-30	25	30	24-19	5	8
20-2	25	35	22-31	25	30	24-20	20	35
20-3	20	30	22-32	25	30			
20-4	20	30	22-35	300	400	25-1	900	1,200
20-5	20	30	22-36	20	25	25-4	700	800
20-6	15	20	22-38	30	40	25-6	1,200	1,500
20-7	15	20	22-39	25	30	25-7	200	300
20-8	8	12	22-40	200	300	25-8	200	300
20-9	20	30	22-41	200	300	25-9	200	300
20-10	40	50	22-42	60	75	25-10	75	100
20-11	30	40	22-43	40	50	25-11	75	100
20-12	30	40	22-45	75	100	25-12	100	150
20-13	25	35	22-46	40	50	25-13	300	400
20-14	15	20				25-15	200	300
20-15	25	35	23-3	150	175	25-16	200	300
			23-6	150	175	25-18	150	200
21-2	15	20	23-7	50	75	25-19	200	300
21-3	15	20	23-8	150	175	25-20	150	200
21-6	20	25	23-9	150	175	25-21	40	50
21-7	8	15	23-10	150	175	25-22	300	400
21-8	25	30	23-11	300	350	25-23	150	200
21-9	15	20	23-12	900	1,000	25-24	300	400
21-10	8	10	23-13	400	500	25-25	150	200
21-11	8	10	23-14	100	125	25-26	200	300
21-12	8	10	23-15	500	700	25-27	200	300
21-13	8	10	23-16	500	600	25-28	75	100
21-14	8	10	23-17	800	1,000	25-29	75	100
21-15	15	20	23-18	125	150	25-30	200	300
21-16	25	30	23-19	350	400	25-31	200	300
21-17	18	20	23-20	800	1,000	25-32	400	500
21-18	10	15	23-21	800	1,000	25-33	800	1,000
21-19	10	15	23-22	200	250	25-34	200	250
21-20	25	35	23-23	40	50	25-36	200	300
21-21	18	20	23-24	50	75	25-37	100	150
21-22	3	5	23-25	125	150	25-38	1,200	1,500
21-23	75	100	23-26	125	150	25-39	600	800
21-24	25	35	23-27	150	175	25-40	1,500	2,000
21-25	15	20	23-28	125	150	25-41	600	800
21-26	30	35	23-29	40	50	25-42	600	800
21-27	25	30	23-30	150	175	25-43	200	225
21-28	20	25	23-31	150	200	25-44	75	100
21-29	40	50	23-32	75	100	25-45	200	225
21-30	20	25	23-33	150	200	25-46	75	100
21-31	20	25	23-35	75	100	25-47	200	250
21-32	75	100	23-36	75	100	25-48	50	60
21-33	75	100	23-37	125	150	25-49	250	300
21-34	75	100	23-38	75	100	25-50	200	250
21-44	15	20	23-39	40	50	25-51	200	250
21-45	10	15	23-40	60	75	25-52	40	50

Figure	Low	High	Figure	Low	High	Figure	Low	High
25-53	15	18	29-14	3	4	P-30	150	200
25-54	15	18	29-15	7	10	P-31	200	225
25-55	20	25	29-16	2	3	P-32	3,000	3,500
25-56	150	200				P-33	275	300
25-59	75	90	30-1	200	300	P-34	500	600
25-60	40	50	30-2	125	135	P-35	500	600
25-61	40	50	30-3	250	400	P-36	500	600
25-63	40	50	30-4	200	225	P-37	100	150
25-66	500	600	30-5	125	150	P-38	100	150
25-67	150	200	30-6	75	100	P-39	100	150
25-68	150	200	30-7	2,000	2,225	P-40	100	150
			30-8	5,000	5,200	P-41	100	150
26-1	1	3	30-9	1,500	2,500	P-42	100	150
26-2	1	3	30-10	3,000	3,500	P-43	150	175
26-3	85	90	30-11	45	50	P-44	65	75
26-4	35	45	30-12	2,000	2,500	P-45	65	75
26-5	85	95	30-13	1,000	1,500	P-46	350	400
26-6	25	35	30-14	35	125	P-47	50	75
26-7	25	35	30-17	75	150	P-48	15	20
						P-49	400	500
27-1	15	20	31-1	60	75	P-50	600	700
27-3	20	25	31 2	60	75	P-51	75	100
27-4	15	20	31-3	15	20	P-54	25	35
27-6	15	20	31-4	35	40	P-55	25	35
27-7	15	20	31-6	100	150	P-56	25	35
			31-6A	75	100	P-57	900	1,200
28-1	2	3	31-7	15	20	P-58	250	300
28-2	1	2	31-7A	35	40	P-59	250	300
28-3	1	3	31-8	35	40	P-60	2,000	2,500
28-4	2	4	31-9	15	20	P-61	1,000	1,200
28-5	1	3	31-10	8	10	P-62	125	150
28-6	1	3	31-12	15	20	P-63	125	150
28-7	1	3				P-64	25	35
28-8	1	3	P-1	1,000	1,200	P-65	10	15
28-9	1	3	P-2	75	100	P-66	10	15
28-10	2	5	P-3	1,000	1,200	P-66A	1	2
28-11	2	5	P-4	1,000	1,200	P-67	30	35
28-12	1	3	P-5	1,000	1,200	P-68	50	75
28-13	1	3	P-6	1,000	1,200	P-69	75	90
28-14	1	3	P-7	1,000	1,200	P-70	175	200
28-15	1	3	P-8	1,000	1,200	P-71	350	400
28-16	1	3	P-9	200	300	P-72	400	500
28-17	1	3	P-10	200	300	P-73	125	150
28-18	1	2	P-11	200	300	P-74	30	40
28-19	1	2	P-12	60	75	P-75	25	30
28-20	1	2	P-13	60	75	P-76	8	10
28-21	2	4	P-14	75	90	P-77	10	12
28-22	2	4	P-15	125	150	P-78	18	20
28-23	1	1	P-16	100	125	P-79	2	3
28-24	1	2	P-17	150	175	P-80	50	75
			P-18L	400	500	P-81	50	75
29-1	3	4	P-18C	100	125	P-82	35	40
29-2	1	2	P-18R	100	125	P-83	35	40
29-3	1	2	P-19	125	150	P-84	50	60
29-4	1	2	P-20	150	175	P-85	25	35
29-5	1	2	P-21	500	600	P-86	75	100
29-6	1	2	P-22	300	400	P-87	75	100
29-7	1	2	P-23	400	500	P-88	4	5
29-8	3	4	P-24	250	300	P-89	3	4
29-9	5	6	P-25	300	350	P-90	3	4
29-10	3	4	P-26	300	350	P-91	1,500	2,000
29-11	3	4	P-27	150	200	P-92	1,200	1,500
29-12	3	4	P-28	90	110	P-93	1,800	2,200
29-13	3	4	P-29	125	150	P-94	2,500	3,000

Return with payment to:

Warman Publishing Co.
P.O. Box 1112, Dept. EZ
Willow Grove, PA 19090

Prices are subject to change without notice. Allow 4-6 weeks for delivery.
Inquire about quantity discounts for dealers, schools and clubs.
Phone (215) 657-1812

Qty.	Title	Price	Total
	Warman's Antiques and Their Prices, 23rd Ed.	$12.95	$
	Warman's English & Continental Pottery & Porcelain	$18.95	$
	Warman's Americana & Collectibles, 3rd Ed.	$13.95	$
	Zalkin's Handbook of Thimbles & Sewing Implements	$24.95	$
	TOTAL OF BOOKS ORDERED		$
	Pa. residents add 6% sales tax		$
	POSTAGE & HANDLING: $2.00 for first book, 50¢ for each additional book		$
	TOTAL AMOUNT ENCLOSED		$

Send check or money order, no C.O.D.

Ship to:

NAME (please print) _____

ADDRESS _____

CITY _____

STATE _____ ZIP _____

EZ

Warman price guides are available from leading book stores and antiques booksellers, or they can be ordered directly from the publisher.

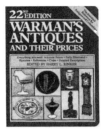

☐ **WARMAN'S ANTIQUES AND THEIR PRICES, 22nd Ed.,** edited by Harry L. Rinker. The standard price reference for the general antiques field. 50,000 items, 1,000 photos and illustrations, histories, references, 100's of American Pattern Glass designs, fully indexed. April, 1988.
Paperback **$11.95**

☐ **WARMAN'S ENGLISH & CONTINENTAL POTTERY & PORCELAIN** by Susan and Al Bagdade. A price and reference guide to the entire field. 200 manufacturers, 1,000's of items, 600 photos and factory marks, plus histories, references and collecting hints. June, 1987.
Paperback **$18.95**

☐ **WARMAN'S AMERICANA & COLLECTIBLES, 3rd Ed.,** edited by Harry L. Rinker. An all new edition of the best-selling price guide and reference in the collectibles field. 592 pages, 600 photos, 25,000 prices, histories, references, clubs, fully indexed. November, 1987.   Paperback **$13.95**

☐ **ZALKIN'S HANDBOOK OF THIMBLES & SEWING IM-PLEMENTS, 1st Ed.** By Estelle Zalkin. A new comprehensive record of everything from thimbles and pin cushions to workboxes. 1,400 objects photographed with their current prices. Sixteen pages in color. Complete text, collecting hints, histories, and much more. August, 1988.
Hardback **$24.95**